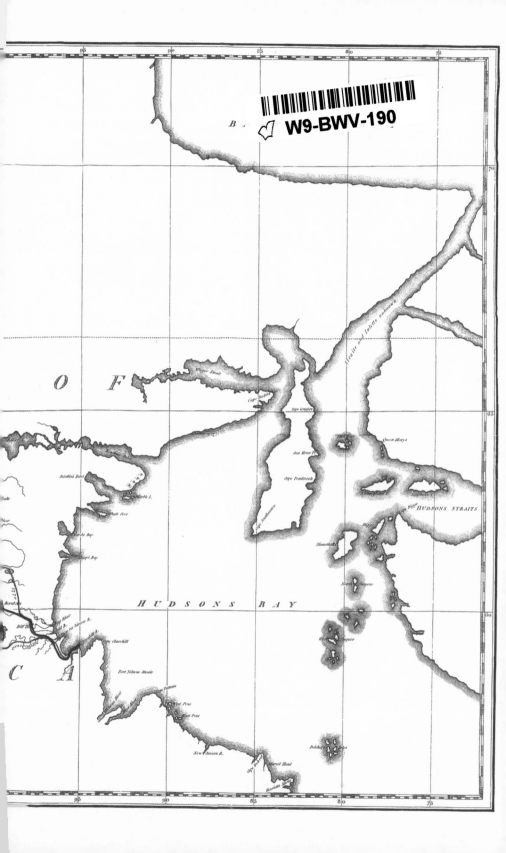

Ancient Mariner

Ken McGoogan

ANCIENT
MARINER

*The Amazing Adventures of Samuel Hearne,
The Sailor Who Walked to the Arctic Ocean*

Harper*Flamingo*Canada   A PHYLLIS BRUCE BOOK

First edition

HarperCollins books may be purchased for educational, business, or sales promotional use through our Special Markets Department.

HarperCollins Publishers Ltd.
2 Bloor Street East, 20th Floor
Toronto, Ontario, Canada
M4W 1A8

www.harpercanada.com

National Library of Canada Cataloguing in Publication

McGoogan, Kenneth, 1947–
Ancient Mariner : the amazing adventures of Samuel Hearne, the sailor who walked to the Arctic Ocean / Ken McGoogan.

"A Phyllis Bruce Book".
Includes bibliographical references and index.
ISBN 0-00-200098-9

1. Hearne, Samuel, 1745–1792 – Journeys – Canada, Northern. 2. Northwest, Canadian – Discovery and exploration. 3. Northwest, Canadian – Description and travel. 4. Indians of North America – Canada, Northern. 5. Inuit – Northwest Territories. I. Title.

FC3212.1.H42M34 2003   917.19'2041
C2003-903766-5

HC 9 8 7 6 5 4 3 2 1

Printed and bound in the United States
Set in Monotype Bell

FOR SHEENA,

MY FELLOW ADVENTURE TRAVELLER

Since then, at an uncertain hour,
That agony returns;
And till my ghastly tale is told.
This heart within me burns.

I pass, like night, from land to land;
I have strange power of speech;
That moment that his face I see,
I know the man that must hear me:
To him my tale I teach.

SAMUEL TAYLOR COLERIDGE
The Rime of the Ancient Mariner

CONTENTS

MAPS

Author's Note

EIGHTEENTH-CENTURY letters and documents tend to be grammatically capricious. For the sake of readability, and where I could do it without changing the meaning, implications, or flavour of the originals, I have modernized spelling, capitalization, and punctuation. Throughout, with the contemporary reader in mind, I have opted for consistency, clarity, and simplicity, preferring "Inuit" to "Eskimo," "Chipewyan Dene" to "Northern Indian," and "Prince of Wales Fort" to "Prince of Wales's Fort." Instead of using footnotes, I have indicated sources within the text.

Prologue

COLERIDGE
AT WORK

LATE IN the evening of November 12, 1797, on the outskirts of the village of Nether Stowey in southwestern England, Samuel Taylor Coleridge sat reading by candlelight in a "book parlour" set aside for his use by a friend. This cozy, low-vaulted chamber, complete with fireplace and well-stocked bookshelves, had become his favourite study. He usually worked here during the day. But earlier this evening, his wife and child having retired, Coleridge had felt moved to pursue an intuition arising from a neighbour's dream. He had returned to the parlour for a brief moment, but found himself instead scratching notes in the margins of a real-life adventure by Samuel Hearne, entitled *A Journey from Prince of Wales's Fort in Hudson's Bay to the Northern Ocean.*

Coleridge had recently composed a literary ballad called "The Three Graves," drawing on what, years from now, he would describe as "Hearne's deeply interesting anecdotes" about witchcraft and superstition among the native peoples of North America. For this theme and its development, he had borrowed the old navigator's tale of the laying on of a curse. Coleridge had changed the particulars, transforming the North American native people into English country folk, but Hearne's supernatural storyline remained unaltered.

Now Coleridge pored over his heavily annotated copy of the mariner's book, uncertain of what he sought. A neighbour, John Cruikshank, had recently described a nightmare about a mysterious skeleton ship manned by strange, tormented figures. While listening, and wondering if he could create a poem around this image, Coleridge had remembered meeting Samuel Hearne six years before, at Christ's

1

Hospital, a Blue Coat School for boys in central London. The occasion had been one of many "stately suppings in public," as his friend Charles Lamb would call them, "where the well-lighted hall, and the confluence of well-dressed company who came to see us, made the whole look more like a concert or assembly, than a scene of plain bread and cheese collation."

The masters had all attended, of course, including that eccentric disciplinarian James Boyer, the grammarian who had introduced Coleridge to poetry, and William Wales, head of the mathematical school, a convivial Yorkshireman who inspired respect because he had sailed with Captain James Cook. The dining hall was hung round with paintings, the most impressive of which was a huge representation by Antonio Verrio of James II, surrounded by courtiers and presiding at a convocation of graduating students.

Arriving late, Coleridge had noticed a tall, weather-beaten stranger gazing intently at this portrait, as if analyzing its very strokes. William Wales had seen him staring. "Ah, Coleridge!" he called. "You've a keen interest in adventure. Come!"

The mathematics master introduced the diffident stranger as an expert navigator and one of his closest friends. During the Seven Years War, Hearne had sailed as a midshipman with Samuel Hood, one of England's famous fighting captains. Later, on behalf of the

Samuel Taylor Coleridge in 1795, as portrayed in Bristol by Pieter van Dyke. The young poet, having encountered Samuel Hearne four years before, was still two years away from writing The Rime of the Ancient Mariner.

Hudson's Bay Company, he had conducted a remarkable journey of exploration, becoming the first European to visit the Arctic coast of North America. He was now preparing a narrative about his voyaging for publication.

Coleridge, whose intuition verged on clairvoyance, registered the stranger as an older figure of extraordinary presence—yet a man not entirely well. Handsome once, perhaps, the visitor was now gaunt, ethereal, almost otherworldly. And yet so eloquent! Hearne spoke in an accent recognizably southwestern, yet oddly inflected because he had lived so long abroad.

Wales drew him out with questions, and soon a small circle had gathered. Hearne spoke with animation of his days in the Royal Navy and grew passionate when, at the urging of Wales, he began describing his journey across the "Barren Lands" of North America to the Arctic coast. Coleridge, who usually listened with a critical ear, found himself swept away as the old navigator evoked the hardship, the hunger, and the awful magic of that endless journey—a journey that had culminated in a massacre that haunted the old man even now, all these years later, and that still he could not recall without wiping away a tear. Hearne felt an irrational guilt that he lived on when so many had perished needlessly.

Now, in 1797, as he sat examining Hearne's *Journey*, Coleridge was struck by the originality of the volume. The navigator had not only immersed himself in a foreign culture, but had made of his experience an unforgettable narrative, even while pioneering as a naturalist. The poet stared off into space, realizing suddenly that he sought not specific images, but a way of entering his projected poem. Perhaps that lay hidden not within the pages of this volume, but in the very figure of its author. The poet rose to pace the floor. Samuel Hearne had been so wracked by guilt that he felt compelled to bear witness—to tell his dark story again and again. Perhaps the poet could work with that? He could take the guilt-ridden navigator and give him a new narrative: the tale of a mysterious skeleton ship. . . .

Part One

MR. MIDSHIPMAN
HEARNE

THE BOY
FROM BEAMINSTER

EARLY ONE EVENING in January 1757, a strapping youth wearing the blue jacket, off-white pantaloons, round tarpaulin hat, and square-buckled shoes favoured by Young Gentlemen of the Royal Navy, the entire sparkling outfit purchased earlier that day, swung down High Street in Portsmouth, wide eyed and incapable of hiding it. After an exhausting stagecoach journey from Beaminster, four days to the west in Dorset, twelve-year-old Samuel Hearne had arrived with his mother the previous evening.

They had spent their first night in Dorchester, seventeen miles southwest of Beaminster, having avoided the journey through Hooke, which was cheaper but meant following a winding, steep, muddy road thick with caravans of walkers, poor people who had been ordered by overseers to move to another parish lest they become a burden. Instead, from the King's Arms in Beaminster, Hearne and his mother had caught the morning stage to Bridport, six miles south. That coach had been slowed by lumbering wagons, but from Bridport they had travelled to Dorchester by six-horse carriage, following the Great West Road that ran from Exeter to London.

On that fine road, a stagecoach might cover thirty miles in a day. Well-to-do travellers in private carriages could hardly do better, not unless they hired fresh post horses every twelve or fifteen miles. Hearne and his mother, journeying by regular coach, had covered twenty-five miles the second day, arriving in Bournemouth too late and too tired to see much.

The third day, on yet another coach, they had rolled steadily eastward through low, flat country, crossing creeks and inlets and

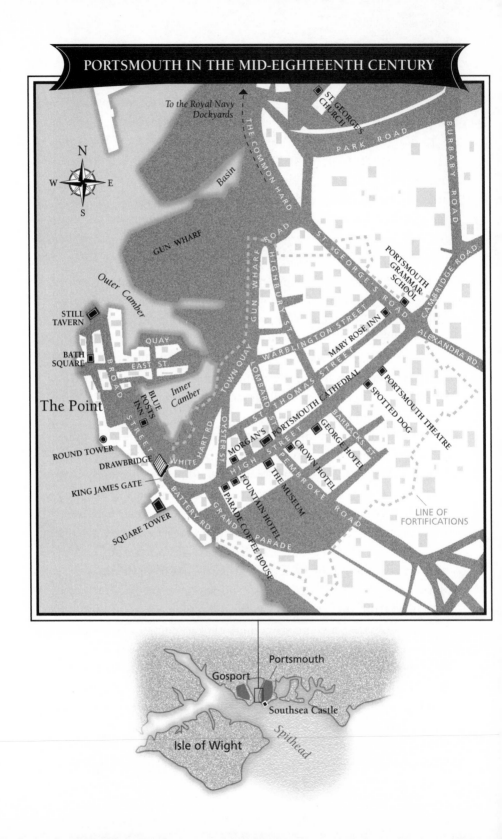

PORTSMOUTH IN THE MID-EIGHTEENTH CENTURY

To the Royal Navy Dockyards

ST GEORGES CHURCH

PARK ROAD

BURBABY ROAD

Basin

THE COMMON HARD

GUN WHARF

Outer Camber

PORTSMOUTH GRAMMAR SCHOOL

CAMBRIDGE ROAD

STILL TAVERN

QUAY

GUN WHARF ROAD

HIGHBURY ST

ALEXANDRA RD

BATH SQUARE

EAST ST.

BROAD STREET

WARBLINGTON STREET

MARY ROSE INN

ST GEORGES ROAD

Inner Camber

The Point

BLUE POSTS INN

TOWN QUAY

LOMBARD ST

ST THOMAS STREET

PORTSMOUTH CATHEDRAL

SPOTTED DOG

PORTSMOUTH THEATRE

ROUND TOWER

DRAWBRIDGE

WHITE HART RD

OYSTER ST

HIGH STREET

MORGAN'S

THE MUSEUM

CROWN HOTEL

PEMBROKE ROAD

GEORGE HOTEL

BARRACKS ST

KING JAMES GATE

BATTERY RD

FOUNTAIN HOTEL

PARADE

LINE OF FORTIFICATIONS

SQUARE TOWER

GRAND PARADE

PARADE COFFEE HOUSE

N
W E
S

Gosport

Portsmouth

Southsea Castle

Isle of Wight

Spithead

resorting three times to ferries before reaching Southampton. There, Hearne had remarked on the crowds, the spacious square, the impressive French cathedral. But even that bustling city had not prepared him for the unruly energy of Portsmouth during another war with France.

Last night, hanging onto the outside of the coach as it turned onto High Street, young Hearne had registered the tumult and din spilling out of shops, taverns, and coffee houses, and wondered, had they arrived during an annual fair? High Street rang with shouts and laughter and the cries of pedlars hawking their wares. Even the sidestreets were choked with people—women selling fruit and men hauling carts piled high with luggage, meat, or vegetables. Hearne saw livestock being driven down an alleyway: cows bawling, chickens squawking.

On descending from the coach at the Globe Inn, just off High Street, they had found themselves surrounded by porters clamouring to know where they were bound and if they needed a room, and offering to take them to "quality premises." Taller than most men despite his youth, Hearne placed a protective arm around his mother, who called out, "The Mary Rose? Anyone from the Mary Rose Inn?"

A burly porter stepped forward and glowered at his competitors until they melted away. The big man loaded their luggage into a one-horse cart and then helped Hearne's mother into the seat. With Hearne walking alongside, the porter led them by way of St. Thomas Street, a slightly quieter roadway. The Mary Rose, grander even than the King's Arms, had been built in 1742. From a posted sign, Hearne learned that the inn took its name from a ship that had sunk off Portsmouth harbour in 1545 while, from the wall of a nearby castle, a horrified King Henry VIII watched through a looking glass.

The next day, with his mother, Hearne plunged into the city, which was virtually encircled by a great stone wall. Not long ago, according to Daniel Defoe, the back entrance had been guarded with a double moat, double palisades, and several "ravelins," or freestanding barricades designed to retard attack. The city posted sentries and nobody could enter or leave after nine o'clock at night. Now, it was far more accessible.

From the Mary Rose Inn, waving off sedan-chair carriers, Hearne and his mother walked into the grey afternoon. They stood and admired the Portsmouth Grammar School, an impressive brick building

Built in 1742, the Mary Rose Inn takes its name from a ship that sank off Portsmouth in 1545 while hundreds watched in horror. The remains of the wreck, recently reclaimed from the sea, are preserved at the naval dockyard.

now fifteen years old, situated almost directly across the road from their inn. Then, swinging down High Street with the crowds, they realized that the town hall doubled as a marketplace and sat right in the middle of the street, traffic flowing past on both sides.

At Oyster Street, they recognized the Globe Inn, where they had debarked, and they continued past the bustling Parade Coffee House. From here, they could see King James Gate, beyond which lay Portsmouth Point, a bent finger of land that sheltered the Camber, the ancient harbour that still served all vessels except those of the Royal Navy. Hearne had expected to carry on but his mother demurred. "No respectable woman would venture through that gate, Samuel. Come! Let's get you fitted out."

Now, not six hours later, as the young man strode alone down High Street marvelling at what a figure he cut, he was making straight for The Point. Having passed the Portsmouth Theatre and the Spotted Dog, where in 1628 the Duke of Buckingham had been murdered, he approached the George Hotel, three storeys high and frequented by senior naval officers. Drawing himself up to his full height, Hearne stepped smartly. Perhaps here he would spot Captain Hood, under whose protection he would join the Royal Navy. Outside the George, three naval officers stood reading a notice and debating its meaning. As Hearne strode past, one of them cried, "Agreed, then—to London I must go!" He climbed into a waiting chaise-and-four and, to the cheers of his fellows, thundered away up High Street.

As Hearne crossed Pembroke Road, he could not help admiring the majestic Portsmouth Cathedral. St. Mary's Church, the glory of Beaminster, simply could not compare. Out front of the Fountain Hotel, cock-hatted junior officers jostled each other, placing wagers on some looming contest. And there, directly across the road, blazed the shop that had fitted him out—a place called Morgan's, with a handwritten sign in the window: "Sailors rigged complete from stem to stern."

Hearne passed the Parade Coffee House, noisier now even than it had been in the afternoon, and at the foot of High Street approached the Square Tower—since the fifteenth century, a semaphore station. He stared up at a bust of King Charles I mounted in a recess, and read the words beneath it: "After his travels through France into Spain and having passed many dangers both on sea and land, he arrived here on the 5th day of October 1623." History was everywhere.

Hearne climbed the stairs to the ramparts and gazed east toward Spithead, a channel mouth ten miles wide, dotted with scores of sailing ships, and separating the mainland from the Isle of Wight. Catching a whiff of sewage on the salt sea breeze, he recalled that Portsmouth Point was sometimes called Spice Island—and realized this was a bad joke.

Before leaving Beaminster, Hearne had rummaged through his dead father's books, among them Defoe's *Tour Through the Whole Island of Great Britain*. The author had described Portsmouth as "the largest fortification, beyond comparison," in the entire country. He had especially admired this harbour entrance, observing that it was guarded from both sides by platforms of powerful guns, including those cannons that Hearne could now see for himself.

From the foot of the stairs, immediately to the west, Broad Street ran through King James Gate, a passageway separating the respectable city from its disreputable quarter—Portsmouth Point. Once, that name had conjured up an ominous warren of pubs and brothels, press gangs and cutthroats. The reputation lingered still, though mitigated by the Royal Navy's well-fortified dockyards, which lay across the Outer Camber to the northeast.

Hearne strode through the Gate and crossed a seventy-five-foot wooden drawbridge suspended above a moat, realizing as he did so that The Point was not really a peninsula but an island. To his left stood the Round Tower, bristling with cannons. Built in 1417, it protected the harbour entrance and anchored the heavy chain that ran across that expanse to Gosport Point. Hearne could see how men had used the capstan, a round drum on a ratchet, to pull the chain taut across the harbour entrance and so prevent hostile ships from entering.

Across Broad Street stood a three-storey hostelry with a series of bright blue pillars flanking the entrances to a tavern and a stable yard. He recalled that the Blue Posts was popular among Young Gentlemen like himself, and indeed, during the next few years, he would come to know the place intimately. One day, Captain Frederick Marryat would write of "the Blue Postesses, where the midshipmen leave their chestesses, call for tea and toastesses, and sometimes forget to pay for the breakfastesses."

Hearne had believed High Street the epitome of bustle, but now he discovered what a crowd could be. He flowed along Broad Street with the mob, amazed at the diversity of shops and businesses—tailors, drapers, pawnbrokers—and astounded at the number of taverns, thirty-five or forty at least. Tough-looking sailors carrying great mugs of beer reeled drunkenly from one alehouse to another. A couple of them jeered at him, hurling a good-natured insult he didn't catch.

Ducking through a "sally port" in the stone wall, Hearne marvelled at the continuing bustle of the Inner Camber, the original, well-sheltered harbour developed by Normans in the twelfth century and then used by Lombard and Saxon traders. Now, barges, launches, and gigs came and went, and boatmen wrangled with customers, some of whom were cursing the boatmen for not pushing off, while others implored them to wait a bit longer.

Back on Broad Street, Hearne continued north to the tip of The Point. Beyond it lay the entrance to the Outer Camber, a floating forest of tall masts and furled sails. In the deepening twilight, a brigantine moved slowly seaward, sails flapping in the breeze, making for the harbour entrance and Spithead. Beyond the Outer Camber, Hearne could see the Royal Navy dockyards, where tomorrow he would meet Captain Hood.

Turning to the noisy spectacle behind him, he noticed a muscular midshipman striding from the Blue Anchor to the Star and Garter, accompanied by several husky seamen, all of them sober and serious. He watched them confront a group of sailors, and deduced that they were gathering their ship's crew, separating men from their sweethearts, who were clearly new found. From out of the Still Tavern, directly ahead, tumbled a trio of young men no older than himself, laughing and waving tankards of beer. With them came several young women—not their sisters. One of the girls called to him, inviting him to join the party.

Ignoring this jovial crew, Hearne started back toward King James Gate, flowing this time through Bath Square, the alternative channel. Glancing down alleyways not quite lost in darkness, he glimpsed such scenes, men and women together, as he had never yet imagined. So this was what his mother had been trying to protect him from.

Hearne realized that before long, he would probably return to The Point with raucous shipmates of his own. But even as he made his way through Bath Square, the steamiest quarter of the wildest seaport in Europe, he vowed never to be distracted. He was joining the Royal Navy not just to have adventures, but also to restore the name Hearne to its rightful lustre. He was joining the Navy to make his mark, and from that nothing would distract him.

AN ARTICLE published in *The European Magazine and London Review* in June 1797, while self-contradictory and not wholly reliable, is an important source on the early life of Samuel Hearne.

Mr. Samuel Hearne was born in the year 1745. He was the son of Mr. Hearne, Secretary to the Waterworks, London Bridge, a very sensible man, and of a respectable family in Somersetshire; he died of fever in his 40th year, and left Mrs. Hearne with this son, then but three years of age [*sic*], and a daughter two years older. Mrs. Hearne, finding her income too small to admit her living in town as she had been accustomed to, retired to Bimmester, in Dorsetshire (her native place), where she lived as a gentlewoman, and was much respected.

Samuel Hearne, Sr., died in January 1750. A record of his burial, at Bunhill Fields, suggests that he was a non-conformist—a Christian who dissented from certain Church of England teachings. He had been born in Somerset in southwestern England, perhaps in Crewkerne, Chard, or Yeovil, towns within fifteen miles of Beaminster. His branch of the Hearne family clearly enjoyed some position and influence, for employment as secretary and engineer to the London Bridge Water Works would be open only to someone of respectable family and advanced education. Many positions like this one also had a property qualification, which meant that incumbents had to own property that generated a minimum income—for example, £100 or £200 a year.

The Water Works, a private company subject to the Metropolitan Water Board, supplied two million gallons of water each day to eight thousand London homes, drawing it from the River Thames and pumping it through wooden pipes made of hollowed logs. While overseeing workers and handling accounts, this capable, ambitious man designed and installed improved waterwheels and also wrote a detailed analysis of the waterworks—"a thing never attempted by any of my predecessors."

At age twenty-seven, the engineer felt sufficiently established to take a wife. There is a record of a marriage taking place on January 7, 1737, at St. Bennett Church in Paul's Wharf, London, between Samuel Hearne and Diana Rown or Rowan. The birth records covering the period when Diana was born have long since disappeared, probably destroyed by fire.

In 1743, Diana gave birth to a daughter, Sarah Hearne. The following year, to accommodate the chief engineer and his growing family, the Water Board bought them a house near the west side of London Bridge, between Thames Street and the river. And there, in 1745, Diana gave birth to her second child, Samuel Hearne, Jr. The future looked bright. Comfortably ensconced near the Thames, the Hearnes would have kept a couple of servants. They would have entertained regularly, and probably attended theatrical performances in the Strand.

Eighteenth-century London was notoriously unhealthy, however. Outbreaks of typhoid, typhus, and smallpox—all contagious, all potentially lethal—frequently swept the city. Late in 1743, when Samuel Hearne, Sr., prepared his last will and testament, he mentioned that he did so in perfect health and sound memory, and "knowing the uncertainty of life and the certainty of death." He bequeathed all his worldly possessions to his "dear and loving wife Diana Hearne," including lands, houses, moneys, household goods, bills, and bonds.

Early in 1750, when Samuel Hearne was nearing five, his engineer father contracted a fever and passed away. For mother and children, this proved not just a human tragedy but an economic disaster. The concept of insurance was still in its infancy. Samuel Hearne, Sr., left some money—his will was "proved" April 14, 1750—but most of his assets remained in property. The Water Works now required its house for the new chief engineer. Diana Hearne took her two children, aged seven and four, and moved back to the town in which she had grown up.

Beaminster (pronounced "Bemminster") lies 130 miles southwest of London in a wide valley at the head of the River Brit. Surrounded by rolling hills, it is today recognized as one of the loveliest old towns in England—a peaceful place of stone cottages, quaint shops, and a parish church built mostly in the fifteenth century whose tower soars

The town of Beaminster, 130 miles southwest of London, has changed little enough in two and a half centuries that even today, Samuel Hearne would recognize this as a photo of the main square, or "fore place."

one hundred feet into the sky. Despite having been devastated by fires in 1644, 1684, and 1781, Beaminster today contains two hundred listed buildings—so many that the town's historic centre has been designated a conservation area. In the nineteenth century, author Thomas Hardy, who lived near Dorchester, seventeen miles away, would use Beaminster as the model for Emminster, the hometown of a central character in *Tess of the D'Urbervilles*.

In the mid-eighteenth century, when Samuel Hearne lived here, the population was just under two thousand, and the surrounding hills, downs, and plains sustained great herds of cows and sheep. For almost five hundred years, Beaminster had been conducting a weekly market, specializing in woollens and various kinds of cloth, as well as shoe-thread, rope, and twine. Outside the town lay villages and hamlets where peasants did the requisite spinning of wool. The master clothiers lived in Beaminster. Each week, they would send servants to bring wool to the spinners and collect finished yarn, which they fitted to the loom in their shops. According to Daniel Defoe, writing in the 1720s, Beaminster specialized in fine medley, or mixed, cloths worn by the better sort of people.

In the 1750s, any boy growing up in Beaminster or nearby Netherbury would attend the Tucker Free School, situated in a one-room schoolhouse on the grounds of St. Mary's Church. This was not fatally constricting: Thomas Spratt, eventually bishop of Rochester, attended this institution. In the seventeenth century, a Beaminster heiress named Frances Tucker had endowed the school with funds, providing for the maintenance of the schoolmaster, for educating poor boys of the parish, and for apprenticing three or four boys annually, "whereof one at least if not two shall be every yeare sent to sea when they are fitted for it."

According to the 1797 article in *The European Magazine and London Review*,

It was her [Mrs. Hearne's] wish to give her children as good an education as the place afforded, and accordingly [she] sent her son to school at a very early period, but his dislike to reading and writing was so great that he made very little progress in either. His masters, indeed, spared neither threats nor persuasion to induce him to learn, but their arguments were thrown away on one

If Bristol-based artist Francis Danby had set out deliberately to evoke the childhood of Samuel Hearne, he could not have improved upon Boys Sailing a Little Boat, *which he painted around 1821.*

who seemed predetermined never to become a learned man; he had, however, a very quick apprehension, and, in his childish sports, showed unusual activity and ingenuity; he was particularly fond of drawing, and though he never had the least instruction in the art, copied with great delicacy and correctness even from nature.

Although the article states that the boy did not enjoy reading and writing, Hearne's later life stands as a convincing rebuttal and suggests that other considerations were at play here. In the mid-eighteenth century, even the finest schools offered learning by rote, insisting that children sit in rows for hours at a time while completing prescribed exercises and drills. In this environment, the imaginative, irrepressible Hearne could only have been bored to desperation and driven to misbehaviour.

Schoolmasters and vicars were doubtless the only "learned men" the boy had yet encountered, and he felt no desire to join their ranks.

17

Nor did he intend to go into business, as some of his mother's friends suggested. Open a clothing shop and remain in Beaminster? Never!

Hearne seized early upon the notion of joining the Navy. At school, he met the younger brothers of boys who had taken that route, and heard stirring stories. A boy of vivid imagination, Hearne took direction from Defoe's *Robinson Crusoe*. Since its publication in 1719, the work had become a staple of leisure reading, and would soon be described by the philosopher Jean-Jacques Rousseau as "the one book that teaches all that books can teach."

At the outset of the novel, Crusoe reveals that his father had hoped he would study law, but he himself would be satisfied with nothing but going to sea. This passion led him to ignore the commands of his father and the entreaties and arguments of his mother and her friends. In a final attempt to make the boy see sense, Crusoe's father called him into his study:

He asked me what Reasons more than a mere wandering Inclination I had for leaving my Father's House and my native Country, where I might be well introduced, and had a Prospect of raising my Fortunes by Application and Industry, with a Life of Ease and Pleasure. He told me it was Men of desperate Fortunes on one hand, or of aspiring, superior Fortunes on the other, who went abroad upon Adventures, to rise by Enterprize, and make themselves famous in Undertakings of a Nature out of the common Road.

To Samuel Hearne, who could scarcely remember his father, Crusoe was a marvellous figure of resolution, self-reliance, and industry—a man whose life of "desperate Fortunes" was easily the most exciting imaginable. Only by going to sea would Hearne stand a chance of regaining the status he felt to be his by birth but which threatened to elude him because of his father's too early demise. In response to his mother's pleas, the headstrong youth remained adamant: he would go to sea.

Diana Hearne, knowing the obstinacy of her son, did what loving mothers have always done in such circumstances. She relented and undertook to help, turning first to her friends and relatives, among them "the seafaring Hoods of Netherbury." Probably she approached Ann Hood, the wife of a Samuel Hood who in 1756 was serving in the

Royal Navy as a purser. Ann Hood maintained close ties with her husband's aunt, Mary Hood, who had grown up in Beaminster and lived not far away in Butleigh, Somerset.

Mary was the wife of the vicar Samuel Hood, who had once served as the Beaminster schoolmaster. She was also the mother of two young officers in the Royal Navy. Might one of these two be willing and able to engage a young man of good family who insisted on going to sea? Late in December 1756, one of Mary's sons—Samuel Hood— responded affirmatively from Portsmouth. He had just returned to England after serving two years along the coast of North America. While awaiting another permanent posting, he would soon undertake a series of temporary commands. He would welcome the services of an energetic Young Gentleman, who would move with him from ship to ship. Could the lad report early in the new year?

In January 1757, as he strode through Portsmouth in his new sailor's outfit, imagining himself a first officer or even a lordly captain enjoying shore leave in a foreign country, and having banished all thoughts of Beaminster, Samuel Hearne could not know it, but he would come to miss the market town he had so eagerly left behind. In the months and years to come, while laying siege to some sweltering Mediterranean port or shivering with cold in the wilds of North America among men and women who spoke no English, Hearne would remember Beaminster with a pang—an instant that would resolve itself, eventually, into a pining he could not now conceive.

Hearne would remember how, when he was seven or eight years old, some leading citizens decided to buy a fire engine. Until then, local firefighting, woefully ineffective, had consisted of teams of men passing buckets of water drawn from a stream. The vestry settled on one of Newsham & Ragg's Fourth Size Engines, which could hold ninety gallons in its cistern. Supplied with water through leather hoses and pumped continuously by hand, this marvel could discharge that same amount once a minute. He would remember the fire engine arriving at the King's Arms in a horse-drawn wagon. Three feet long and eighteen inches wide, the contraption had four solid wheels and, in case a blaze proved difficult to access, poles extending from each side so that men could carry it like a sedan chair. He would remember workmen building an engine house beside the market house, and digging up the Fore Place to create a covered reservoir and several watercourses.

Beaminster provided Hearne with more than memories. Because it proclaims its antiquity in every street and building, this old market town gave the receptive youth a sense of history. Coming of age here made Hearne aware that he belonged to a collective life process that extended back through the Middle Ages into Roman times and beyond.

In the seventh century, the town had emerged into public records as Bebingmynster, which means "minster," or church, of Bebbe, an Anglo-Saxon female name. Six hundred years later, in 1284, Beaminster acquired the rights to conduct a weekly market and an annual three-day fair—and so became not just another village but a market town. At the heart of that town, facing out across the Fore Place, stood the market house, an impressive stone building fronted by mighty pillars. In the various stalls, people bought and sold not only milk, butter, and cheese, but hemp, flax, and linen goods, as well as sailcloth, sackcloth, shoe-thread, rope, and twine.

Near the middle of the Fore Place stood a carved market cross, which had been erected in the thirteenth or fourteenth century. Beside the market house stood the shambles, where butchers plied their trade beneath awnings, hacking off prime cuts of meat and tossing offal into the streams that still ran through town.

By the mid-eighteenth century, both the market house and the shambles had recovered from the two devastating fires of the previous century. The most dramatic was the fire that broke out on Palm Sunday in 1644, during the Civil War. Strongly Parliamentarian, Beaminster had been occupied by Royalist troops, some of whom started the blaze by firing muskets into thatched roofs. Within two hours, more than two-thirds of the town's two hundred houses had been reduced to ashes. The image of this conflagration burned brightly enough in local memory that any youth of imagination would carry it forever in his mind's eye.

Young Hearne also knew something about the Monmouth Rebellion of 1685, when many Beaminster men, opposed on principle to king and hierarchy, supported the duke of Monmouth in his claim to the throne. This support came mainly from non-conformist families like Hearne's own—people who had left the Church of England to worship as Presbyterian dissenters. When the uprising was ruthlessly quashed, nineteen Beaminster men found "wanting from their Homes in the tyme of the Rebellion" were tried at Dorchester by the infamous Judge Jeffries. Among them was one John Hearn, Jr. Four Beaminster men convicted of treason were sentenced to transportation. On a frigate bound for Barbados, one of them died. Several other local men were hanged, and young Hearne had heard rumours that their remains had been strung up at St. Mary's Church.

Beaminster was also a town of alehouses. Years from now, sheltering from a howling snowstorm in a moosehide tent, Hearne would make a game of remembering their names and find that he could recall Nag's Head, Red Lyon, New Inn, Half Moon, Shoulder of Mutton, White Horse, Fountain, White Hart, Bull, George, Swan, Crown & Greyhound, Hare & Hounds, Rising Sun, Lace, Three Horseshoes, Green Dragon, White Dog, Blew Ball, Valiant Soldier, and King's Arms—more than twenty.

He would remember the last with special fondness. The King's Arms, a three-storey stone cottage that overlooked the Fore Place, was Beaminster's chief inn and coaching house. There, one grey morning in January 1757, Hearne and his mother had waited for the first of the stagecoaches that would take them, via Bridport, Dorchester, and Southampton, to Portsmouth, where he would join the Royal Navy. At the King's Arms, twelve-year-old Hearne had stood looking around, sobered by the awareness that he was saying goodbye to Beaminster. What he didn't realize, of course, was that he would carry this place, the only hometown he would ever know, to the farthest reaches of European civilization and beyond. Samuel Hearne would carry Beaminster wherever he went, and for as long as he lived.

Now, in Portsmouth, while his mother perched in a chair by the window, the twelve-year-old paced restlessly around a waiting room in the Admiralty offices. One hour before, emerging from the Mary Rose into a steady drizzle, Hearne and his mother had reluctantly

St. George's Church, sturdily built by dockyard shipwrights, has endured into the twenty-first century. The foundation stone was laid May 11, 1753, and the edifice was still new when Hearne first saw it four years later.

piled into a coach. His mother had tried to distract him, drawing his attention to the impressiveness of St. George's Church, recently built by dockyard shipwrights, and then to the countless small boats at anchor off The Common Hard, the road that led to the naval base. Young Hearne was so excited he could hardly concentrate.

At the dockyard gate, the only way through the wall that surrounded the naval yards, a uniformed guard, after ascertaining their business, had directed them to proceed along a cobblestone walk to the right, past the porter's lodge and the pay office. All the activity, Hearne could see, lay in the other direction, to the left along the waterfront, which was lined with workshops, rope-houses, and storehouses. Judging from the number of visible masts, the harbour was choked with ships.

Finally, having located and entered the red-brick building that housed the Admiralty offices, they had been directed into this drawing room, splendidly decorated with maps and globes and paintings of His Majesty's ships. Here they waited for Captain Samuel Hood—a man regarded, back in Beaminster, as an almost mythical figure.

From his mother's friends, the Hoods of Netherbury, they had heard wonderful stories about the captain. Seventeen years before, when Samuel Hood had been fifteen and living with his parents in Butleigh, twenty-five miles north of Beaminster, a Captain Thomas Smith had providentially entered his life. This famous officer, popularly known as Tom of Ten Thousand, had been travelling from Plymouth to London when his carriage had broken down in Butleigh village, a tiny place without an inn. Hood's father, the local vicar, had insisted that the captain spend the night at their cottage.

After dinner, Captain Smith entertained his hosts with stories of life at sea. Samuel and his younger brother, Alexander, sat enthralled. Before leaving, the captain offered to take one of the boys to sea. Under his protection, the youth would train to become a Sea Officer. He would be a Young Gentleman who "walked the quarterdeck." Because he intended to follow his father into the Church, Samuel declined. His younger brother, Alexander, joyously accepted the invitation, and soon boarded HMS *Romney* as a captain's servant—an officer-in-training. When Alexander sent letters describing life aboard ship—so eventful, so exciting—Samuel abandoned all thought of the Church and followed after his brother.

He remained aboard the *Romney* after Smith left, and progressed steadily through the ranks. Then, a general peace brought widespread staff reductions. In 1749, as a first lieutenant waiting to be recalled to active duty, Hood married Susannah Linzee, the daughter of a prominent surgeon who was also mayor of Portsmouth. Before long, he was recalled.

More recently, England and France had entered into a period of hostilities that would eventually be known as the Seven Years War (1756–63). Having achieved a captaincy, Hood had won several victories off the coast of North America—victories that produced considerable prize money, in which his crew shared. Just the year before, in the West Indies, Captain Hood had wreaked havoc among the French merchant fleet, shutting down commercial shipping out of Santo Domingo and capturing more than a hundred prisoners. That story had reached even Beaminster.

In mid-December, after serving two years abroad, Hood had arrived back in Portsmouth. He consulted with Admiral Edward

Boscawen, one of several powerful friends, and applied to take temporary command of any ship whose captain was drawn away by a high-profile court martial currently underway.

In *The Admirals Hood*, Dorothy Hood describes her relative: "Samuel was tall, and no one could ever have thought him good-looking, with a nose as big as Wellington's and not so well shaped." She adds, however, that Hood had more education than the average naval officer, and as he grew older, his "manners and conversation were both of a superior order, the former amounting to high courtesy." Elsewhere, she observes that his letters "reveal a strong, lovable personality." In *Men of the Wooden Walls*, naval historian Frank C. Bowen qualifies this: "[Hood's] portraits do not suggest a very pleasant personality with his long face and nose, but he was a prime fighting seaman, always cool-headed in an emergency."

Now, through a door to which Hearne had paid no attention, Captain Samuel Hood arrived—tall and hawk nosed and, though still in his early thirties, hugely self-confident and decidedly intimidating. It is not difficult to imagine the scene that ensued. Hearne's mother, having blushingly introduced herself—she was not much older than Hood—handed the captain letters from his aunt and his parents. Hood thanked her but scarcely glanced at these before setting them aside for later perusal.

He invited his visitors to join him at a table. "As you may have heard, Mrs. Hearne," he said, "I have been given temporary command of the *Torbay*—the first of several such appointments that will arise, I have reason to believe, as a result of the court martial of Admiral John Byng."

"A terrible business."

"Terrible but necessary, Mrs. Hearne." Hood glanced up from hunting through his satchel. "Cowardice cannot be allowed to undermine the dignity of the Royal Navy."

"Quite so, Captain."

The officer resumed his search. "When the court martial is finished, I will again take command of my own vessel." He produced the papers he sought, laid them on the table, and looked finally at Samuel Hearne. "So this young man wishes to enter His Majesty's Service."

"I do, Sir. I hope to make my mark in the world."

"It's not an easy life, the Royal Navy. Not for the weak or faint hearted."

"Sir, I am neither."

Turning again to Mrs. Hearne, Captain Hood said, "You do understand that a Young Gentleman is expected to keep up appearances? And that Samuel will require an allowance?"

"Twenty-five pounds a year?"

"Thirty."

"Of course, Captain." Probably, the widow Hearne would be able to draw on some monies set aside at the Tucker School for the express purpose of enabling boys to begin a naval career. Yet she could not resist adding, "My husband did not leave me destitute."

Captain Hood nodded. "I have drawn up the requisite papers. Please look them over and sign where indicated."

As Mrs. Hearne did so, the captain turned again to her son. "The Royal Navy is the greatest fighting force the world has ever known because it is built upon discipline and respect for rules and regulations. To make progress, you must learn to obey your superiors. You must remain attentive to orders, and zealous in pursuit of duty. Aboard my ship, Young Gentlemen set the tone."

"Yes, Sir."

Hearne's mother finished signing the documents. The captain scrawled a note and handed it to young Hearne. "This will get you into the dockyard," he said. "Report to the *Torbay* tomorrow at noon. Once aboard ship, ask for Mr. Neville, the gunner. Give him this note and do what he says."

Captain Hood returned his papers to his satchel and rose to his feet. "You must excuse me, Mrs. Hearne, but my presence is urgently required elsewhere. I believe you know the way out."

"We do, Captain. And thank you again."

Captain Hood bowed stiffly, spun on his heel, and disappeared out the door.

Samuel Hearne noticed that his mother wore an odd expression. Misreading it, he said, "Don't be sad, Mother. I will write you letters. I'm on my way to becoming a Sea Officer! Father would be proud, don't you think?"

"Very proud, Samuel. Very proud, indeed."

2

THE YOUNG
GENTLEMAN

By THE MID-NINETEENTH century, class-conscious Britain would develop a reputation as highly stratified—a land of social barriers. But in Samuel Hearne's day, compared with its European contemporaries, English society remained remarkably fluid. The gentlemanly condition, which reflected aristocratic codes of behaviour and involved the wearing of linen waistcoats, flamboyant hats, and square-buckled shoes, could be assumed by birth, but could also be attained through wealth or professional distinction. Even relatively poor individuals could achieve gentlemanly status by entering the naval service.

And so, in Jane Austen's *Persuasion*, a nobleman strenuously objects to the Royal Navy "as being the means of bringing persons of obscure birth into undue distinction, and raising them to honours which their fathers and grandfathers never dreamt of. . . . A man is in greater danger in the navy of being insulted by the rise of one whose father his father might have disdained to speak to . . . than in any other line."

Nevertheless, the vast majority of commissioned officers came from upper-middle-class or middle-class backgrounds. They were "gentleman-born" or "near-gentleman born." As someone whose father had held not a sinecure but a responsible position demanding education and ability, Samuel Hearne fell into the latter category. And so he joined the navy as a "captain's servant"—a confusing term best understood, according to naval historian Michael Lewis, as "captain's protégé." Essentially an officer-in-training, such a one would become "an officer and a gentleman" only when he received the King's Commission that made him a lieutenant. Until then, he would remain a Young Gentleman or, loosely speaking, a "midshipman"—someone who enjoyed the privilege of "walking the quarterdeck" at the rear of the ship.

Every young man who entered the Service under the nominal protection of a captain, and so entertained realistic hopes of becoming a commissioned officer, was "quarterdeck." Those who joined without such protection and expectations were "lower deck." Unlike the lower-deck boys, who received a wage, albeit a pittance, the Young Gentlemen received nothing. Their nominal earnings showed up in the ship's records, but these went directly to the ship's captain. As Lewis explains in his *Social History of the Navy*, this was an apprenticeship system:

Just as "the master" in commerce and the mechanical trades took apprentices in order to initiate them into his craft, ultimately to set them up on their own, the while lodging and feeding them, and receiving some payment from the learners' parents, so the Captain took on such protégés as he cared to select, on the understanding that he would teach them *his* craft and—tacitly—do his best when the time came to launch them out as officers like himself: at the same time seeing that they were boarded and fed, and even being paid for his pains.

In 1757, as an ordinary captain, Samuel Hood was entitled to four "servants" or protégés, and filling that quota meant money in his pocket. These Young Gentlemen were obliged to live up to their claims of gentlemanly status. In lieu of a salary, they were expected to receive an allowance from home—at this time, perhaps £30 a year. Some captains, bent on keeping up the style of their vessels, insisted that their "volunteers" receive more. Out of this, the young midshipmen would have to pay not only for clothes, but sometimes additionally for "messing expenses" and an additional fee for the schoolmaster.

Had Samuel Hearne been slightly older when he first went aboard, he probably would have followed a grinning midshipman down a ladder into darkness. At the foot of the ladder, he might well have encountered a throng of ordinary seamen, great swarthy fellows cursing and laughing as, with a pedlar, they bargained for food—bread and red herrings, cherries and clotted cream, and, most popular of all, cases of strong beer.

The grinning midshipman would have beckoned him onward. Young Hearne, increasingly dismayed and striving to ignore the stench of putrid cheese and rancid butter, would have followed the older boy down yet another ladder to the orlop, or lowest deck. There, he would have stood gazing around at his new quarters in the so-called after cockpit—a wretched hole near the mainmast, windowless, airless, dark as a dungeon, and measuring roughly eight feet long, six feet wide, and just over five feet high. In this hole, a board served as dining table. Someone might have fixed a wooden shelf to the wall and placed on it a candle and a chunk of cold salt pork.

Because he was only twelve, Hearne was spared the after cockpit, at least initially. On arriving aboard the *Torbay*, clutching his note from Captain Hood, he was taken in hand either by the gunner, usually a steady man, or else by the schoolmaster, who was charged with furthering his education. He was led to the gunroom, which was situated near the wardroom, where the officers were quartered and which usually had at least a few windows. Hearne's arrival there, even before he

Mr. Midshipman Hearne spent most of his naval career sailing on frigates resembling this fifty-gun two-decker. Frigates were the speediest, most versatile warships, and were especially effective as convoy scouts and escorts.

realized it, proclaimed him a captain's protégé: a Young Gentleman who could walk the quarterdeck.

Nevertheless, during his first night aboard ship, when twelve-year-old Hearne lay alone in his hammock listening to the creaking of the ship and the banter of rough men, he undoubtedly thought of his mother and of their cozy home back in Beaminster, and wondered, "What have I done?"

ACCORDING TO its popular image, the eighteenth-century Royal Navy offered nothing but hardship and misery. Samuel Johnson famously observed, "As to the sailor, when you look down from the quarter deck to the space below, you see the utmost extent of human misery; such crowding, such filth, such stench."

Yet the reality of naval life was complex. Commissioned officers could fare extremely well, and given a commander of some integrity—Captain Hood, for example—even the youngest midshipmen, the "captain's servants," could find some pleasure in His Majesty's Service. Hearne quickly perceived that the most presentable midshipmen received the pleasant duties, such as rowing ashore parties of ladies who had come aboard to dine.

Some captains—and the ambitious Hood was almost certainly among them—insisted that no commissioned officer should appear on deck without a wig, a sword, and a shirt with ruffles, and that no midshipman or petty officer should present himself in a checked shirt or dirty linen. The fastidious young Hearne happily adapted. A strapping, good-looking youth, he enjoyed donning his tarpaulin hat and parading around the quarterdeck with a dirk in his belt. Unlike the ordinary seamen, he had regular access to water for shaving, and he practised this daily ritual so assiduously that he would eventually continue it even in the wilds.

As an officer-in-training, Hearne performed no menial duties— cooked no meals, cleaned no sheets. Indeed, even a twelve-year-old "middie" soon found himself giving orders, or at least relaying them, to adult seamen. The gulf between these Young Gentlemen and the men of the lower deck is captured by Simon Leech in *A Voice from the*

Main Deck. An ordinary seaman, Leech joined the Royal Navy half a century after Hearne, but the relationship he describes was well established by 1757: "In performing the work assigned to me, which consisted in helping the seamen take in provisions, powder and shot, I felt the insults and tyranny of the midshipmen. These little minions of power ordered and drove me around like a dog, nor did I and the other boys dare interpose a word. They were officers; their word was our law, and woe betide the presumptuous boy that dared refuse implicit obedience."

On a Royal Navy ship, those who walked the quarterdeck shared a distinct collective life. Yet the crowded conditions made complete segregation impossible. The ordinary seamen, some of whom might well have been press-ganged aboard, usually included some tough customers. While in harbour, sailors would bring their "wives" aboard. As one naval surgeon observed, nobody inquired after details of the marriage: "The simple declaration was considered as sufficient to constitute a nautical and temporary union ... authorized by long established custom as practised from time immemorial in His Majesty's Navy." A well-bred newcomer might shrink from such depravities, as from the brutality, the drunkenness, and the foul language, but he could not remain unaware of them.

Artist W.J. Higgins did not create A Scene Between Decks *until 1833—seven decades after Hearne did most of his sailing. Clearly, the raucousness of life in port had changed little in the interim.*

A career in the Royal Navy also tested a man's constitution, especially his immune system. A few months before Hearne entered the service, the sixty-four-gun *Stirling Castle* had arrived in Portsmouth carrying 480 sick men, including 225 who had been rounded up by press gangs. When the diseased had been sent ashore, 160 men remained aboard. During the entire Seven Years War, only 1,500 British sailors would be killed in action; 133,708 would die of illness or some disease, most often scurvy, typhus, or yellow fever, the scourge of the West Indies.

The better officers strove to improve conditions. In November 1759 Captain Hood wrote to the Admiralty, "I shall use my best diligence in cleaning and refitting the ship. . . . I shall be obliged to smoke her, she swarms so very abundantly with Ratts. Indeed, it would otherwise be quite necessary to throw out the Ballast . . . which . . . from the length of time it has been in, is so very dirty that I am afraid it would affect the health of my Ship's Company [should it be taken on] another Cruise without washing."

The diet and filth made some men sick, and bad ventilation also gave rise to illness. Typically, at a certain hour each morning, a boy would travel from deck to deck ringing a small bell, and in rhymes composed for the occasion, invite all those who had sores to appear before the mast to be treated by one of the surgeon's mates. In 1761, while Hearne was still sailing with Hood, an officer named William Thompson would publish *An Appeal to the Public* complaining of conditions—and be promptly drummed out of the service.

DURING HIS first years in the Royal Navy, Samuel Hearne shared a mess with half a dozen boys of roughly his own age, eating his meals and hanging his hammock in the gunroom. Every day for three or four hours, he would attend classes, most of them conducted by the schoolmaster. Some schoolmasters came up through the master's branch aboard ship and, lacking much formal education, would content themselves with teaching such skills as setting up rigging, weighing anchor, taking in sails, box-hauling, club-hauling, laying to under different sails, sending down spars in a gale, working off a lee shore in a gale, sounding, sailing in sudden shifting squalls, warping along shore in a chase, hoisting out boats, and anchoring in a crowded harbour in blowing weather.

Other schoolmasters were legitimate scholars, cultivated men who had got into trouble ashore—drinking, gambling, running up debts, making free with the wrong woman. Having incurred the wrath of the powerful, these secretive "mystery men" entered His Majesty's Service to escape a worse fate. One such was Andrew McBride, described by a contemporary as "one of the finest mathematicians in Europe: an excellent writer in prose and verse, an able disputant, and possessed of a mind remarkable for the strictest integrity." An alcoholic, McBride served for years, mostly in the Caribbean, before succumbing to drink and fever. Another notable schoolmaster served on HMS *Gloucester*. He claimed to be a London-born Irishman forced to leave Paris after landing in debt. A chaplain wrote that this man spoke French fluently, "had the manners and address of a gentleman, was a good mathematician and arithmetician, wrote a beautiful hand, conversed with very happy choice of expression, quoted various authors, poets, philosophers and orators; criticized with judgment and novelty of feeling statuary, architecture and painting—and played the violin finely; he, besides, impressed everyone with respect by his air of genteel and humble melancholy."

Samuel Hearne probably never met this individual. But he almost certainly came under the influence of a schoolmaster of this type, an educated man (Hood would have accepted none other) who introduced him to the world of ideas and awakened in him the insatiable curiosity and love of learning that distinguished his later life. Hearne remained under the direct guidance of this petty officer probably until June 1760, when at fifteen, a Young Gentleman now "rated" Ordinary Seaman, he began slinging his hammock not in the gunroom but in the after cockpit on the orlop dock—the midshipmen's mess.

Those who ate and slept there in the dank, overcrowded darkness ranged in age from fifteen to forty or more. Most were Young Gentlemen, but some were ordinary seamen who had progressed through the ranks and served as master's mates, captain's clerks, or assistant surgeons. The makeup of the mess varied, but throughout the Navy, as Michael Lewis observes, the cockpit was "notorious for noisy, riotous and not always pleasant orgies." Worse, because it was located near the surgeon's cabin, the cockpit would serve during naval battles as surgery, operating room, and amputating theatre, with the surgeon practising his bloody craft on the nearest sea-chest.

In these environs, with a guttering candle holding out against the darkness of below-decks, midshipmen would crowd around a rough table to eat, perching on lockers and benches, the shelves around them overflowing not just with plates and glasses, knives and forks, but with dirty stockings and shirts and foul-looking tablecloths, clothes brushes and shoe brushes, cocked hats, dirks, quadrants, and pairs of boots.

The typical meal included a bowl of soup, a chunk of salt pork, and a piece of rock-hard cheese. The diners would begin by devouring small sea biscuits, or "midshipman's nuts," plucking them from a tin bread-basket and washing them down with a "large-jack" of beer. The ship's biscuit, according to the naturalist Sir Joseph Banks, "could be a surprisingly lively insect menagerie." He identified five distinct weevils that lived, burrowed, mated, and multiplied in the hardtack, all tangier than mustard and available at twenty per bite.

Hearne and other middies would find "bargemen" in their soup—tiny reptiles, smooth and black-headed, that tasted cold. Some men augmented their Spartan diet with "millers," skinned rats caught in the bowels of the ship and available for five pence each. When a ship had been at sea for a few months, the fare would get worse. Like the ordinary seamen, midshipmen would discover their bread full of maggots, their beer tasting of sewage (its having been stored in leaky caskets), and their pork so rotten that the requisite boiling in alcohol would reduce it to shreds and crumbs that had to be eaten with a spoon. After drinking the liquid leavings, men would fall ill.

Nor were these a middie's only trials and tribulations. Tyranny reigned in the after cockpit. Young men would be left "to find their own level" while sharing crowded quarters with those several years older. Sooner or later, a sensitive fifteen-year-old would probably find himself confronted by a bully of nineteen or twenty. Knuckling under would not be an option—certainly not for a spirited lad like Hearne.

But fighting back and bloodying an older boy's nose could lead to a mock trial and a "cobbing." Several boys would hold the miscreant over the mess table, pressing his face against it, while others would beat him with a worsted stocking filled with wet sand. Usually the surgeon's assistant would be there to watch for signs of cold sweat and fainting, at which point he would call a halt to the proceedings. The brightest, most articulate boys soon discerned that the best solution to a looming confrontation with a superior force might be to talk your way out of it—an approach that would later serve Hearne well in still more difficult circumstances.

By age sixteen or seventeen, the tall, muscular Hearne would have begun emerging as a leader. Never the toughest or the most aggressive of the Young Gentlemen, almost certainly he was the smartest—not to mention the most decent. If the younger midshipmen needed a champion, invariably they turned to Hearne. If a prank threatened to get out of hand, Hearne would step forward and call for restraint. When a bully went too far, Hearne could be relied upon to intercede. By this time, as well, Hearne would have gained a reputation as an imaginative storyteller. Late at night, when the young men traded anecdotes and ghost stories by the flickering light of a candle, Hearne would spin the final yarn, if only because nobody wished to follow him.

A REGAL PRESENCE, a commander accustomed to exercising god-like authority, Captain Samuel Hood inevitably became the focus, for those who served under him, of endless discussion. Before Samuel Hearne had served long in the Royal Navy, he knew that the captain had got embroiled in a controversy off the coast of North America two years before. The insatiably curious Hearne, already given to soliciting as many versions of a story as he could, pieced together a tale that made him wonder if Captain Hood was the kind of man he himself wished to become.

In HMS *Jamaica*, the captain had been anchored at Charleston, South Carolina, when he received a distress call from Admiral Edward Boscawen in Nova Scotia, where a typhus epidemic was ravaging the British forces. The ambitious Hood, anxious to impress the senior officer, rounded up as many volunteers as he could and sailed to Halifax.

Desperate for manpower—the epidemic would kill more than two

This is probably the most flattering of all portraits of Samuel, Lord Hood (1724–1816), the quintessential Royal Navy man of the eighteenth century. Under him served both Horatio Nelson and Samuel Hearne.

thousand men—Boscawen requisitioned thirty-eight of the new recruits. Hood returned to Charleston, intending to renew his attacks on the French merchant fleet, for which he needed twenty sailors. He advertised as usual but received not a single application. Potential recruits had heard accounts of the epidemic in Nova Scotia and feared that the *Jamaica* would sail not to the balmy Caribbean, as promised, but to the typhus-ridden north.

Captain Hood advertised a second time, underscoring his intention to capture French ships. This would mean considerable prize money—easily the most important inducement for securing volunteers. Capture a single enemy vessel and every man aboard stood to double his year's pay. In addition, he promised volunteers the option of being discharged in Charleston after two months. Unbelievably, there were still no takers.

Now out of patience, Hood sent an armed press gang into colonial Charleston "to pick up all stragglers." The majority of sailors brought aboard, however, proved to be merchant crewmen exempt from impressment, and their various captains claimed them. Nine sailors were ordered to join the *Jamaica*. Fearing a trip to typhus country, they mutinied, seizing their ship's boat and leaving their captain alone in his rudderless craft. Hood sent armed men to hunt the mutineers.

This precipitated a waterfront riot. A mob threw bricks at Hood's men, who managed to retreat with five prisoners. Next morning, merchant mariners retrieved four of the five, but Hood refused to surrender the ringleader, a seaman called Irish whom he intended to punish "for his audacious behaviour in throwing stones at and arming himself against the King's servants." He put Irish in chains while he considered his punishment.

Meanwhile, he wrote to James Glen, the British-appointed governor of South Carolina, complaining of his continuing difficulties in recruiting seamen, and also of the rough treatment his men had encountered: "I have been in many parts of the world, sir, but never in one belonging to the King, my master, where so little regard is paid to His Majesty's ships as I have experienced here."

The governor did not respond. After two weeks, Hood sent a lieutenant ashore to demand a written reply that he could then forward to the Admiralty. Still no response. Finally, early in January, Governor Glen sent word that his constables had searched local "tippling houses" and found sufficient recruits. Knowing Charleston, Glen had deduced that most of the toughs who inhabited the waterfront had fled to Georgia but that, over Christmas, they would drift back into town.

Now, the only problem was the seaman Irish, whose friends and relatives had retained the services of a shrewd lawyer named John Rattray. The unhappy sailor had tried to escape by jumping ship. Hood had declared him a mutineer and clapped him in leg irons. He proposed to try Irish for desertion and make an example of him: he would hang the man from the yardarm.

Rattray enlisted the aid of visiting native people, who had come to Charleston to negotiate treaties. One of the leaders, an eloquent man called the Gun Merchant, publicly deplored the idea that a sailor could be put to death not for murder or some other great crime, but "for an offense that no man would be punished for by the customs of our nation." He called for clemency, and the governor promised to try again.

The following day he relayed the native leader's appeal. And he found an argument that Hood could accept: clemency would benefit His Majesty's Service. It would be far wiser "to oblige these two powerful nations [the Cherokee and the Creek] than to make fifty such examples. . . . Your refusal cannot fail to be productive of much mischief, which if you do not prevent you must bear the blame of."

Captain Hood relented. He released the impudent Irishman into the arms of his weeping wife—but not before he'd had the sailor flogged so severely that he had to be carried ashore.

ON MARCH 14, 1757, when he was two months into the Royal Navy, Samuel Hearne stood on the quarterdeck of HMS *Torbay* gazing seaward, oblivious to the rain. It was just past noon, and great white-capped waves were rolling through the harbour, rocking even the largest ships before smashing into the stone walls that surrounded Portsmouth. Peering into the distance, the Young Gentleman could just discern the dark outlines of ships and boats near Spithead, at the mouth of the harbour. Somewhere in that shadowy throng, HMS *Monarch* lay at anchor.

Every senior naval officer in Portsmouth had gone to attend the event looming aboard that ship. As prescribed by standing regulations, they had donned full-dress uniforms and made their way to the appointed vessel. Unable to board for sheer numbers, they stood at oars in the gusting drizzle. Despite the weather, scores of small boats, both commercial and pleasure craft, had ventured out among the Navy launches. Hearne had even seen men rowing doggedly seaward, simply to be present near the climactic scene of this dark drama.

At a quarter to one, Hearne spotted the *Torbay*'s launch approaching out of the fog, returning with Captain Hood. From the grim look on the captain's face and also the way he sat, arms folded across his chest, Hearne knew that the deed had been done. As he watched the launch approach, he remembered the captain reddening at the mention of a Frenchman named Voltaire, and telling one of his lieutenants, "The Royal Navy can brook no dereliction, no cowardice."

Hearne wondered at the captain's anger. For much of the past year, all England had been furiously arguing about a lost naval battle, a disaster most Englishmen blamed on Admiral John Byng. In May 1756, while attempting to relieve the French siege of St. Philip's Castle on the island of Minorca, Byng had engaged a fleet roughly equal to his own in numbers—twelve French vessels to thirteen English.

Led by the duc de Richelieu, this French fleet had settled into a defensive formation. As the English approached in their traditional line of battle, Byng halted briefly to realign the rear of his fleet. This proved to be a tactical error. The French decimated the leading British vessels, rendering them incapable of rejoining the fray. While Byng tried to regroup, Richelieu wisely remained in a defensive posture.

During the night, the two fleets drifted apart. The next morning, the wind changed direction. For four days, the prevailing winds prevented Byng from renewing his attack. The delay enabled the French to capture nearby Port Mahon, considered indispensable to the war effort. Finally, after calling a council of war, Byng returned to Gibraltar with the remains of his fleet.

When news of this defeat reached home, England reacted with outrage. The Admiralty dispatched a replacement and had Admiral Byng arrested and brought home in disgrace. Throughout the English countryside, Byng was burned in effigy. Admiral Edward Boscawen, Captain Hood's friend, told his wife, "Our disgrace in the Mediterranean has so filled my spirits that I could not sleep all night. What shall we come to?"

By July the influential politician Robert Walpole was writing, "The clamour is extreme, we are humbled, disgraced, angry." A Sussex shopkeeper named Thomas Turner observed in his diary, "Never did the English nation suffer a greater blot."

In July 1756, when Byng arrived in Portsmouth, an enraged mob had to be restrained from attacking him. The disgraced admiral spent the next several months in jail awaiting trial. The court martial began on December 28, 1756, with thirteen senior naval officers sequestered aboard a vessel in Portsmouth harbour.

By now, the fury had abated. Somebody had to take the blame, however, for the naval disaster, and if it wasn't the admiral, it might well be those who had sent him to the Mediterranean with too small a fleet. In certain powerful circles—those frequented by Admiral Boscawen, for example—this notion did not sit well.

As the court martial dragged on into the new year, the Admiralty received petitions for clemency. In January 1757, as Hearne was entering the Navy, the celebrated Voltaire had got involved. An anglophile who had lived in England and who subsequently sparked a revival of European interest in British intellectuals, the French polemicist came out strongly against the scapegoating of Byng. He enlisted the aid of the duc de Richelieu, who had commanded the French forces at Minorca. To Byng, in English, he wrote, "Sir, though I am almost unknown to you, I think it is my duty to send you a copy of the letter I have just received from the Marshal duc de Richelieu. Honour, humanity, and equity order me to convey it to your hands. This noble and unexpected testimony from one of the most candid as well as the most generous of my countrymen, makes me presume your judges will do you the same justice." He enclosed the letter from Richelieu, who argued that Byng had done all that could be expected: "When two men of honour fight together, one of them must be worsted, but it does not count to his discredit. . . . I consider that it is generally agreed that had the English persisted in the engagement, they would have lost their entire fleet. There has never been such an act of injustice as now directed against Admiral Byng, and every officer and man of honour ought to take note of it."

These letters, intercepted and then sent back and forth between English officials, soon appeared in *Scot's Magazine* and other periodicals. Robert Walpole, formerly as outraged as anyone, now strongly opposed the execution of Byng. None of this registered with the Royal Navy.

After sitting continuously for one full month and enquiring of the Admiralty whether they might be given the discretionary power to stipulate a lesser penalty than that prescribed by law—the answer was no—the officers of the court martial returned their verdict. They found Admiral Byng guilty of failing to do his utmost to relieve St. Philip's Castle. They judged this to be a neglect of duty that fell under the twelfth Article of War, which carried an automatic death penalty. The court martial appended an "urgent representation" to the Admiralty for mercy, describing their anguish "in finding ourselves under a necessity of condemning a man to death, from the great severity of the Twelfth Article of War . . . which admits of no mitigation, even if the crime should be committed by an error of judgment only, and therefore for our own conscience's sake, as well as in justice to the prisoner, we pray your Lordships in the most earnest manner to recommend [Byng] to His Majesty's clemency."

By now, however, too many powerful people wanted Byng dead. Before the trial had even begun Boscawen had declared, "We shall have a majority, and he will be condemned." Admiral John Byng would die by firing squad.

In the days following March 14, 1757, given the exhaustive discussion in newspapers and periodicals and the endless back-and-forth of Navy men living in close quarters, Samuel Hearne pieced together a vivid image of how the dark business ended. On the last morning of his life, Admiral Byng rose at five and had his valet shave him. Then he dressed carefully, donning a white waistcoat and stockings, a plain grey coat and breeches, and an elaborate white periwig.

Byng ate breakfast, spent an hour alone in a stateroom writing a last testament, and at nine o'clock received four friends. They brought word that, after all, he would be executed on the quarterdeck, universally recognized as the preserve of officers. The previous day, on learning that Boscawen had ordered him shot on the forecastle, the usually stoic Byng had grown furious, protesting that this represented an indignity to his birth, his family, and his rank in the service. That evening one of his friends had protested to Boscawen, who had grudgingly relented. Now Byng received news of the change with some relief.

As the appointed hour drew near, Byng handed the marshal of the Admiralty a final statement, in which he forgave his enemies and prophesied his own vindication: "If my crime is an error of judgment, or differing in opinion from my judges, and if yet the error of judgment should be on their side—God forgive them, as I do, and may the distress of their minds, and the uneasiness of their consciences, which in justice to me they have represented, be relieved and subside, as my sentiment has done."

At a few minutes before noon, a dignified and composed Admiral Byng led the way from the stateroom to the quarterdeck. The day was dark, the rain steady. On the poop deck, a large contingent of marines stood at arms; in the rigging, scores of seamen perched in orderly rows. In the centre of the quarterdeck stood nine marines in scarlet jackets, three rows of three, muskets in hand. Before them on the deck lay a cushion with sawdust around it, both sodden with rain.

In each of his hands, Admiral Byng carried a neatly folded white handkerchief. He knelt on the cushion, tucked one handkerchief into a pocket, and blindfolded himself with the other. The ship's captain ordered the marines to take their positions. The nine advanced two paces. The front rank knelt and the second rank crouched behind them. The third rank stood erect, muskets in hand, ready if necessary. Admiral Byng reached into his pocket, took out the second white handkerchief, and held it aloft in his right hand.

The captain said, "Cock your firelocks."

The six marines did so.

The captain said, "Present!"

The six brought their muskets to their shoulders. The three nearest muzzles were not two feet from the breast of the kneeling and blind-folded figure at the heart of the action. Admiral John Byng remained motionless. He whispered a few inaudible words then released the white handkerchief. The six marines fired. One shot missed and rico-cheted away. Five struck home. Byng toppled onto his side and did not move again.

In the weeks, months, and even years that followed this day, the imaginative Samuel Hearne would revisit this event again and again, struggling to understand how such an execution could be justified. To him, it seemed . . . shameful. But at the time, summoned by the sound of piping, he hurried to join the other middies in welcoming the captain aboard the *Torbay*. He reminded himself that he owed his very pres-ence to the extended court martial of Admiral Byng because it had cre-ated this temporary posting for Captain Hood. Hearne struggled, and not for the last time, to put the cold-blooded execution out of mind.

3

BLOOD, SMOKE, AND FIRE

LARGE-SCALE naval engagements had become predictable. An admiral of the fleet would lead thirty or more "ships of the line" into a major action, all of them classified, or "rated," according to firepower. In the late 1750s, three-decker first and second rates were armed with ninety or more cannons, while third and fourth rates, the bulk of the fleet, carried sixty-four or seventy-four guns. Vessels in the "line of battle," organized into vanguard, centre, and rear, were expected to remain in formation.

Besides these massive battle ships, the Navy relied heavily on thirty-two gun frigates, which were faster and more mobile—perfect for the ambitious Captain Hood. As on the larger vessels, most of the guns were mounted to broadside, pointing outward from the sides of the ship. A thirty-two-pound cannon had a range of one mile and required a crew of thirteen.

Samuel Hearne learned early how to fire these cannons, which recoiled several yards across the deck. A century before, a well-trained crew could fire one round every four or five minutes. Now, thanks to flintlock firing mechanisms, an efficient crew could fire once a minute. Each thirteen-man crew handled two cannons, one to starboard, one to port. The crew's first captain, assisted by a second, would supervise every firing. Within three or four years, having mastered the rudiments and having served as both second and first gun captain, Mr. Midshipman Hearne commanded six guns, three on each side.

When a ship's captain signalled to clear for action, the effect, according to Captain Marryat, was like that of "a match laid to a long train of gunpowder." Men raced to their battle stations. The junior

Eighteenth-century sea battles were brutal affairs that produced less smoke than suggested in this work by Philip de Loutherbourg. Here, HMS Brunswick *takes on two French warships, one of which, the* Achille, *is losing the last of her masts.*

officers stood with their divisions, their swords drawn, while the captain himself commanded the quarterdeck, assisted by the first lieutenant, the lieutenant of marines, and a party of men with small firearms. The boatswain raced to the forecastle and the gunner to the magazine, from where he would send up powder by way of boys called "powder monkeys."

The carpenter and his mates stood ready to repair any damage with shot plugs, oakum, and tallow. The captains of the guns, priming boxes buckled to their waists, checked shot and wads, while crewmen opened boxes filled with canisters and grapeshot. According to one eyewitness, "When everything was cleared, the ports open, the matches lighted, the guns run out, then we gave them three such cheers as are only to be heard in a British man-of-war."

In battle, the French preferred to attack and disable the rigging, so rendering the opponent immobile. The "English way" was to hold fire until the ship was within range of pistol shot, or even closer, and then to fire devastating broadsides into the enemy hull. Next would come

When Samuel Hearne served under him, Captain Samuel Hood was still making his reputation by seizing French vessels—an activity that usually involved boarding the enemy ship despite stiff resistance. In this painting by Philip de Loutherbourg, French sailors fight back while British tars pour into their corvette.

boarding and seizing control. Taking an enemy vessel was a brutal business, but in this Captain Hood specialized.

An hours-long chase would culminate in the crunch of ship against ship. As the battle was joined, the smoke of the guns would obscure visibility. In the thick of battle, seamen would struggle to improvise rigging to keep their ships mobile, swaying up spars and topmasts the size of large trees while cannons roared and shot whistled around their heads. From both sides, marine sharpshooters would try to pick off senior officers.

When the smoke cleared, a sword-waving lieutenant would lead a boarding party over the bulwarks into the enemy vessel. Often this first wave of men would be driven back by a blaze of fire, with men taking musket balls in the chest and stomach. The second wave might reach the deck. Then would ensue a sword-to-sword, knife-to-knife encounter, with sailors hacking away at each other—an infernal scene of slaughter amidst fire, smoke, and uproar. Some men would lose a limb or be sliced in half by cannonballs, while others would be crushed by falling spars or burned to death.

One French vessel, having begun an engagement with forty-seven men, surrendered after eight were killed and sixteen wounded. Of an initial twenty-four men on the attacking British ship, eleven had been killed or disabled. Those injured in major battles would eventually be transferred to a hospital ship, where they would end up lying below decks in hammocks fourteen inches apart, deprived of sunlight and fresh air, gagging at the stench of festering wounds. Dead bodies, thrown overboard, would be devoured by sharks and carrion crows— a spectacle that survivors would not soon forget.

ON MAY 14, 1757, after not four months in the Navy, Samuel Hearne got his first taste of action. With Captain Hood, he had transferred from the *Torbay* to the *Tartar* and then to the *Antelope*. While cruising off the north coast of France, the fifty-gun *Antelope* encountered the French *Aquilon*, also fifty guns, and drove her aground over a reef in Audierne Bay. Hood battered the stranded vessel into a total wreck, though not without losses: "I had three men killed and thirteen wounded, and was much shattered in my rigging and sails." During the battle, Hearne had seen clusters of iron balls whirl past his head. He had seen these apple-sized balls smash one fellow's kneecap, slice off another's arm, and turn a friendly quarterdeck figure into a man-gled red mass of torn flesh.

Horrified, the twelve-year-old threw up over the side.

The schoolmaster told him, "You'll get used it."

Hearne wasn't convinced.

The following week, the *Antelope* captured two privateers, one of which was carrying wine, brandy, and flour from Bordeaux to Canada. Hood took prisoners and brought them to Portsmouth. There he divided the spoils among his crew. At this time, a captain received three-eighths of all prize monies; midshipmen like Hearne, along with junior warrant officers, warrant officers' mates, and marine sergeants, shared equally in another one-eighth—which could still be a consid-erable sum.

According to the 1797 article in *The European Magazine and London Review*, "They had a warm engagement soon after [Hearne] entered, and took several prizes. The captain told him he could have his share, but he begged, in a very affectionate manner, it should be given to his mother, and she should know best what to do with it."

In July, Hearne moved with Captain Hood to the *Bideford*, a twenty-gun frigate that spent the autumn cruising with the fleet in the Bay of Biscay. Early in 1758, Hood gained command of HMS *Vestal*, a powerful thirty-two-gun frigate. Thirty-five feet wide and 175 feet long, the *Vestal* could accommodate 254 men. A full complement included 18 forecastle men, 21 foretop men, 24 maintop men, 9 mizzentop men, 9 carpenter's crew, and 5 quartermasters. In March 1758, the ship carried 210, yet soon took an active part in the destruction of French fortifications on the Isle of Aix. The frigate spent the remainder of the year cruising the Bay of Biscay between Ushant, an island off the coast of Britanny, and Cape Clear on the northern coast of Spain.

On February 12, 1759, the *Vestal* departed for North America as part of a squadron led by Commodore Charles Holmes. Ten days out of Portsmouth, at six o'clock in the morning, the ship was sailing ahead of the squadron as a scout when one of her men spotted a strange sail in the distance. The *Vestal* gave chase and finally, at two-thirty in the

This painting by Thomas Butterworth depicts a British frigate pursuing a French cutter during the Napoleonic wars of the early 1800s. This single-deck frigate closely resembled HMS Vestal, *on which, as a midshipman, Samuel Hearne chased many an enemy ship.*

afternoon, overtook the larger and heavier *Bellona*, another thirty-two-gun frigate. After a desperate running battle that lasted three hours, the *Bellona* struck her colours, signalling surrender by lowering her flag. She had been dismasted. Only the foremast remained standing, without yardarm or topmast, and that, too, soon toppled over the side. When the *Vestal* came alongside, her own topmasts fell over. Had there been the least breeze, the badly damaged lower masts would have followed.

The *Bellona* had been returning to France from the island of Martinique. In his 1798 biography of navy officers, John Charnock wrote, "The slaughter on board the French ship was considerable, more than thirty of her crew lying dead on the deck when the lieutenant of the *Vestal* took possession of her, exclusive of those whom they had disencumbered themselves of, during the action, by throwing into the sea. The *Vestal* had only five men killed [among them the bosun's mate] and twenty-two wounded; but was otherwise very materially damaged."

Obliged to return for repairs, and also to bring in the badly damaged *Bellona*, the *Vestal* arrived in Portsmouth on March 3. Hood sent prisoners ashore and the wounded to hospital. The following day, according to his logbook, he "came to anchor with the small bower, slipt the cable, came alongside the prize, got the powder out, sent on shore our damaged masts, sent on shore the sails and rigging." Besides the powder, the plunder from the *Bellona*—which carried 14 officers and 191 seamen—included guns, furniture, and two elephant tusks.

The *Bellona* constituted a major prize. Admiral Lord Anson introduced Captain Hood to King George II, who happened to be visiting Portsmouth, and somebody composed a suitably rousing song:

> Our frigate the *Vestal*, both lofty and good,
> And bravely commanded by bold Captain Hood;
> Espy'd a French frigate, to whom we gave chase,
> Who strove for to run, but we forc'd her to face.
> Our gallant commander, 'midst blood, smoke and fire,
> Like great Alexander, did never retire;
> With courage he acted, with prudence he sway'd,
> His words were rever'd, and his orders obey'd.

London newspapers began warning that, with most army troops stationed abroad—27,000 in North America, 10,000 in Germany, 5,000 in Gibraltar, 4,000 in Africa—Great Britain stood vulnerable to an invasion from across the English Channel. William Pitt, the principal secretary of state, had assigned the Royal Navy to blockade the entire northwest coast of France, from Le Havre to south of Brest. As long as that blockade held, he saw no chance of invasion. But then the English discovered that the crafty French were preparing to ferry a multitude of troops across the channel from Le Havre using a flotilla of flat-bottomed transport boats.

In July 1759, with Hearne aboard, the *Vestal* took a leading role in bombarding and destroying this flotilla. Rear Admiral George Rodney, wishing to observe the action at close quarters, directed the operation from the *Vestal*. Afterward, Rodney praised three frigate captains, including Hood, noting that without them he "should have found it extremely difficult and tedious to have anchored the bomb-vessels properly; but these gentlemen, during the night, placed them in a position to effectually bombard the invasion flotilla."

Following this decisive action, the *Vestal* resumed its role in maintaining the blockade. Then, in April 1760, complaining of ill health, Captain Hood asked that the frigate be dispatched to warmer climes—specifically, to the Mediterranean.

That request was granted. During the next three years, the *Vestal* returned to Portsmouth for several refittings. But until April 1763, when the Treaty of Paris ended the Seven Years War, Hearne served mostly in the Mediterranean, enjoying shore leave in the port cities of Italy, Greece, Turkey, and North Africa. He experienced the best that the Royal Navy had to offer.

BY THE TIME the war ended, Mr. Midshipman Hearne had also experienced the worst. He had survived terrifying storms at sea, seen mainsails ripped apart by howling winds, and heard the fearful din as gun carriages broke loose and rolled dangerously around the deck. He had braved the quarterdeck in pounding rain amidst the clanking of chain pumps and the shouts of lieutenants trying to make themselves heard. He had seen the sea towering above the main mast, and the ship hanging poised between giant waves, and one of the main braces snapping like a twig so that two sailors, sent aloft to unfurl a caught sail, went spinning from the yardarm into the sea, never to surface again.

Hearne had seen midshipmen "sent to the masthead" for fighting, giving them three or four hours aloft to regret their misconduct. He had seen ordinary seamen clapped in irons for insolence while their companions waited sullenly to take their turn in the bilbos. And he had seen pressed men brought aboard ship in handcuffs—though not in any great numbers, because Hood's reputation as a maker of prize money attracted plenty of volunteers.

Even so, Hearne had encountered hundreds of pressed men. Royal Navy captains were charged with raising their own crews—even by conducting, if they deemed it necessary, violent conscriptions. Theoretically, they were confined to pressing only seafaring men between the ages of eighteen and fifty-four. In practice, any able-bodied man was in jeopardy unless his attire "unmistakeably proclaimed the gentleman"—and even then, the preacher John Wesley was once hauled aboard a ship (though later released).

Starting in 1755, two years before Hearne joined, presses frequently swept the streets and alleys of dockyard towns, not just in England but in the colonies. Led by the toughest midshipmen, armed gangs would board colliers, fishing vessels, and trading ships to induct sailors. By 1770, only 20 per cent of the Royal Navy's ordinary sailors would be volunteers.

Why such a lack of enthusiasm? Dangerously won prize money aside, merchant seamen earned more than those in the Navy. They enjoyed greater freedom and faced far less discipline, far fewer punishments. Without convening a court martial, a Royal Navy captain could order a man beaten by a bosun's mate wielding a rope's end—a practice so common it would not even turn up in the ship's log. For answering back, a seaman could suffer "gagging." He would be seated with his legs clamped in irons and his hands bound behind his back, all according to navy regulations. His jaws would be pried open and an iron bit forced into his mouth. And there he would remain until the captain decided otherwise.

A petty thief would "run the gauntlet." Stripped to the waist, tied into a wooden tub, he would be hauled around on a grate while crew members lashed him with knotted ropes. During this exercise, the bosun and his mates would employ not a rope but a cat-o'-nine-tails, a whip comprising nine thick, three-foot lashes of knotted cords. They would use this same "cat" to administer a flogging. Without court martial, sailors could be given up to twelve lashes for drunkenness, insubordination, stealing, quarrelling, or neglect of duty.

A piper would summon "all hands to witness punishment." The miscreant would be stripped to the waist and lashed to a grating by his knees and wrists. A bosun's mate would be ordered to begin cutting the man's back. He might tire and weaken after applying six to twelve of the best, and if more had been ordered, a second mate would be called forward to continue the punishment. The most vindictive captains had been known to use court martials to pursue up to 150 lashes.

Around this time, one seventy-four-gun ship of the line recorded 187 misdemeanours in a year, an average total. Of those, 123 involved drunkenness, which usually elicited a dozen lashes, with a repeat offence drawing twice that. One quarter of the trespasses were forgiven, but that still meant 140 floggings—three a week. The typical frigate, considerably smaller, would record one or two floggings per week.

Eighteenth-century captains differed greatly. At one end of the spectrum, Captain Cuthbert Collingwood shunned flogging in favour of excommunication. He would isolate wrongdoers and employ them in extra duty. At the other end, the sadistic Captain Hugh Pigot made a game of flogging the last man down from aloft; eventually, his half-crazed crewmen mutinied and murdered both him and his officers.

Fortunately for Samuel Hearne, Captain Hood stood closer in attitude to Collingwood than to Pigot. According to Frank C. Bowen, "He was respected by the lower deck, who understood just what he wanted and obeyed him willingly. He was cantankerous and a merciless critic, although very touchy when criticized himself. . . ." Sir William Hotham, who served with the long-lived Hood decades after Hearne did, observed, "Without the least disposition to severity, there was a something about him which made his inferior officers stand in awe of him."

Canadian historian Richard Glover surmises that Hood

was probably a kindly and paternal master. . . . His logs reveal a real concern for his men's well-being, for the cleanliness of their quarters and the goodness of their food and drink. His punishments were rather few, and not very severe for an age that had few inhibitions about making generous use of the cat-o'-nine-tails; according to his muster-rolls desertion from his ship was pleasantly infrequent. Under such a captain the young Hearne's situation in the Navy was perhaps much more like that of a boy under a good housemaster in a boarding-school than might at first appear.

Glover leans to generosity. The ambitious Hood was a decent man but a hard one, if only because to rise in the Royal Navy he had to be. Yet Hood was not a warped man—not a man like Captain William Bligh, whose cruelties engendered the mutiny on the *Bounty*, or like Captain Edward Edwards, who savagely punished some of those mutineers. Fiercely loyal to His Majesty's Service, Hood stood guard against the slightest threat to the standards of the Royal Navy. Admiral Horatio Nelson, to whom Hood taught tactics, would one day defend him against political attack by calling him "the best officer, taking him altogether, that England has to boast of." Eventually, Hood would take a seat in the British parliament, declaring, "I am neither Whig nor Tory, but only a naval officer."

Late in 1759, while blockading the coast of France, Captain Hood learned of an impending event that he was duty-bound to attend. And so, in the *Vestal*, he joined the fleet off Brest. By this time, almost three years into the Navy, Hearne would have witnessed not just severe flogging but "flogging through the fleet."

This punishment, meted out for major crimes like desertion, was almost the equivalent of a death sentence. Each ship in the fleet would send a boat to the malefactor's vessel, along with a guard of marines. The prisoner would be placed in a launch, together with a master-at-arms and a doctor. He would be stripped to the waist and lashed by his wrists to a capstan bar. An officer would read the sentence and order the bosun's mates to do their duty. They would apply the cat-o'-nine-tails to the man's back. After twenty-five lashes administered by four different mates, the prisoner would be cut down.

While serving in the Royal Navy, Hearne inevitably witnessed more than a few flog-gings. Here, a seaman has been lashed to a grating for punishment. With the marines drawn up on the quarterdeck above, a second seaman has stripped off his shirt and stepped forward to insist that he himself is the culprit. Caught up in such a scene, Hearne would have stood among the junior officers at the lower left.

He would sit with a blanket wrapped around his shoulders while, to the doleful piping of "The Rogue's March," the boats rowed to the next ship in the line. There, while sailors looked on from above, as required, another four bosun's mates would apply twenty-five lashes. This procedure would be repeated until the prisoner had been flogged alongside every ship in the fleet—an exercise that would last at least half a day. If the man passed out and could not be revived by any means, he would be taken to sick bay. If he recovered, the floggings would be resumed until the sentence was completed. In a few cases, the victim survived.

On this occasion, off Brest, a court martial had settled on a more certain course. Two ordinary seamen, overheard speaking of mutiny, had been sentenced to hang from the yardarm. They had been clamped in irons and confined to a cabin. At length, the fatal morning arrived. At eight, the cannons boomed, and the master-at-arms brought the prisoners to the quarterdeck.

Two boats from each ship in attendance lay alongside, several men in each—among them, Mr. Midshipman Hearne. On the vessels nearby, crew members in white trousers and blue jackets hung in clusters from the rigging. On the quarterdeck, guards of marines stood along each gangway.

A shrill whistle signalled: "All hands attend punishment."

In eerie silence, seamen climbed ladders. Soon the prisoners stood in the middle of the quarterdeck. The captain read the sentence and the order for execution. The chaplain, near tears, contributed psalms and prayers. The prisoners were asked if they were ready. One requested a glass of wine and drank it off at a gulp. The other asked to address the ship's company. Given permission to do so, he told those who had begun the talk of sedition, "You have made fools of us. Let our fate be a warning."

Marines pinioned the arms of both prisoners, and the chaplain read a funeral service as guards marched the men to the forecastle at the front of the ship. Here, a platform had been erected. A tail block had been attached at the extremity of each yardarm, and through it ran a rope. One end reached the platform, while the other ran along the yard and then down onto the main deck. The guns were primed and ready to fire. At the fore of the ship, directly beneath the scaffold, a noose was made fast around the neck of each prisoner.

The condemned men, weak in the knees, mounted the platform. A lieutenant pulled white caps over their faces. On the main deck, twenty or thirty men responded to an order by picking up the end of each rope. The captain waved his white handkerchief. A cannon boomed. The men on the main deck hauled on the ropes and, in an instant, the two sailors were swinging by their necks, kicking and squirming, one at the end of each yardarm.

These hangings did not trouble Captain Hood, who saw in them only the final movement of justice. But they disturbed the impressionable Hearne, still just fourteen, calling forth thoughts of Admiral John Byng. Under the tutelage of the schoolmaster, the wide-eyed boy had become an independent-minded youth. What was he to make of these hangings? Two young fellows, neither of them clever, clearly followers rather than leaders, had been strung up merely for grumbling.

Hearne could not help wondering: Was this justice? He knew better than to articulate this question. He knew what Captain Hood thought and that he would gain or change nothing by voicing dissent. As long as he stayed in the Royal Navy, he would have to bear silent witness to ruthless injustice. For the first time he wondered, could he do it?

FOUR YEARS LATER, in April 1763, an eighteen-year-old midshipman wearing knee-length breeches, square-buckled shoes, and a three-quarter-length coat, his blond hair hidden beneath his stylish black tricorn, stood at the railing of HMS *Vestal* as she sailed toward Portsmouth harbour. An experienced sailor with a gift for navigation, Samuel Hearne could hardly wait to step ashore and begin his new life.

At Spithead, the *Vestal* entered the usual floating forest of masts, and the young man watched several merchant vessels negotiate a careful exit from the harbour. He reflected with some excitement that few of those ships were embarking on anything like the transformative voyage he himself was about to undertake.

Hearne had requested a letter of reference from Captain Hood. Now, as he stood on the starboard side of the quarterdeck enjoying the breeze, he waited, hoping to catch the captain's eye. Circumstance had played a role in bringing him to this crossroads. As a result of the Peace of Paris, the Royal Navy was dramatically reducing its deployments of both ships and men. With the *Vestal* bound for drydock, Hood himself would have no vessel to command—not for a while, anyway.

Commissioned officers, the captain among them, would receive half pay while they waited for another posting. But Hearne had no commission. Nor was he old enough, at eighteen, to take the examination that could lead to one. He knew very well that midshipmen had found various ways around the age requirement, but courage and ability could take a man only so far. In the end, he would still need friends with "quarterdeck interest."

To confirm the truth of this, Hearne needed only to contemplate the career of Captain Hood. By marrying the influential daughter of the mayor of Portsmouth, Hood had gained intimate access to some of the most powerful families in England. This had enabled him to secure command of the *Jamaica*, which he had then used to create a bond with the powerful Boscawen. That relationship had spawned subsequent postings, and so it went—the politics of advancement in the Royal Navy.

Many a midshipman, lacking powerful friends and relations, had passed the ordinary examination for lieutenant then waited a long, weary time for a vacancy and never found one. Samuel Hearne would have known Billy Culmer, who began sailing with Hood at the same time as himself and who, in 1791, would claim to be the oldest midshipman in the Navy. As J.A. Gardner writes, "it remains conceivable that even poor Billy had once been a real 'young gentleman,' who hoped to become a lieutenant, and was merely an extreme instance of what happened to those who commanded no influence."

Samuel Hearne was no Billy Culmer. Sooner or later, Captain Hood would acquire another ship. If Hearne waited, he could rejoin Hood, who would, when the time came, contrive to get him his commission. The captain had virtually promised as much, and Hearne knew him to be a man of his word. All he had to do was bide his time—but waiting did not suit him.

Looking back, Hearne decided he had no cause for complaint. The *Dictionary of National Biography* summarizes his naval career with the broad-brush description, "served as a midshipman in the royal navy." But the muster rolls and logbooks at the Public Records Office provide greater detail and explode the mistaken notion that Hearne was "never more than an ordinary seaman."

After joining Hood in January 1757, Hearne had moved with him through the *Torbay*, the *Tartar*, the *Antelope*, and the *Bideford* to the *Vestal* (as of March 8, 1758). For just over three years, ending in June 1760, Hearne sailed as a "captain's servant." On June 18, 1760, at age fifteen, Hearne became an ordinary seaman, in which capacity he continued for fifteen months. On September 1, 1761, he was promoted to able-bodied seaman, and on June 25, 1762, at age seventeen, to quartermaster's mate.

The rapidity of Hearne's advancement testifies to his status as a Young Gentleman. The true able-bodied seaman was the most skilled sailor aboard ship. He came from the lower deck and had to serve three years as an ordinary seaman and be at least eighteen—and even then, to be rated an "AB" he had to be exceptional. To become a quartermaster's mate, he required still more skill and experience.

For officers-in-training like Hearne, these ratings signalled preparations to face the oral examination necessary to qualify for a commission. They also suggested what special skills a Young Gentleman had
acquired. Hearne had been serving in the master's line, which was
responsible for navigation and conducting a ship from one port to the
next. The master and his mates managed the sails, maintained the rigging, sails, and stores, and kept the logbooks. As a quartermaster's
mate, Hearne also supervised the stowing of ballast and provisions in
the hold and the coiling of cables on their platforms. Finally, he kept
the time and helped steer the ship, an activity that, Hollywood por-
trayals to the contrary, required at least two men at the wheel.

By the end of the century, the master's mate—rated immediately
above the quartermaster—would become an intermediate position
between midshipman and lieutenant. In 1763, having established
himself in this line, Hearne was on his way to becoming a commissioned officer. If the war had continued, given his abilities and barring
the unforeseen, and even without notable quarterdeck interest, he
could probably have made lieutenant within a couple of years, and certainly within three or four. But then what?

Then, almost certainly, he would have languished in obscurity—
not just for lack of connections, and certainly not for lack of ability,
but because, in the end, clever and resolute and articulate as he was,
Hearne would not have been able to hide his true nature for much
longer. He was a born dissenter, a natural challenger of authority, an
inveterate rejecter of brutishness and cruelty.

How had he come to this? Any Royal Navy ship could count at least
a couple of well-educated men among its officers. In conjunction with
the schoolmaster, they would conduct formal classes for young midshipmen, teaching professional skills such as trigonometry and navigation, but also, depending on their backgrounds, ranging afield to
treat literature and French, without which, many argued, no officer
could declare himself a gentleman.

These officers encouraged younger men, lending out their books
and even their cabins for study. All his life, Hearne sought and found
mentors, and there can be no doubt that while sailing with Captain
Hood, he discovered at least one to direct his newly awakened passion

for learning. One naval historian observes that Hood himself, though cantankerous and crotchety, could be kind to young officers who did their duty: "They turned to him for advice in their difficulties, and that advice was generously given without stint."

Yet it seems unlikely that Hearne became one of Hood's favourites, if only because temperamentally the two men were so radically different. At this point, Hood was consumed with fighting a war and advancing his own career. It is far more likely—indeed, virtually certain—that either the *Vestal*'s schoolmaster or one of Hood's lieutenants guided the midshipman's education.

Like other men his age, Hearne had arrived in the Royal Navy knowing the works of Daniel Defoe. While sailing around the English Channel and the Mediterranean Sea, he would also have encountered and enjoyed *Roderick Random* by Tobias Smollett—the first serious novelist to draw on first-hand experience of the Royal Navy for his most vivid characters and scenes. Yet even Hearne's enthusiasm for Smollett could not compare with his passion for the work of the iconoclastic Voltaire, hailed by many as the foremost intellectual of the age. Hearne might not have read *Candide* as early as 1759, when it appeared in English, but he had certainly perused it by 1762, when in France the book was banned and publicly burned.

In *Candide*, young Hearne discovered much of interest, but he especially admired the passage devoted to Admiral John Byng:

At Portsmouth the shore was crowded with people eagerly watching a big man who was kneeling on the deck of a man-of-war, with a bandage over his eyes. In front of him stood four soldiers, each of whom phlegmatically fired three bullets into the big man's skull. The crowd then dispersed, with an air of satisfaction.

"What is all this," said Candide. "What demon has the mastery of the world?" He inquired who the big man was. "An admiral," he was told.

"And why was that admiral killed?"

"Because he did not kill enough men himself. He fought an engagement with a French admiral, and it is thought that he did not sufficiently close with him."

"But surely, then, the French admiral was as far from him as he was from the other?"

"That is undeniable. But in this country, it is found requisite now and then to kill an admiral, in order to encourage the others."

Candide was so shocked that he would not set foot on shore.

By April 1763, though he made no claims as an intellectual, Samuel Hearne had come under the influence of Voltaire. And as he sailed into Portsmouth, he thought of the hanging of the two would-be mutineers off Brest, dupes rather than ringleaders. Those hangings, he felt, constituted cruel and unusual punishment. And the shooting of Admiral Byng verged on judicial murder.

During the past few months, Hearne had also begun to question the wisdom of the endless warring against the French, certain of whom he so admired. Finally, he had come to suspect the truth: he could not remain much longer in the Royal Navy. The signing of the Treaty of Paris had affected only his timing.

But now, at last, Captain Hood stepped onto the quarterdeck.

Protocol demanded that all those on deck move to the other side, but as the midshipman started forward (and just as he had hoped), the captain called. "Mr. Hearne?"

Hood led the midshipman into his cabin, where he shuffled through papers and extracted a handwritten page. "That reference you requested, Mr. Hearne."

"Thank you very much, Sir. This will make a great difference."

"In time, you would have made a fine officer."

Hearne wondered fleetingly if the captain knew him at all. Yet this, he realized, was the closest Hood could come to offering a blessing. "Thank you, Sir."

"You are travelling to London, then."

"To enter the merchant service, yes—though first I will visit my mother in Beaminster."

"Greatest city in the world, London." Hood clasped his hands behind his back and gazed out the window at the sea. "Also, the most expensive." He glanced at the young man. "Don't give away all your prize money, Mr. Hearne."

"No, sir."

"Very well, Mr. Hearne. That will be all."

Hearne saluted smartly. As he emerged onto the quarterdeck, he felt a rush of exhilaration. The sun shone no more brightly than before, and the white sails snapped no more briskly—but he was free! A great burden had been lifted from his shoulders. He was eighteen years old, a young man bound for the greatest city in the world. He was free.

4

CANDIDE
IN LONDON

ARRIVING FROM the southwest in a crowded stagecoach, his triangular black hat cocked at a jaunty angle, his stockings gartered just below the knee, his knee-length coat open to display his brocade waistcoat, Samuel Hearne entered the most populous centre in western Europe, a raucous metropolis of 750,000. Rivalled in size and vitality only by Paris, London was ten times larger than any other city in England. One in ten English people made their home here, and each year, some 9,000 immigrants turned up from elsewhere in the country, attracted by jobs and high wages, 30 per cent of them from as far away as Beaminster. Tax officials had recently determined that London contained 21,600 retail outlets—one-seventh of the combined total of England and Wales.

Even so, London covered only fifteen square miles, and the same year Hearne arrived with £20 or £30 stitched into his clothing, two gentlemen walked the perimeter of the city in seven hours. Most Londoners lived within reach of open country. From the roof of a building at the western edge of the city, a newcomer could look out and see green fields to the north and west; to the south, he would see marshes, market gardens, and the River Thames; and to the east, the Thames again, with docks and wharves and myriad sailing ships, beyond which lay the fields of Kent and Essex. While looking out in late spring or summer, when the sky was relatively free of the suffocating coal smoke, the rooftop spectator could not help but notice that this was a city of monuments and church spires, with Westminster Abbey, the Tower, and the dome of St. Paul's Cathedral standing tall amongst the more modest spires of almost three hundred places of worship.

Westminster Abbey, originally the abbey church of a monastery, had become a major London landmark by the mid-eighteenth century. This view of the west front was done in the 1800s by Thomas H. Shepherd.

Yet the glory of London, as Samuel Johnson observed, consisted not in its monuments, streets, and squares, and not in its churches, but in "the multiplicity of human habitations which are crowded together." Mansions in once-fashionable districts had been supplanted by inns, taverns, and coffee houses. The Strand was lined with booksellers and print shops, with milliners and haberdashers and goldsmiths, their front windows alive with elaborate displays, their brightly painted shop signs lying flat against their storefronts in accordance with a statute passed the previous year, the result of people having been injured by falling signs. Even the side streets were thick with pedlars, fruit sellers, and card sharps, and loud with the clip-clop of horses' hooves, the clank of metal carriage wheels on cobblestone, the bell-ringing of scavengers, and the yodelling cries of milk women, the whole infernal racket punctuated by the clamour of puppeteers, street dancers, and strolling players.

The upper classes travelled around London by horse-drawn landau, the ostentatious among them employing "running footmen" to trot ahead of these carriages brandishing white canes to clear traffic. Rather than walk three blocks, or even across a muddy street—thereby risking a "beau-trap," a shaky pavement stone that would splash white silk stockings—gentlemen used sedan chairs as short-haul taxis, and teams of chairmen would skim along footpaths carrying these decorated encumbrances on their shoulders, splashing through puddles of water and urine, and warning pedestrians to move out of the way by crying, "Have care!" or "By your leave, Sir!" If rain were falling—no unusual circumstance—they would trundle the sedan chair right into a building rather than inconvenience their customers.

After securing lodgings in a rooming house, the eighteen-year-old Hearne began exploring a world in which labourers earned ten shillings a week while lords, betting on "the mains" at Whitehall cockpit, would gamble away hundreds and even thousands of pounds in a single evening. This was a world in which educated men would fight a duel to the death over the pronunciation of a Greek phrase, while the children of the poor would have their teeth extracted for sale to the toothless rich. A world in which a gentleman who owned an enamelled snuffbox for each night of the week would bathe only twice a year, and elegant ladies would purchase ivory-handled back-scratchers to battle the lice that tormented them.

By contemporary Western standards, London was filthy. The flush toilet would not be invented until 1775, so even the wealthy used chamber pots and basement cesspits that would be emptied, eventually, by nightsoil men. Few Londoners could afford this service, and many would wait until dark, then toss garbage and slops into the streets and back alleys. Dead dogs, cats, and even horses would be left to decay by the roadside, and open cesspits gave rise to cholera.

Epidemics swept London regularly. Besides cholera and typhus, or jail fever, which was carried by water and which probably killed Hearne's father, they included diphtheria, dysentery, scarlet fever, whooping cough, tuberculosis, measles, and mumps, all of which could be treated—ineffectively—with nothing but tender loving care. Medical procedures were harrowing at best—mainly bloodletting and cupping, which involved placing small heated cups on the back and then lancing the ensuing blisters. There were no antibiotics, no anaesthetics.

Visitors complained that London stank—not just of cesspits, but also of thick, black coal smoke, which enshrouded the city for months at a time. This all-encompassing smoke was the result of coal fires used not only to heat homes, but also by tradesmen working in glasshouses and earthenware factories, in blacksmith shops and gunsmith shops and dyer's yards. Worst of all was the stench of communal graves. Dug deep enough to accommodate seven layers of coffins with three or four coffins in each tier, these pits would be left open until full. As the coffins piled up and the corpses putrefied, spreading dangerous effluvia, the smell would get so bad that ministers would conduct services only at a distance.

Against this backdrop, David Garrick was transforming British theatre, Joshua Reynolds was painting portraits that would earn him a knighthood, and Samuel Johnson was creating the Literary Club, which began meeting weekly at the Turk's Head Coffee House in Soho. Even the middling sort of Londoner could visit Ranelagh or Vauxhall, those glittering pleasure gardens, or see the king's recently acquired elephant exercising in St. James's Park. Other popular entertainments included cockfighting, badger-baiting, and, eight times a year, on designated holidays, festive public hangings.

At Tyburn, where Marble Arch now stands, a permanent gallows had been steadily in use for two centuries. In the 1760s, 246 people would swing from "Tyburn tree," an average of 25 a year. These hangings drew crowds of 30,000 or more. Condemned prisoners, having been kept in rat-infested Newgate prison, would be transported down Oxford Road, a rough highway that passed through the slums of St. Giles. For two hours, while chained in open carts, they would be subjected to derision and physical abuse. At the hangings, spectators who wanted a better look could rent powerful spy glasses.

FOR ALMOST two hundred years, London Bridge Water Works had been providing most of the city's drinking water. This engineering marvel drew the sustaining liquid from the River Thames, a waterway that, according to Smollett, was thick with the filth of London and Westminster—with not just human excrement, but "all the drugs, minerals, and poisons used in mechanics and manufacture, enriched with the putrefying carcasses of beasts and men, and mixed with the scourings of all the wash-tubs, kennels, and common sewers within the bills of mortality."

Because his father had once run the entire system, Samuel Hearne took a special interest. Standing at the north end of the London Bridge, he studied the twenty-foot waterwheels, calculating that they rotated six times a minute. For the functioning of this complex machinery his father had borne final responsibility, contending against freak tides and bad weather. During the winter just past, ice had jammed the waterwheels to a halt. And now, as in his father's day, the wooden water pipes proved a constant trial. Created out of elm trees in seven-foot lengths, they seeped continually and needed to be replaced every twenty years. As well, frozen pipes would burst and require immediate action. The Water Works inspector, who would have reported to Hearne's father, had the power to seize and remove carriages or horses that blocked the way.

Hearne walked to the middle of London Bridge. Standing at the railing, looking back at the city, he tried and failed to locate the house in which he had lived his first few years. His father's position at the Water Works would have generated an annual income of several

When Samuel Hearne looked north from London Bridge, he saw a view resembling this one—although artist Gordon Home has greatly exaggerated the width of the street, which was at most twenty feet. The clock of St. Magnus the Martyr bears ornamental features later blown off in a gale.

hundred pounds. Securing that post would have required not only family connections, but payment of a considerable sum, probably a couple of thousand pounds. That way forward did not lie open.

How to proceed? If his father had lived, Hearne would probably have joined the ranks of professional men—lawyers, clergymen, teachers, physicians—who moved easily among the landed gentry and the wealthy merchants. But clever and talented as he was, he lacked both connections and formal qualifications. He felt attracted to Fleet Street, where countless scribblers and pamphleteers eked out a living, but at eighteen he did not have the literary skill to succeed there.

A few ex-midshipmen had sought work as gentleman's valets, having heard that with "vails," or tips, they could easily earn £50 a year. Most had trouble finding positions, however, because as former officers-in-training, they were known to aspire to gentleman status. Valets needed to know their place. Hearne had acquired the requisite fastidiousness—the fondness for clean linen, polished shoes, and powdered wigs—but felt repelled by the idea of relying on tipping, a practice the wealthy James Boswell characterized as "unhospitable, troublesome and ungracious."

On his way to London Bridge, Hearne had walked along docks and quays overflowing with warehousemen, watermen, dockers, porters, packers, seamen, shipbuilders, coal brewers, and lightmen. Thousands of Londoners—one-quarter of the city's workforce—were employed along the river, either at the 140 wharves or among the 2,500 service craft (lighters, barges, billy boys).

Standing on that bridge, Hearne had only to lift his eyes from the waterwheels to see his way forward. The River Thames, wider and shallower than it is today, was a forest of masts. London had long since surpassed Amsterdam as the world's leading centre of trade and commerce. The port handled three-quarters of British trade, which meant exporting not just woollens, but increasing amounts of grain, metalwares, foodstuffs, lead, and tin, as well as cloth and manufactured goods. From Europe, England imported linen, flax, hemp, timber, and iron; from the Mediterranean, silk, wine, fruit, oil, and brandy; and from India, calico, silk, pepper, and other spices. Coal came to London from Newcastle and Sunderland; spruce and fir from

London Bridge can be seen in the background of this painting by J.T. Serres, which suggests the importance of the River Thames to England's economy. In Hearne's day, the British merchant marine included 2,000 ocean-going vessels and 7,000 that plied coastal waters.

Norway and the Baltic countries; iron from Sweden; sugar, molasses, and tobacco from the West Indies.

Britain had 9,000 merchant ships at sea—2,000 ocean-going vessels and 7,000 "coasters." At times, the Thames became so crowded that the queue of ships anchored in mid-channel, waiting to be unloaded by lighters, often extended for miles. By the end of the century, 800 British ships would be trading to the Baltic, 600 trading to North America, 400 to the Mediterranean, and 700 to the West Indies. The Newcastle coal trade occupied another 500 vessels. Then there were the fisheries: 700 vessels with 4,000 fishermen were at work in the Newfoundland cod fishery, while the Greenland and South Pacific whale fisheries occupied 150 ships averaging 300 tons.

A few great trading companies dominated this vast trade: the East India Company, the Levant Company, the Russian Company, the South Sea Company, and the Hudson's Bay Company. Each of these kept a head office in London; the East India Company had its in Leadenhall Street, and that of the Hudson's Bay Company was in

Fenchurch Street. Not long after arriving in London, Hearne probably made his way to the Marine Coffee House in Birchin Lane, which attracted merchant mariners. Certainly, he went to Lloyd's Coffee House in Lombard Street, corner of Abchurch Lane.

For seventy years, Lloyd's had been catering to merchants, shipowners, and shipmasters, who gathered daily to exchange news and information. Eventually, because it attracted underwriters of marine insurance, the coffee house would give rise to Lloyd's of London, the world-famous insurance company. Already, Edward Lloyd's handwritten "ship's lists" had evolved into a printed "Lloyd's List" which offered news of ship arrivals and departures—and so of possible hirings.

In 1763, Samuel Hearne probably worked through Lloyd's. If he had found employment with a major commercial operation—the East India Company or the South Sea Company, for example—the record would mention it. We do know that in 1766 Hearne secured a first mate's posting on a ship owned by another leading concern. To qualify for that posting, Hearne must have started working in 1763 with one or more smaller companies. During the next three years, while based in London, he diligently worked his way upward, probably to the captaincy of a small vessel, certainly to the position of first mate, the minimum he would have required to secure a major posting.

EIGHTEEN MONTHS after he arrived in London, Samuel Hearne noticed a new sprightliness in the letters he received from his mother. Having perused two or three lively missives, he overcame the natural incredulity of a son and understood that Diana Hearne was being courted by a businessman originally from London. She had met Samuel Paine through mutual friends. A widower, somewhat older, Paine was a prosperous dyer who visited Beaminster frequently to acquire cloth. He lived now in the town of Peckham, just south of London and west of Greenwich, where his properties included two houses.

When he recovered from his initial astonishment, Hearne responded with enthusiasm. If his mother remarried and moved to Peckham, so near London, he would be able to visit her far more frequently. Where Beaminster required a journey of several days each way, Peckham he could reach in a few hours. This, of course, his mother had already realized. He pointed it out anyway, then went about his business.

SAMUEL HEARNE'S London was a city of five thousand coffee houses. These had proliferated in recent decades as a result of a change in national habits—a dramatic increase in coffee consumption promoted by the East India Company, purveyors of various fine roasts. Coffee houses served as hubs of social activity, transmitting news and information and functioning as postal centres and lost-property offices and business addresses, as doctors' consulting rooms, matrimonial agencies, Masonic lodges, auction houses, and gambling dens, and sometimes even as "temples of Venus," in which case the sign out front would feature a woman's arm or hand holding a coffee pot.

Most coffee houses sold not only coffee but also chocolate, wine, and brandy, providing these from a small bar in one corner of a candlelit room. Most were simple affairs, with bare wooden floors, and tables with benches or Windsor chairs, although some provided booths or snugs for more intimate conversation. Coffee houses catered to particular clienteles, some attracting scholars and wits, others actors, newspapermen, or politicians. Some offered games of chess, draughts, or backgammon, others hasty-pudding-eating contests and gambling.

Booksellers frequented coffee houses in Paternoster Row. Gentlemen of fashion visited those near Pall Mall, with Whigs going to the St. James and Tories to the Cocoa-Tree. Authors gravitated to Covent Garden and Temple Bar. Many people gave priority to coffee houses over lodgings, inspiring the expression, "He lodges at home but lives at the coffee house."

In the more eclectic coffee houses, where gentlemen rubbed shoulders with merchants and ambitious young mariners, Samuel Hearne exercised his passion for storytelling and political discussion. Intellectual currents were swirling into the English metropolis from abroad, especially from France, whose culture was giving shape and texture to the Enlightenment. Having escaped from the rigidities and suppressions of the Royal Navy, Hearne found himself furiously debating the merits of Denis Diderot and Jean-Jacques Rousseau while venerating, above all, the thinker who so dominated the intellectual climate of the times that later scholars would call it the Age of Voltaire.

A brilliant satirist, Voltaire decried superstition, fanaticism, and oppression while encouraging the habit of critical thought. An admirer of older cultures—Greek, Roman, Indian, Chinese—Voltaire presented himself not as a Frenchman, but as a citizen of the world. His wildly successful *Candide*, an attack on the fatalistic notion that everything works out for the best, had been inspired by the destruction of Lisbon in 1755, when an earthquake not only destroyed churches, monuments, and irreplaceable works of art, but killed tens of thousands of innocent people. How could such an event be reconciled with the loving kindness of a Christian god?

In 1762, outraged church authorities banned and burned the subversive *Candide*, so guaranteeing increased demand for it. Three years later, as Hearne followed the story in London newspapers and talked about it in coffee shops, Voltaire denounced an even worse outrage: the gruesome murder of Jean François Lefebvre, chevalier de La Barre, who had been found guilty of irreverence for failing to bare his head and kneel at the passage of a religious procession. After torturing the man, his Christian judges tore out his tongue, cut off his head, and committed his body to the flames. With his body, they burned a copy of Voltaire's *Philosophical Dictionary*, which they identified as the cause of the sacrilege.

Voltaire had published the *Dictionary* the previous year. It was not a conventional dictionary, but a collection of essays, alphabetically organized, whose incendiary topics included Apocalypse, Atheism, Baptism, Beauty, Character, Chinese Catechism, Christianity, Destiny, God, Equality, Prejudice, Religion, and War. Voltaire wished to see organized Christianity, which he called the "Christ-worshipping superstition," eradicated root and branch.

The eloquence and ferocity of Voltaire's attack on Christianity would not be equalled until 1883, when Friedrich Nietzsche published *Thus Spake Zarathustra*. Even so, Voltaire stopped short of embracing atheism, which he declared "the vice of clever people even as superstition is the vice of fools." He remained a skeptical deist, willing to entertain the idea of God as the ultimate embodiment of a rational, all-pervasive order, while denying revealed religion—whether Christianity, Islam, or Hinduism—and rejecting the notion that God, a supreme being, would intervene in the natural order.

This complex, subtle thinker would be denounced as iniquitous in February 1766 by no less a personage than Samuel Johnson, an articulate provincial who, holding forth at the Mitre Tavern, spoke for much of England. Dr. Johnson did not, however, speak for a certain ex-midshipman with a mind of his own.

WITHOUT PRETENDING to be an intellectual, Samuel Hearne admired Voltaire's humanism, eloquence, and courage. But it was in a different field that he yearned to emulate the Frenchman's spirit of adventure. Early in 1766, at Lloyd's Coffee House, he heard that the Hudson's Bay Company was seeking to hire an adventurous young mariner. And on visiting the head office in Fenchurch Street, he determined that the Company was planning to expand its whaling

To Samuel Hearne, nothing could have been more commonplace than this view of A Quay on the Thames at London, *done by Samuel Scott around 1756. The cargo of rum, tea, sugar and oil strewn about the quay, and under inspection by a tricorn-hatted customs officer, undoubtedly came from the merchantman in the background.*

operations out of Prince of Wales Fort, the most imposing fortification on Hudson Bay.

To the ambitious Hearne, this sounded intriguing. On February 12, 1766, he returned for a second interview. Would the HBC be willing to offer him the captaincy of one of its sloops? The answer was no, not immediately; both vessels had captains already. However, given his experience and capabilities, especially as a navigator, the Company was prepared to hire him as a first mate at an annual salary of £25. When an opening arose, assuming that his services proved satisfactory, the HBC would promote him to captain. He could sail with the first supply ship at the end of May.

This offer fit his plans perfectly. Hearne had recently received a letter from his mother announcing that she was to marry Samuel Paine. She and his sister, Sarah, still unwed at twenty-two, would take up residence in nearby Peckham. The young adventurer would be able to attend his mother's wedding and help her to relocate, then return to London with time to spare. He accepted the quill pen, dipped it in black ink, and, in his neat, artistic hand, signed the proffered agreement.

Afterward, swinging through the streets of London, Samuel Hearne could scarcely contain his mounting excitement. Hudson Bay! The wilds of North America! He started to run. He was embarking on the adventure of a lifetime.

Part Two

MAKER OF HISTORY

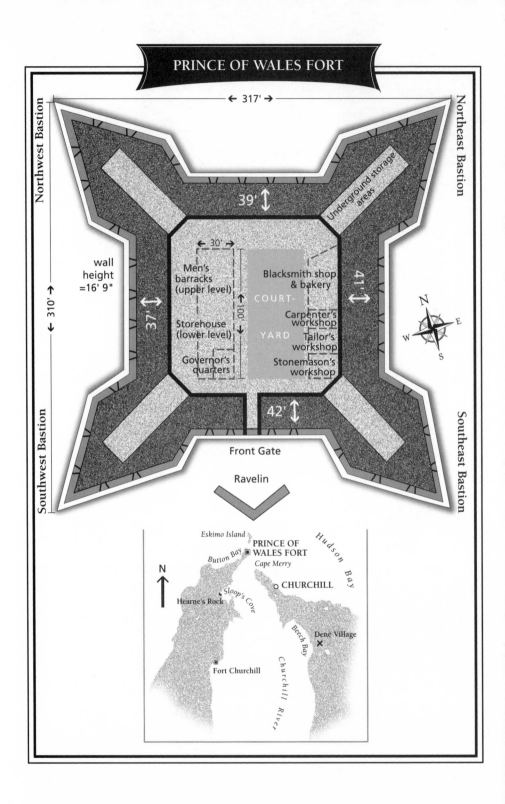

PRINCE OF WALES FORT

← 317' →

Northwest Bastion

Northeast Bastion

39' ↕

Underground storage areas

wall height =16' 9"

← 310' →

37 ↕

← 30' →

Men's barracks (upper level)

Storehouse (lower level)

Governor's quarters

100'

COURT-YARD

Blacksmith shop & bakery

Carpenter's workshop

Tailor's workshop

Stonemason's workshop

41' ↕

N
W E
S

42' ↕

Front Gate

Southwest Bastion

Southeast Bastion

Ravelin

Eskimo Island

Button Bay

Hearne's Rock

Sloop's Cove

PRINCE OF WALES FORT

Cape Merry

Hudson Bay

CHURCHILL

N ↑

Beech Bay

Dene Village ×

Fort Churchill

Churchill River

5

PRINCE OF WALES FORT

FAR, FAR AWAY from the cockfights and witty conversation of Dr. Johnson's London, and farther still from the book burnings and iniquities of Voltaire's Europe, accessible only by ship after a journey of several weeks, situated on the west coast of Hudson Bay on a windswept promontory, the most formidable stone fortress in North America sat guarding the great northwest from which, for the past century, native peoples had been harvesting furs to trade with the Hudson's Bay Company.

For four thousand years, hunters and fishers had frequented the mammal-rich Churchill River area, and three well-rooted aboriginal peoples—the Cree, the Dene, and the Inuit—had contended over it for centuries. The first European to winter here was Jens Munck, a Danish explorer who arrived with two ships in 1619, seeking the Northwest Passage that would lead from the Atlantic Ocean to the fabled riches of Cathay. Munck established a camp five miles up the Churchill River, a waterway that eventually took its name from John Churchill, first duke of Marlborough, who served as governor of the Hudson's Bay Company.

Munck chose the site because it lay just beyond the point to which heavy tides drove salt water upriver from the Bay, so leaving potable fresh water immediately accessible. During the ensuing winter, however, the explorer lost sixty-one men—almost his entire crew—to scurvy, trichinosis, and exposure. With two fellow survivors, he made it back to Europe. In 1624, Munck published an account of his ordeal, a tale so horrific that for decades it discouraged potential explorers. Finally, in 1689, the Hudson's Bay Company dispatched one of its best men to the area, hoping to increase trade with native peoples from the far northwest. At Munck's old campsite, Henry Kelsey began to build a trading post, but it caught fire and burned to the ground.

Almost three decades later, in 1717, the HBC sent the dauntless James Knight north from York Fort to re-establish what was called Fort Churchill. After a single season, he reported to London that his home base was "bad but this is ten times worse." Knight hung on at Churchill as relations deteriorated between England and France, not least because the two powers were competing for furs. In 1731, drawing on a plan devised by Captain Christopher Middleton, the HBC's Governing Committee decided to build an impregnable fortress to which all of its servants could withdraw in the event of all-out war. It decreed the construction of Prince of Wales Fort at the entrance to the Churchill River, where stone and slaked lime for mortar were readily available.

The following year, the Company sent two dozen tradesmen and labourers to begin the job. They laid the first stone on June 3, 1732. Governor Richard Norton, who had neither military nor engineering experience, predicted that, using four teams of oxen and eighty-four men, he could complete construction within six or seven years. In fact, when Samuel Hearne arrived in 1766, the massive stone fort—roughly one hundred yards square, with four corner bastions, numerous parapets, and embrasures for forty cannons—remained a work-in-progress, and would for another five years.

Why did building it take so long? In addition to contending with small work crews, short construction seasons, and the need to hunt food, cut wood, haul water, and conduct trade, the untrained first governor made mistakes—decreeing, for example, that the width of the ramparts be reduced from forty-two to twenty-five feet. His error became evident—and had to be rectified at considerable cost—when, on first firing a cannon, he watched it recoil off the too narrow rampart. As well, the frigid winters caused the ground to freeze and heave, wreaking havoc with completed work. In 1751 Governor Joseph Isbister reported, "My self & one of our Men had like to have been Killed by a piece of ye Old Wale sudenlly Shuting and tumbling down."

By that time, the HBC had developed its white whale (beluga) fishery out of Churchill. In 1765, the London committee decided that, while expanding its coastal fur trade, it would develop a black whale (bowhead) fishery, using Marble Island as a northerly base. Each summer, the Company sent one or two sloops up the coast to trade with the Inuit, who refused to visit the massive stone fortress because so many of their traditional Dene enemies lived nearby. Now those HBC vessels would function additionally as black-whalers. During the next seven years, the Company would sink over £20,000 into this project. It would add a one-hundred-ton brigantine to its fleet and hire a capable, experienced, and ambitious young mariner—Samuel Hearne—to serve initially on the sloop *Churchill.*

By THE TIME Hearne arrived, Prince of Wales Fort had become one of the most important fur-trading posts in Rupert's Land. In *The Fur Trade in Canada*, historian Harold Innis notes that around 1770—by which time most "Forts" were also called "Factories"—the HBC kept over sixty men there, with forty-two at York Factory, twenty-five at Moose Factory, and smaller complements at other posts. As for profitability, the Hudson's Bay Company measured production in "made beaver," or cured skins of adult beavers. Some historians have contended that Prince of Wales Fort outstripped all trading posts, with annual returns of up to forty thousand made beaver. Others put York Factory on top with thirty-three thousand and accord fewer than ten thousand to the more northerly post.

Company ships arrived annually from England to leave supplies and trading goods and to collect furs. On August 7, 1766, Hearne arrived aboard the *Prince Rupert.* He sailed into the Churchill River, almost one mile wide at its mouth, passing between the imposing fort and a six-cannon battery at Cape Merry, to anchor three miles upriver near Sloop's Cove. Debarking into a launch, Hearne made his way back to the almost square fort, which measured 310 feet north to south and 317 feet east to west. The top of the parapets stood nearly 17 feet high, and the stone walls varied in thickness from 37 to 42 feet.

Passing through the front gates, Hearne entered a courtyard paved

with cobblestones. To his left, covered with a flat roof of lead sheet-
ing, sat a two-storey stone building a hundred feet long. At the front,
the governor's quarters occupied most of the ground floor and proclaimed the man's importance; the rest of the building comprised a
workroom and storehouse for trade goods, furs, and food stuffs, and
also the men's quarters, with the barracks, or sleeping area, upstairs.
To Hearne's right stood a series of smaller stone buildings—adjoin-
ing workshops for the stonemason, the tailor, the carpenter, and the
blacksmith. The powder magazine and various storage areas, including a root cellar, were located underground near each of the four bastions.

In most newcomers, Prince of Wales Fort inspired a false sense of
security. Hearne had grown up in the Royal Navy, however, and recognized that the fort was virtually defenceless, if only because it
lacked a well to supply fresh water. In addition, each of the forty
mounted cannons required a crew of ten or twelve men, and he could
see that the fort housed only a fraction of that number. Nor had any of
these men—blacksmiths and masons, tailors and labourers—received
any military training. Probably this would never matter. Why would
anyone attack a fort guarding an apparently empty wilderness, whose
vastness he found staggering?

THE ROLLING LANDS that lay beyond Prince of Wales Fort, Samuel
Hearne soon discovered, were less empty than they appeared. Tens of
thousands of native people, most of them nomadic hunters, inhabited
this so-called Grand North, as distinct from the Petit Nord around
the bottom of Hudson Bay. Among them, the basic unit of social
organization was the extended family or band, which usually ranged
in size from eight to twenty persons—more in the case of some peoples. At various times of year, these households, some of which
included people of different language groups, would congregate to
hunt caribou or bring furs to an HBC post.

Among the aboriginal peoples, the European fur-traders identified
certain linguistic groupings as "tribes," an approach that obscured
the pre-eminence of the autonomous band and gave rise to debatable

generalizations. Roughly speaking, and allowing for diversity as a result of intermarriages and adoptions, as well as for occasional Assiniboine and Ojibwa families, some two thousand Swampy Cree dominated the area around Churchill and made up the vast majority of the "Homeguard Indians."

These Algonquian-speaking people were closely related to the Plains, Rocky, and Woodlands or Thickwoods Cree who lived farther west, and with them constituted the "Western Cree," as distinct from those who lived east of Hudson Bay. The Swampy Cree were skilful hunters and discerning traders who knew enough to demand muskets that worked in winter, and who sometimes played the French traders against the English. The Western Cree were the first to serve as middlemen to the fur trade, and while eventually they armed the Blackfoot of the plains and mountains, they first made good use of firearms to solidify their position. By the time Hearne arrived in the 1760s, they numbered thirty thousand and ranged westward from Churchill to Lake Athabasca and south as far as present-day Alberta and James Bay, intermingling with other peoples.

The lands to the north and west of this vast, Algonquian-speaking area were dominated by the so-called Northern Indians. These Dene, as they called themselves, were Athapaskan-speaking peoples descended from a culture extending back at least six thousand years. Long-time enemies of the Cree, whose name derives from the French *Christenaux*, the Dene had begun uneasily coexisting with them in the early 1700s. Related peoples roamed the boreal forests and tundra from Hudson Bay to the Pacific Coast, and from Lake Athabasca to the Arctic coast, crossing into Inuit-dominated areas in the north. They hunted and fished through most of the present-day Northwest Territories and parts of Inuit-controlled Nunavut.

Identifiable subgroups of the Dene, who spoke mutually intelligible Northern Athapaskan dialects, included the Chipewyan, Dogrib, Slavey, Hare, and Gwich'in or Loucheux. Hearne would have most contact with the Chipewyan, whose name derives from an Algonquian-Cree word, *chipwayanewok*, referring to their customary wearing of beaver-skin shirts whose backs narrowed to a point at the bottom—like contemporary tails. The Yellowknife or "Copper Indians"—so called because they used copper tools—were a regional

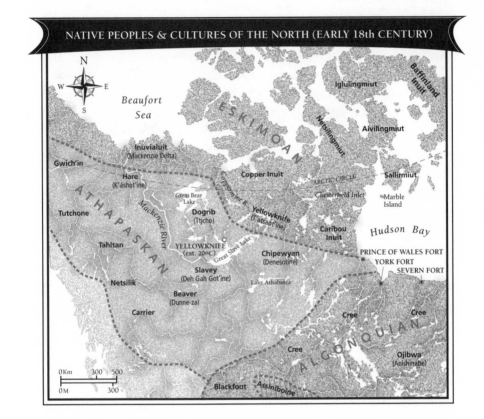

Beaufort
Sea

ESKIMOAN

Iglulingmiut

Baffin Island
Inuit

Netsilingmiut

Aivilingmiut

Inuvialuit
(Mackenzie Delta)

Gwich'in

Hare
(K'ásho't'ine)

Copper Inuit

Coppermine R.

ARCTIC CIRCLE

Sallirmiut

Great Bear
Lake

Dogrib
(Tłı̨chǫ)

Yellowknife
(T'atsaot'ine)

Chesterfield Inlet

Marble
Island

Tutchone

ATHAPASKAN

Mackenzie River

YELLOWKNIFE
(est. 20th C)

Great Slave Lake

Caribou
Inuit

Hudson Bay

Tahltan

Chipewyan
(Denesǫłıné)

PRINCE OF WALES FORT

YORK FORT

SEVERN FORT

Netsilik

Slavey
(Deh Gah Got'ine)

Lake Athabasca

Beaver
(Dunne-za)

Carrier

Cree

Cree

Cree

ALGONQUIAN

Ojibwa
(Anishinabe)

Blackfoot   Assiniboine

0 Km   300   500
0 M   300

subgroup of the Chipewyan who contested territories traditionally controlled by the Inuit. All of the Dene were related to the Navajo and Apache, whose ancestors had followed the bison south in the 1400s.

The Dene, like the Cree, responded to the demands of the environment by functioning mainly as autonomous families. The local bands were usually larger than those of the Cree and might include the families of from 6 to 28 hunters, or 30 to 140 persons in all; sometimes these would gather as regional bands of 300 or more. Such groupings were often culturally diverse as a result of intermarriages, adoptions, and the practice of stealing wives. At the time of Hearne's arrival, several Chipewyan bands were serving as fur-trade middlemen for groups who lived farther west.

In the treeless, frozen lands that lay still farther north lived a third aboriginal people. The Inuit extended across the Arctic from present-day Baffin Island to the Beaufort Sea. Most anthropologists and archaeologists believe their ancestors arrived in North America from Asia later than ancestral Indians, and perhaps as recently as four thousand years ago. In the eighteenth and nineteenth centuries they were called "Esquimaux," though later they rejected this as deriving from an Algonquian-Cree word meaning "eaters of raw meat." The various subgroups of Inuit spoke one of two related languages: in the west, a branch of Yup'ik, and in the east, including north of Churchill, a dialect of Inuktitut. The Inuit, too, hunted caribou, but also fish and sea mammals such as seals, walruses, and even whales.

Inuit people had sometimes visited Churchill to acquire wood for boats, but they did not enjoy friendly relations with the Dene, who had acquired European muskets and who jealously guarded their role as middlemen. The Inuit declined to risk their lives for the sake of metal goods, and so the HBC had begun sending a sloop north along the coast to trade for furs. One of these vessels was the *Churchill*, to which Hearne had been posted as first mate.

In 1766, he arrived too late to voyage north. But, having been discharged from the *Prince Rupert* on August 22—he had been listed as a gunner—Hearne sailed south to York Fort in the *Churchill*, a trip that kept him busy through September. After helping to stow the sloop in her winter quarters, a creek that lay roughly a quarter mile upriver from the fort, Hearne spent the ensuing winter getting to know his surroundings. Soon he could distinguish among native peoples. Besides the "Homeguard" or Swampy Cree, he identified the "Upland Indians" (Western Cree and Assiniboine), the "Northern Indians" (Chipewyan Dene), and the "Far Indians," who comprised other Dene, but especially Dogrib and Hare. All were distinct from the "Athapuscow Indians," the Athabasca Cree of the Mackenzie River Valley.

During his first few winters on the Bay, while many of his fellow officers gambled or drank or did both, the relentlessly curious Hearne began learning Cree, regarded by many as the root Algonquian language. In summer, while sailing with two Inuit boys training as interpreters, he mastered the rudiments of Inuktitut. To these languages he would later add several dialects of Athapaskan as spoken by various Dene groups.

PRINCE OF WALES FORT had developed a social stratification typical of HBC establishments. Its usual complement of forty to fifty men fell into three classes: officers, tradesmen, and labourers. Officer positions were sometimes vacant or doubled up; besides sloop captains and first mates like Hearne, these included a governor or master, a deputy or second-in-command, a surgeon, an accountant, a steward, and a clerk-writer. Tradesmen included an armourer, a shipwright, a blacksmith, two stonemasons, a bricklayer, a carpenter, a cooper (maker of casks and barrels), a tailor, and three harpooners. The two dozen other men were labourers and ordinary seamen.

During the winter, the junior officers would help procure firewood and shovel drifting snow, but the best hunters—a group Hearne soon joined—spent much of their time shooting and netting partridges, snaring rabbits, and fishing. Despite the novelty of these occupations, the ex-midshipman felt entirely at home with the Company's quasi-military approach, as described by Andrew Graham: "The inferior officers, tradesmen and all others are regularly kept at duty . . . and are victualed etc in the same manner and form as on board a King's ship or foreign merchantman; the Servants are rung out and in to duty by a bell, they work from 6 to 6 in summer, and from 9 to 2 in winter, being

Samuel Hearne did not draw A Northwest View of Prince of Wales's Fort in Hudson's Bay, North America, *until 1777. But the scenery had changed little from the time he had arrived at Churchill, in late 1766. The artist's precise sketch gave rise to this engraving, which is easily the most important depiction of this time and place.*

allowed an hour to breakfast, and the same time to dinner; a regular watch is kept in the night by two men three hours at a time."

Prince of Wales Fort was both a military installation and a "factory," so designated because the Hudson's Bay Company wanted its outposts to be productive sites, as self-sufficient as possible, and not just depots for European goods. Work life revolved around trading, hunting, fishing, and whaling, and was typically pre-industrial, with short periods of intense labour—at ship-time, for example—followed by long periods of relative ease. Hearne discovered that fishing in winter—mostly for *tickameeg*, or whitefish, and "salmon," or Arctic char—was cold, hard work that involved cutting holes in the ice and running nets between them.

He had arrived at Prince of Wales Fort early enough in the season to realize that because of the summertime heat and humidity, mosquitoes and blackflies might pose a problem. He would not experience the magnitude of the challenge, however, until the following summer, when he began readying HBC sloops to sail north, and found himself tormented to the point of plunging into the river. A study of northern biting flies conducted in 1952 determined that during an intensive attack, mosquitoes can inflict 280 bites on an exposed forearm in a minute. Blackflies could prove just as difficult, swarming into ears, eyes, noses, mouths, and even down throats.

That first year, Hearne did experience the wind and hail of autumn, though nothing to compare with the worst seasons on record. In 1746, a hailstorm had smashed all the windows on the northwest side of the fort, and hailstones reached four inches in circumference. In 1759, violent winds blew the wooden parapet off the ramparts on one wall and knocked down most of the palisade outside the fort.

Yet even the winds of autumn did not prepare the young Englishman for the ferocity of his first winter. In the courtyard the snowdrifts reached shoulder height—and still the white stuff continued to fall. Snowdrifts here had been known to exceed twenty-four feet. This winter was not especially bad, though men had to shovel snow off rooftops to prevent collapse and to dig tunnels to move from the barracks to workshops. At times, the drifting got so bad that men had to dig their way out of second-storey windows.

Hearne learned that conditions could be worse. If the snow cover were too thin, as occasionally happened, the men could not use the "great sledge" to haul firewood but would have to carry the wood on their backs. And with temperatures often hovering for weeks on end at minus 50 or 60 degrees Fahrenheit, firewood remained a constant necessity. In January, the cold prevented mortar from setting, and masons repairing walls had to cover their work every evening with horse dung to prevent frost damage.

At any time of year, the work could be dangerous. Hearne saw no accidents that first winter. But the following September, a seaman named Richard Chirgwen was crushed to death while putting up a sloop for winter, when a jack screw gave out and the vessel slid off its blocks. The December after that, a junior officer was seriously injured in a hunting accident. He had been chasing a wounded partridge when it flew into the trigger string of a fixed gun, which fired and hit him in the feet and legs.

Hearne could understand why, faced with such conditions, some men escaped Hudson Bay at first opportunity. He could also see why so many signed on again and again. Those who remained, he decided, valued the outdoors life, especially the hunting and fishing. They had no place to spend money, and so could save almost every shilling they earned; and they worked hard only sporadically, enjoying long periods of leisure. They played football, they skated, they arm-wrestled and fought.

Yet because the work was usually so physical, most recreations were sedentary. These followed the pattern of pre-industrial England, and drinking was prominent among them. The most popular beverage was "bumbo," which combined rum with sugar, water, and nutmeg. On Wednesday and Saturday, each man received a quart of brandy and the governor would invite the officers into his quarters for a bowl of rum or brandy punch. The men drank spruce beer and other strong beers at mealtimes, and the officers sometimes enjoyed wine. Occasionally, drinking led to raucous behaviour and fist fights, but Hearne, as an ex-Navy man, had seen it all before.

He regarded drinking as a waste of time. Nor did he care much for gambling, another popular pastime—although he was interested to discover that Bay men had taught the Homeguard Indians to play cards, dice, checkers, and dominoes. These games had become so popular that in a rudimentary Cree-English dictionary compiled by James Isham, Hearne found Algonquian words for king, queen, knave, and ace and for the four suits, clubs, hearts, diamonds, and spades.

Some of the Bay men did a lot of reading. The library included *Pilgrim's Progress* and *The Epistles of Pliny the Younger*, along with miscellaneous works of philosophy, language, and medicine, collections of poetry, and comic plays. Hearne had brought favourite books by Defoe and Voltaire.

Some HBC men kept domestic animals—sheep, hogs, cattle, horses. Many tended gardens to augment staples imported from England, which included flour, sugar, and oatmeal. Early attempts to grow grains had failed, and the men had abandoned oats, barley, and corn in favour of hardy crops like turnips and cabbage. Dandelions were plentiful and could be used, Hearne would observe, to make "an early salad, long before anything can be produced in the gardens." He would also mention uses for the local berries, turning gooseberries into tarts and pies, heath berries into a drink, and juniper berries into a brandy cordial.

Even so, at this northerly latitude the growing season was brief, and the Company sent more provisions to Prince of Wales Fort than to any other outpost. Generally, the men ate as well or better than they would have in Britain, and certainly better than the men in the Royal Navy. Still, they frequently protested, and had been known to riot over inedible salt salmon, rotten partridge, and uncooked bread. The governor and his officers never complained, doubtless because, as Andrew Graham observed, their "table is always handsomely supplied with provisions, very seldom having less than three dishes; and on particular occasions fourteen or sixteen."

If protests became a problem, the remedies were invariably corporeal, as Hearne witnessed on more than one occasion. Andrew Graham had written that the fort's governing council of officers "act for their interest taking care to follow all just and legal methods, strictly abiding by the laws of old England." Riotous peacebreakers, he explained, would suffer a caning or, on the advice of the Governing Council, a whipping "which last is inflicted always on him or them who steals or pilfers from the neighbours; the Chief and Council messes together and are also in the Captains mess out and home, excepting bad behaviour has rendered them incapable of being looked on as Gentlemen." To Hearne, after seven years in the Royal Navy, such punishments appeared mild.

The greatest source of tension at Prince of Wales Fort was the HBC policy regarding women—a policy with which Hearne would soon come into conflict. In summarizing it, Graham, for many years the master at York Fort, made clear the Company's old-familiar double standard, one set of rules of officers, another for ordinary men:

No European women are allowed to be brought to Hudson's Bay, and no person is allowed to have any correspondence with the natives without the chief's orders, not even to go into an Indian tent, and the natives are not permitted to come within the forts but when their business requires, and then they are conducted to the chief's house or trading room, where all business with them is transacted, however the factors for the most part at proper times allow an officer to take in an Indian lady to his apartment, but by no means or on any account whatever to harbour her within the fort at night, however the factors keep a bedfellow within the fort at all times, and have carried several of their children home [to England].

Company supply ships docked three miles up the Churchill River beyond the fort in an excellent natural harbour called Sloop's Cove. One sunny afternoon, after spending a final night aboard the *Churchill*, supervising preparations for departure, Samuel Hearne spent two hours chiselling his name, in twelve-inch-high letters, onto a large flat rock: "Sl Hearne, July ye 1, 1767." With that gesture, he encapsulated what he proposed to do in these northern wilds: to make his mark. The next morning, with Hudson Bay at last free of ice, and as second-in-command to a crew of half a dozen men, the twenty-two-year-old first mate sailed north up the coast, hunting whales and seeking Inuit, or "Esquimaux," with whom to trade European goods for furs.

Because he had been raised in Beaminster, where the oldest buildings dated back centuries, Samuel Hearne arrived in Hudson Bay with a keen sense of history, and of continuity through time. Hence, his ambition to leave his mark for posterity, the first evidence of which—a precise chiselling he undertook on July 1, 1767—survives to this day at "Hearne's Rock."

Along with the carpenters and shipwrights, Hearne had been working sixteen-hour days, preparing the eight-man sloop and stocking it with knives, chisels, and other goods. He had also supervised major repairs to the sloop *Success*, whose ordinary seamen had refused to sail until they were completed. Whale fishing mandated even longer hours than usual, with days beginning at three in the morning and extending until seven or eight at night. In any given season, HBC whalers would harvest between seventy and one hundred beluga whales, reducing them to valuable blubber and oil. The London committee hoped for still greater returns from the black whale fishery.

During a typical thirty-six-day voyage, an eight-man crew would consume considerable food, eating beef on ten days, pork another ten days, geese on six days, fresh fish on seven days, and fresh venison on three days. The sailors acquired the fish and venison by trading as they travelled. They would also devour 280 pounds of flour, 60 pounds of bread, and such "luxuries" as plums and molasses, this last required for a popular fur-trade dish called "grout," made by sweetening thick oatmeal with molasses. As well, they would drink 63 gallons of beer.

Sailing north, Hearne worked with two young Inuit men, learning the rudiments of their language and teaching them English as part of a Company plan to increase trade. The HBC was hoping to develop Marble Island, ten miles off the west coast of Hudson Bay near Chesterfield Inlet, as a forward base for the black whale fishery. It would spend £20,000 on this venture before finally abandoning it as uneconomical.

In the summer of 1767, as small boats from the *Success* searched for whales around Marble Island, one of them chanced upon wreckage from a two-ship expedition led by James Knight. Arriving a short while later, and despite a threatening storm, Samuel Hearne went ashore and examined guns, anchors, cables, bricks, a smith's anvil, and other articles. Eventually, he would offer a memorable reconstruction of the expedition's mysterious fate, challenging the earliest, most racist interpretations of the disaster with a version more sympathetic to the native peoples.

A stubborn old codger, James Knight had sailed from London in

1719 with a crew of forty men aboard two ships: the eighty-ton frigate *Albany* and the forty-ton sloop *Discovery*. Knight had a two-fold mission: first, north of 64 degrees, he proposed to discover the Straits of Anian, which supposedly led to a Northwest Passage through the continent; second, he intended to find vast quantities of gold and copper that, he passionately believed, existed near the Neetha-san-san-dazey, the Far-Off Metal River.

Knight and his men sailed into Hudson Bay and were never heard from again.

For this old warrior the HBC undertook only a desultory search. In 1721, Henry Kelsey—no friend to Knight—sailed north to Marble Island and found tools and metal implements that suggested a shipwreck. The following year, Captain John Scroggs discovered more wreckage and concluded that both ships had sunk: "Every man was killed by the Eskimos." His journals have been lost and so details are lacking today, but the HBC wrote off Knight's ships and let stand the verdict of Scroggs.

Enter Samuel Hearne in 1767. Besides the remains of a house, he discovered "the bottoms of the ship and sloop, which lie sunk in about five fathoms of water, toward the head of the harbour." The logbooks of both sloop captains mention that during a fierce lightning storm, Hearne and a few men also found graves. Captain Joseph Stevens of the *Success* noted that "on their digging up part of a soft raising ground they found ye sculls & bones of different human bodies." And according to Magnus Johnston, captain of the *Churchill*, "They had found a great number of graves, one of which Mr. Hearne caused the people to dig up in order to see if they find any thing remarkable—but could not—only the bones of a stout man who without doubt is one of the unhappy sufferers."

Back on the *Churchill*, the Inuit men vehemently denied that their people would have attacked Knight and his men, who presented no threat and were far better armed. Eventually, Hearne concluded that Scroggs, who had visited Marble Island decades before, "finding himself greatly embarrassed with shoals and rocks, returned to Prince of Wales's Fort without making any certain discovery respecting the above ship or sloop; for all the marks he saw among the Esquimaux at

Whale Cove scarcely amounted to the spoils which might have been made from a trifling accident, and consequently could not be considered as signs of a total shipwreck."

The following summer, the HBC whalers again visited Marble Island, Stevens in the *Success* and Hearne commanding the still smaller *Speedwell*. This time, they discovered the figurehead of the *Albany*, and also some guns and other relics, all of which they sent to London as evidence that Knight and his men, as Hearne put it, "had been lost on that inhospitable island, where neither stick nor stump was to be seen, and which lies near sixteen miles from the main land. Indeed the main is little better, being a jumble of barren hills and rocks, destitute of every kind of herbage except moss and grass; and at that part, the woods are several hundreds of miles from the sea-side."

In 1769, Hearne visited Marble Island once more. This time he sailed as first mate on the *Charlotte*, the brigantine sent out from London expressly to expand the black whale fishery. Years later, writing in London, he would describe how, while rowing around looking for whales, he spotted several Inuit people on the island. Perceiving that a couple of them "were greatly advanced in years," he went ashore and interviewed two men at length. By now, Hearne had developed considerable fluency in Inuktitut. He also had the help of an Inuit youth with whom he had sailed annually. Later, he described the narrative he elicited as "full, clear, and unreserved."

Knight's two ships had reached Marble Island late in the fall of 1719. The larger of the two vessels sustained heavy damage as it entered the shallow harbour. As forty or fifty men set about building a large house, the Inuit retreated to their winter quarters on the mainland. When they returned the following summer, they found the Englishmen greatly reduced in numbers. Those who survived looked unwell but remained busily employed, though the Inuit could not easily describe what they were doing. Hearne surmised that the Englishmen were lengthening the longboat, because near the ruins of the house he had noticed a great quantity of oak chips.

Sickness and famine continued to decimate the English. By winter, only twenty remained. The Inuit now erected their own camp on Marble Island, building snowhuts on the opposite side of the harbour and providing the visitors with whale blubber, seal flesh, and oil. In the spring of 1721, the Inuit paddled to the mainland to hunt. That summer, when they returned, Hearne wrote later,

they only found five of the English alive, and those were in such distress for provisions that they eagerly eat the seal's flesh and whale's blubber quite raw, as they purchased it from the natives. This disordered them so much, that three of them died in a few days, and the other two, though very weak, made a shift to bury them. Those two survived many days after the rest, and frequently went to the top of an adjacent rock, and earnestly looked to the South and the East, as if in expectation of some vessels coming to their relief. After continuing there a considerable time together, and nothing appearing in sight, they sat down close together, and wept bitterly. At length one of the two died, and the other's strength was so far exhausted, that he fell down and died also, in attempting to dig a grave for his companion. The skulls and other large bones of those two men are now lying above-ground close to the house. The longest liver was, according to the Esquimaux account, always employed in working of iron into implements for them; probably he was the armourer, or smith.

For decades, and indeed centuries, Samuel Hearne's reconstruction of the expedition's fate stood as definitive. Who could argue with

This fanciful, Victorian depiction of the two final survivors of the James Knight expedition is familiar to anyone interested in northern exploration. It is a product of Samuel Hearne's imagination projected through time, and testifies to the explorer's visionary power and storytelling abilities.

eyewitnesses? And who could forget those pathetic final survivors, scanning the horizon for salvation?

The only problem with Hearne's reconstruction is that he made it up. The logbooks of the HBC ships on location in 1769 make no mention of the first mate's encounter with "eyewitnesses." This looks more than suspicious given the detailed reports of previous visits to Marble Island, as well as the continuing interest in the fate of the Knight expedition. What really happened is that two decades later, while sitting at his writing desk in London, Hearne conjured both eyewitnesses and survivors out of his imagination. He created a fiction.

In *Dead Silence: The Greatest Mystery in Arctic Discovery*, authors John Geiger and Owen Beattie make this case. But they misjudge Hearne's motivations, suggesting that he fictionalized his narrative for monetary reasons; in fact, having visited Marble Island and perused the relevant journals, and drawing on his long experience of the people and land, Hearne honestly believed he had solved the enduring mystery of Knight's fate. To communicate his understanding as fully as possible—to tell as much of the truth as he knew—he invented eyewitnesses and survivors. The result, as Geiger and Beattie observe, was "the most haunting vision of failed discovery in the pageant of Arctic exploration."

From the vantage point of the twenty-first century, we can see that Hearne oversimplified the expedition's fate. Knight and some of his men may well have made it to the mainland, started for the Far-Off Metal River, and perished in the Barren Lands. Whatever really happened, Hearne's memorable yarn reveals him to be a born storyteller. It ends with the dramatic observation that the last survivor was "probably the armourer or the smith"—an intuitive master stroke that increases the illusion of authenticity. Yet if Hearne fabricated eyewitnesses and survivors to communicate the truth of his vision, as now seems certain, the salient passage hinges on such detailed knowledge of when he was where, exactly—summer 1769, Marble Island—that his authorship of the evocative reconstruction is beyond dispute.

* * *

DURING HIS FIRST years at Prince of Wales Fort, while still in his early twenties, Samuel Hearne met three men who would profoundly influence his life. The first was the naturalist Andrew Graham, who, when Hearne arrived in Hudson Bay, was serving as master at Severn House, a small post south of York Fort at the mouth of the Severn River. A dozen years older than Hearne, Graham had joined the Company at sixteen. He had sailed for three years on the *Churchill*, then worked at York Fort as assistant writer, clerk, and accountant before becoming bookkeeper and second-in-command (1759–61). Promoted to run Severn House, Graham filled in as temporary chief at York Fort in 1765–66.

Hearne met him at Severn after trekking south on snowshoes. Graham communicated his passion for wildlife to the younger man, who was always eager to learn. In 1769–70, while on furlough in London, Graham had met the naturalist Thomas Pennant, author of *British Zoology*. After returning to Hudson Bay, Graham not only began seriously to collect natural history specimens, but encouraged other HBC officers to do the same. C. Stuart Houston, a present-day Canadian naturalist, writes that Graham "made a permanent mark in the annals of natural history as one of the early naturalists in North America to collect specimens (including five new species) and provide observations on bird and mammal behaviour." Later, Samuel Hearne would build on his mentor's work to become, in the words of historian Richard Glover, "a much better naturalist than Graham . . . head and shoulders superior to every other North American naturalist who preceded Audubon."

The second major influence on young Hearne was the brilliant mathematician and astronomer William Wales, who arrived at Prince of Wales Fort in August 1768 to observe the transit of the planet Venus across the face of the sun. This event, scheduled to occur June 3, 1769, would not recur for another 115 years. Accurately observed, the transit would enable mathematicians to use trigonometry to calculate both the diameter of the sun and its distance from earth. On arrival at the Fort, Wales took up residence in a stone hut measuring nine feet square—a dwelling so cold that, during the winter, his breath formed ice on the walls.

The thirty-four-year-old scientist, the first scientist to winter in

Hudson Bay, had brought along an assistant but was happy to oblige Hearne's insatiable curiosity. Wales taught the young sailor the finer points of astronomical observation, and the two men developed a firm friendship that not only flourished at Prince of Wales Fort, but flowered again in London, decades later.

While crossing the Atlantic, Wales had discovered to his horror that the specially made timepiece supplied by the Royal Society did not work but gained nine and a half minutes each day. A resourceful man, he carved a sundial out of limestone—an outmoded technology, but one that would, given enough sunlight, ensure the accuracy of his readings. On June 3, 1769, Hearne rejoiced with Wales when the sky cleared long enough to enable them to observe the Transit of Venus, and to use both timepieces.

In August, Wales returned to London on a Company ship, and the following spring, he appeared twice before the Royal Society to report his observations and to read a perceptive fifty-page journal about life on the Bay, incorporating details of climate, clothing, and diet. The Society was impressed enough that in 1772, it sent Wales as astronomer on the second Pacific voyage of Captain James Cook. On his return in 1775 he became master of the mathematical school at Christ's Hospital, London, and the following year he was elected a fellow of the Royal Society.

The third man to shape Hearne's views was Moses Norton, governor of Prince of Wales Fort. Here, the relationship began in wary respect, evolved into mutual dislike, and flowered, certainly on Hearne's side, into contempt and hatred. Moses Norton was the son of ex-governor Richard Norton and one of his Cree wives. As a boy, Moses had spent nine years in England. There, judging from spelling problems involving the letter H, he probably acquired a Cockney accent.

In 1762, after serving a long apprenticeship aboard HBC ships, Moses Norton became chief of Prince of Wales Fort. Within two years, judging from his "general letter" of 1764 to the London committee, he had inspired a threat of legal action: "Last year when ye ship was here I was provoked to strike Thos. Johnson for his denying to do his duty for wch have had a lawyers letter sined Tomlinson wch letter and a certificate of ye whole affare have sent to your hons, inclosed in ye packet."

Fur-trade scholar Richard Glover suggests that historian E.E. Rich was generous in ascribing to Norton "uncommon energy and perception." Norton's projects included sending two moose to London, where the single survivor devoured a fortune in food before the Company disposed of the creature as a gift to King George III. Norton also conceived and engineered the black whale fishery that brought Hearne to Hudson Bay. One century later, bowheads would be profitably hunted farther north, around Southampton Island, but Norton kept his whalers near Marble Island. As a result, during the seven years ending in 1772, when the wildly expensive project was abandoned, HBC whalers caught a total of four bowheads.

In 1765, Moses Norton had engaged two "Northern Indians," Idotliazee and Matonabbee, to locate the source of the copper that had so obsessed James Knight and in search of which his own father had once travelled. In 1768, just as Norton was leaving for a furlough in London, the two Dene men arrived at Prince of Wales Fort carrying copper samples and a rough map purporting to identify their source, "far to the northward where the sun don't set." The map was fictitious, but nobody knew that in London, where the public was much taken with a book called *The American Traveller*, in which author Alexander Cluny falsely alleged that, while exploring in the Grand North, he had chanced upon great lumps of virgin copper.

Given these favourable circumstances, Norton persuaded the Company to send an overland expedition to find the source of those copper samples, searching northward to 70 degrees. Such an undertaking would serve the additional public relations purpose of ostensibly searching for the Northwest Passage. Besides, Norton knew just the man for the job.

Samuel Hearne was muscular and energetic, intelligent and resourceful, an excellent hunter. He got along well with native people, and spoke their languages with astonishing fluency. He also had a stubborn streak: he would neither shrink from a challenge nor quit at the first sign of difficulty. Hearne had been badgering Norton for advancement, by which he meant the captaincy of a ship, but the young man was ambitious enough that he could be persuaded. Because he had studied navigation in the Royal Navy, Hearne could take readings of latitude and longitude; not only that, but Norton had granted him permission, just as he left for London, to study with that visiting mathematician, William Wales.

Late in 1769, when Norton returned to Prince of Wales Fort, he summoned Hearne to his quarters. He described the overland project and, unrolling his fictitious map onto a table, asked, "What do you say, 'earne? Is this journey not the opportunity you've been wanting?"

HAVING WORKED three years in Hudson Bay and having devoted himself to reading, studying, and drawing when other men were drinking or gambling, the twenty-four-year-old Hearne had learned considerable fur-trade history. He knew that in 1690, the HBC's Henry Kelsey had journeyed westward from York Fort across the Great Plains, travelling with native people for two years and becoming the first European to describe the buffalo and the grizzly bear. And because his friend Andrew Graham was even now revising the official report, Hearne also knew the saga of Anthony Henday. In 1754, just fifteen years before, Henday had travelled inland with a party of Cree, among them a woman who served as his cook, interpreter, and "bed-fellow." After wintering in the west, possibly within sight of the Rockies, and encountering Blackfoot who rode horses, Henday returned to York Fort and received a handsome reward.

Hearne had also heard the story of William Stuart, a Cree-speaking protégé of James Knight. In 1715, with 150 Homeguard Cree, Stuart had travelled northwest on a peacemaking mission. Knight had charged him with guarding the expedition leader, the "Slave Woman" Thanadelthur, an extraordinary Dene woman rightly celebrated for her courage, perseverance, and resourcefulness. In the barrens beyond Churchill, beset by sickness and fierce weather and reduced to eating dog meat, the large party had broken into small groups to hunt more effectively.

Committed to remaining with Thanadelthur, Stuart wrote to Knight at York Fort: "We are in a starving condition at this time. We still push on in our journey. We have eat nothing this eight days. I do not think I shall see you any more but I have a good heart." The Cree man who carried the letter to Knight reported that Stuart "weeps

very much to think of their misfortunes and for fear of being starved."
Not long afterward, Stuart and Thanadelthur managed to find game,
but then they stumbled upon a camp containing the dead bodies of
nine Chipewyan people—a camp raided, obviously, by a group of their
fellow travellers.

Fearing retribution, their own party of Homeguard Cree refused to
continue westward. They agreed to wait with Stuart while Thanadelthur carried on alone. Incredibly, after ten days she returned with a
large party of Dene who had been gathering to wreak revenge, and
then established a lasting peace between the two peoples. Stuart made
it back to York Fort, but four years after that horrific winter in the
Barrens, at forty-one, he died a raving "lunatick."

Now, in 1769, poring over a rough map in the governor's quarters
at Prince of Wales Fort—the map drawn by Matonabbee—Samuel
Hearne thrilled to the adventure of these stories, ignoring all their
ominous aspects. The whale fishery did not look promising. In this
overland adventure he felt there was "a greater probability of making
some returns, and giving satisfaction to my employers." Indeed, he
believed this quest might provide the opportunity he had been seeking since boyhood: a chance to make his name. If it involved not a voyage but an overland journey, and if the occasion presented itself
through a man he distrusted, what of that?

To the governor Samuel Hearne said, "If there is copper to be
found, Mr. Norton, I will find it. If there is a Passage to be discovered,
I will discover it. How soon can I leave?"

6

THE FAR-OFF
METAL RIVER

—————————————

THE FRENCH PHILOSOPHER Jean-Jacques Rousseau, writing about first-person narratives of faraway places, regretted that most explorers did not reflect upon their experiences, but merely described. While insisting that observation took precedence over interpretation, he abhorred "unphilosophic travelers, complacent in their Eurocentric prejudices," and called for a new kind of explorer, a combination philosopher and scientific researcher: "Suppose that these new Hercules, on their return from these memorable journeys, then wrote at leisure the natural, moral and political history of what they had seen; we ourselves would see a new world spring from under their pens, and we should learn thereby to know our own world."

Samuel Hearne did not pretend to be a philosopher embarked on a "glorious voyage" inspired solely by the quest for knowledge. He functioned in the real world, where the HBC wanted to make money and he himself sought recognition. Yet his book, *A Journey to the Northern Ocean*, has long been recognized as a classic of northern exploration literature. Indeed, it is usually considered the first such classic, not only because of its humanist perspective and factual, hard-science observations on flora and fauna, but also for its discerning portrait of a people whose way of life has long since disappeared.

The London committee of the Hudson's Bay Company, convinced that a northern expedition could prove immensely lucrative—imagine a thriving copper mine!—sent Hearne the best astronomical instruments available, including a portable Hadley's quadrant. In a letter to Hearne dated May 25, 1769, the committee wrote that, as the projected journey required someone who could take geographical observations and chart rivers, "we have fixed upon you (especially as it is represented to us to be your own inclination) to conduct this journey, with proper assistants."

The Company promised Hearne "a gratuity proportionable to the trouble and fatigue" he might undergo, and also raised his wages and placed him in Council at Prince of Wales Fort, in effect recognizing him as a senior officer. The Committee added that "we should have been ready to advance you to the command of the *Charlotte*, according to your request, if a matter of more immediate consequence had not intervened." Command of the two-masted *Charlotte*, which Hearne described as "a fine brig of one hundred tons," went instead to Joseph Stevens. Hearne had served with Stevens as first mate on the *Success* and regarded him as "a man of the least merit I ever knew."

Yet Hearne had no inclination to nurse resentment. To him had fallen the more challenging task, a quest that might lead to a place in the history books. He began preparing. First, he chose two HBC men to accompany him, mainly to handle the heavier work: William Isbester, a sailor, and Thomas Merriman, a landsman. From among the Homeguard Cree, Moses Norton hired two additional men to

In the vicinity of Prince of Wales Fort, as at York Fort and elsewhere, the Homeguard Cree lived in camps like this one, depicted in the mid-nineteenth century by E.N. Kendall of the Royal Navy.

assist him. And when, early in November, a party of Dene arrived to trade, Norton engaged them to serve as guides.

This band, led by Captain Chawchinahaw, included six or eight hunters plus wives and children. Norton stipulated that Hearne, the two HBC men, and the two Swampy Cree men would bring no women, and alluded to this, using the code of the times, in his written orders: "It is sincerely recommended to you and your companions to treat the natives with civility, so as not to give them any room for complaint or disgust, as they have strict orders not to give you the least offence."

Playing to the Committee, Norton depicted a situation in which this entire party—the Company servants, the Cree, and the Dene—would handle the hunting and fishing and also transport Hearne's baggage, which included trading goods, presents, and two years' worth of ammunition. Chawchinahaw would lead Hearne as far as Athapuscow Lake, where, according to Norton, "Captain Matonabbee is to meet you in the spring of 1770."

This "Athapuscow Lake" would confuse mapmakers for two decades, until finally they would understand that not one but two massive lakes lay hundreds of miles west of Churchill: Lake Athabasca and, a couple of hundred miles northwest, Great Slave Lake. Matonabbee, the most outstanding of all Dene leaders, was one of two men who, the previous spring, had approached Norton with a tale of rich copper deposits near the Far-Off Metal River and had provided him with a rough map and two chunks of copper. Years later, Hearne would observe that his projected meeting with Matonabbee, which Norton concocted to convince his superiors in London,

was barely probable, as Matonabbee at the time had not any information of this journey being set on foot, much less had he received orders to join me at the place and time here appointed, and had we accidentally met, he would by no means have undertaken the Journey without first going to the Factory, and there making his agreement with the Governor; for no Indian is fond of per- forming any particular service for the English, without first knowing what is to be his reward.

According to Norton, Matonabbee would guide Hearne from Athapuscow Lake to the Far-Off Metal River, which ran through three rich copper mines. This northern river was "supposed by the Indians to empty itself into some ocean." Hearne was to follow the waterway to its mouth, determining latitude, longitude, and navigability, and also whether the HBC might there establish a fort or settlement "with any degree of safety, or benefit to the Company."

Either way, Hearne would "take possession of [the area] on behalf of the Hudson's Bay Company, by cutting [his] name on some of the rocks, as also the date of the year, month, etc." Norton obviously remained impressed with the way, two years before, the historically minded Hearne had chiselled his name into a rock slab at Sloop's Cove—and yet he provided him no cutting tools.

Besides claiming land, looking for metals, and judging the feasibility of establishing a mine, Hearne was expected to determine "either by [his] own travels, or by information from the Indians, whether there is a passage through this continent." In England, the dream of a Northwest Passage had been revived by that mendacious book *The American Traveller*. But here, having himself sailed north and explored the only conceivable opening to a passage, the dead-end Chesterfield Inlet, Norton suspected the truth, and he indicated that Hearne's journey would be "useful to prevent further doubts from arising hereafter respecting a passage out of Hudson's Bay into the Western Ocean."

Hearne spent September and October 1769 preparing the expedition. He drew a large empty map on a deerskin parchment, measuring out 12 degrees of latitude north and 30 degrees of longitude west from Prince of Wales Fort. He sketched the west coast of Hudson Bay onto the map and proposed to fill the interior as he travelled. He also prepared numerous smaller pieces of parchment using a larger scale, on which he would indicate daily courses and distances as well as lakes and rivers. Together with his journal and the ammunition, tools, tobacco, knives, and other implements needed for a journey that would last two years, Hearne would carry a considerable load. From the outset, he determined to travel like the native peoples, relying on the country to provide food and clothing: "I only took the shirt and clothes I then had on, one spare coat, a pair of drawers, and so much cloth as would make me two or three pair of Indian stockings, which together with a blanket for bedding, composed the whole of my stock of clothing."

On November 6, 1769, a day both sunny and mild, Samuel Hearne said his goodbyes to Moses Norton and his friends and, encouraged by a booming seven-gun salute, set out to travel overland farther west and north than any previous explorer—indeed, to venture into territory never yet visited by any European.

DURING HIS FIRST winter in Rupert's Land, the tall, strong, and athletic Samuel Hearne had trekked south to Severn and York forts, mastering the art of travelling on snowshoes. In summer, while engaged in the whale fishery, he had sailed north as far as Marble Island, winning praise for initiative and competence. Having grown up in the Royal Navy, he was no stranger to firearms, and he had quickly become an efficient hunter. He had dealt continuously with Cree, Dene, and Inuit people, and had begun mastering their languages—Algonquian, Athapaskan, and Inuktitut. Twenty-four years old, resourceful and observant, Hearne was as well suited for this expedition as any European could have been. Yet the undertaking itself was so ambitious, the projected journey into the unknown so much longer and more arduous than any yet accomplished, that in retrospect it appears wildly over-ambitious.

The western subarctic into which Samuel Hearne ventured is one of the most extreme and challenging environments on earth. This vast region covers more than one million square miles, reaching from Hudson Bay to the Rocky Mountains and the Alaska coast, and from the northern Great Plains to the Arctic. In these cold, forbidding lands, temperatures average above freezing for only three months each year; in winter, they range between 14 and 8 degrees Fahrenheit, with lows reaching 37 degrees below zero. In the most northerly areas, those toward which Hearne would travel, the sun remains below the horizon for months at a time, and hunters do their work in chilly twilight. For several weeks in summer, by way of contrast, the sun scarcely falls below the horizon; daylight is perpetual, and disoriented newcomers have trouble sleeping. Temperatures reach 100 or 105 degrees Fahrenheit—stultifying heat.

This is a land of boreal forests. Except for stretches of birch and

This pen and ink by Charles William Jefferys—Samuel Hearne on His Journey to the Coppermine, 1770—finds the explorer looking warmer, snugger, and calmer than he usually felt. It is notable for its evocation of the aurora borealis, or northern lights, which made a strong impression on him—and, through him, on Samuel Taylor Coleridge.

aspen, which shed their leaves annually, most trees are conifers, cone-bearers that remain green year-round—spruce, pine, fir, tamarack. Here, too, are thousands of streams and scores of freshwater lakes, some of them among the largest in the world. Major rivers include the Mackenzie, Peace, Churchill, Yukon, and Athabasca.

A rough, wavering treeline runs through this vast region from east to west, marking the division between taiga, or swampy coniferous forest, and tundra, the treeless marshy ground beneath which lies permafrost. In this landscape, travel is difficult and hazardous, especially in spring and autumn, when ice on the lakes and rivers is either melting or freezing over. Fish and game could be plentiful, but might be scarce, and starvation remained a constant threat. This harsh environment has never supported more than 100,000 people at one time.

The western subarctic would test Samuel Hearne as few people have been tested—not just in physical endurance, but in resolution and commitment, in the abilities to persevere, to recuperate and rally after a setback, and to begin again after a crushing defeat. The expedition would test Hearne's physicality, but more than that, it would test his character.

The first harbinger turned up two days out of the fort, when one of the Dene hunters deserted. He had been hauling a sixty-pound sledge piled with general baggage and, because mild weather had turned the snow thick and heavy, had been having a difficult time. The man had waited until everyone slept, then disappeared into the night. Because the other men were already heavily laden, Hearne undertook to haul the sledge himself, and from that point on, besides taking observations, writing in his journal, and hunting, he always did a full share of the heavy work.

At this season, many small groups of Dene were transporting furs to Prince of Wales Fort. Three days out, after crossing the Seal River, Hearne and his men encountered the first of them, and traded for venison and other food. But as their provisions dwindled in the treeless country where no animals could be successfully hunted, Hearne began to suspect that Captain Chawchinahaw had not taken the expedition to heart—indeed, that the native leader was trying to discourage him from continuing.

He asked Chawchinahaw when the party might expect to reach the main woods, which would contain game, and was told four or five days. But as temperatures fell and the cold became intense, the travellers remained in the barrens north of Churchill, hauling sledges over rough, stony country where, for lack of trees and wood, the party could repair nothing. Finally, after almost two weeks, the men turned southwest. After a few days, they reached the low, scrubby woods that marked the edge of the treeline, and camped by the side of a lake. The women fished and the hunters killed three deer. These provided two or three solid meals, and then Chawchinahaw led the way northwest through low, scrubby pines and stunted junipers. The men saw animal tracks, including those of deer and muskox, and killed a few partridges—not nearly enough to stave off hunger.

Late in November, Chawchinahaw suggested that the party return to the fort. Hearne flatly refused. He insisted the trading captain, who had received some advance payment, complete his part of the bargain. During recent days, Hearne and his two HBC men had eaten considerably less than the others because the Dene were leading and so had more opportunity to kill partridges, rabbits, and other small game. As well, they had already taken most of the flour, oatmeal, and other English provisions out of the common stock.

One of the two Cree men, Makachy, had brought his Dene wife, and these two frequently resorted to the tents of the leaders and ate with them. The band treated Hearne with some respect, but they were contemptuous of Isbester and Merriman: "knowing them to be but common men, [they] used them so indifferently, particularly in scarce times, that I was under some apprehension of their being starved to death."

Chawchinahaw had calculated that once the Englishmen got a taste of rough-country travelling, they would abandon their foolish quest and retreat to the fort, so absolving him of his promise. Now, realizing that Hearne would not give up in the face of hardship, the band leader changed strategy. He ordered several of his men to desert in the night, taking hatchets, ice-chisels, iron tools, and bags of ammunition. In the morning, when Hearne confronted him, Chawchinahaw denied all knowledge of what had transpired. But he declared that it would not be prudent to continue farther and announced that he and his countrymen were striking off in another direction to join their wives and families.

"What then?" Hearne demanded angrily. "Do you mean to desert us here?"

Chawchinahaw said that was precisely what he intended to do. Gesturing southeast, he suggested that Hearne find the Seal River and follow it to the fort. He and his men then collected their gear and walked off to the southwest. They made "the woods ring with their laughter, and left us to consider of our unhappy situation, near two hundred miles from Prince of Wales Fort, all heavily laden, and our strength and spirits greatly reduced by hunger and fatigue."

Later that morning, having reduced their baggage to a bare minimum, Hearne and his party—two HBC men plus two Cree men and their wives—made their way to the Seal River. For the next few days, they followed that waterway southeast, hunting as they went. The game became so abundant that the travellers gradually regained both strength and spirits. They spent a few days with a lone Dene man they encountered, and hunted beaver with him, then resumed following the river.

On December 11, just over one month since departing to the boom, boom, boom of a seven-gun salute, Hearne arrived back at Prince of Wales Fort—"to my own great mortification, and to the no small surprise of the Governor, who had placed great confidence in the abilities and conduct of Chawchinahaw."

SAMUEL HEARNE told Moses Norton that he wished to depart again as soon as possible—but with a more trustworthy guide. During his one-month absence from Prince of Wales Fort, several Dene men had arrived and been hired to hunt partridges. One of them, a band leader named Conne-e-quese, had travelled near the Far-Off Metal River and knew how to get there. Seeing no prospect of finding a superior candidate, Hearne agreed to travel with him—not just to Athapuscow Lake, but to the mouth of the fabulous river.

While making preparations to leave this second time, and having now gained first-hand experience of travelling with the Dene, Hearne suggested that he should employ some native women as helpers—women who would serve him as they served their own partners.

Norton refused. Best to avoid encumbrances. The governor denied him women, Hearne later observed, "though he well knew we could not do without their assistance," not only for hauling baggage, but for pitching tents, acquiring firewood, and dressing skins for clothing.

Instead of women, Norton said, Hearne should bring a couple of HBC men to handle the menial tasks. The young officer protested that even the most capable traders did not know how to repair snowshoes or create tents from patches of deerskin. Also, he had seen Chawchinahaw treat Company servants so contemptuously that he had feared for their lives. Merriman, having arrived with a terrible cold, wished to remain at the fort. Isbester was ready to go again, but Hearne decided that rather than become responsible for Isbester's well-being, he himself would travel as the sole European. Norton tried to reinstall Makachy, but Hearne considered the man "a sly artful villain" and insisted instead on two other Cree men. The governor supplied him

In this watercolour by Peter Rindisbacher, a Swampy Cree man returns from the hunt with his family. The three walkers are clothed Homeguard style, in leggings and moccasins. Hearne's two Cree companions would have resembled the father, who carries a musket, a powder horn, and three geese.

with ammunition and trading goods and urged him to proceed as quickly as possible.

On February 23, 1770, Hearne left Prince of Wales Fort with three Dene hunters and their families and with two capable Homeguard Cree men. By now, the snow lay so deep on the ramparts that few of the cannons could be seen, much less fired. There could be no seven-gun salute, but the governor, officers, and men gathered out front of the fort and sent Hearne on his way with three rousing cheers. The travellers followed the Seal River westward. The weather was "remarkably boisterous and changeable," and blowing snow forced them to camp for two and three days at a stretch.

Deer were plentiful along the river, but the travellers were so heavily laden they could not carry much meat. For the first couple of weeks, they rarely went to bed without eating. Then came a day when they hunted from dawn until dusk and found not a single partridge. The following morning, they camped by a lake, cut holes in the ice, and, using nets, caught a few fish. They moved several more times. Five miles up a small river, they found a spot where the nets, run carefully under the ice from one hole to another, produced trout, pike, tittymeg, and a "coarse fish" called methy.

Conne-e-quese proposed to remain here until mid-May, when the geese began to fly. Questioned by Hearne, he explained that the weather was too cold to emerge from the woods onto the exposed tundra, while following the woods southwest would mean good hunting but would take them out of their way. Remaining made sense to Hearne, who settled on an elevated point overlooking a large lake and pitched his moosehide tent with greater care than usual. The fish were plentiful, he writes, and "the Indians had too much philosophy about them" to go hunting for partridge. Hearne checked his bearings and updated his journal and charts. He built traps, caught a few martens, and, by way of saving ammunition, set snares for partridges.

Hearne devotes a couple of hundred words to the techniques of snaring martens and partridges. Such naturalistic detail is one of the hallmarks of his book. This discussion follows a precise, 450-word description of pitching a Cree tent in winter: "It is first necessary to search for a level piece of dry ground; which cannot be ascertained but by thrusting a stick through the snow down to the ground, all over the proposed part." He describes how moss must be cut up and removed because of the danger of fire, and then how poles must be procured: "If one of the poles should not happen to be forked, two of them are tied together near the top, then raised erect, and their butts or lower ends extended as wide as the proposed diameter of the tent; the other poles are then set round at equal distances from each other, and in such order, that their lower ends form a complete circle, which gives boundaries to the tent on all sides."

Readers today find this attention to detail excessive. As a man of the Enlightenment, however, Hearne was bent on delivering the close observation and reflection that Rousseau demanded of the ideal explorer. Two hundred yards from his "spring residence," a small waterfall ran fast enough that it created in the frozen lake an area of open water roughly one mile long and half a mile wide. Here the Dene set fishing nets, and Hearne described at length how they did so.

On April 1, the fish suddenly disappeared. Conne-e-quese immediately went hunting. The other men continued to tend the empty nets, and sat around smoking and dozing. Over the next ten days, by hunting until after dark, Conne-e-quese managed to produce a few partridges, but not nearly enough to feed a party this size. Then he was gone until midnight, when, to the joy of all, he returned carrying the most succulent parts of two deer. Within minutes, the camp was a hive of activity, as the suddenly wide-awake men lit a fire and cooked up a broth.

Early the next morning, leaving the camp as it stood, Hearne and the others followed Conne-e-quese to the deer carcasses. One man skinned the animals while another made a hut, or barracado, out of young pine trees. That afternoon, hunters returned having killed two more deer. During the next few days, the party killed five more deer and three beaver, and then spent several days in what Hearne regretted as "feasting and gluttony." To his dismay, the men became "indolent and unthinking" about the fishnets and allowed many fine fish to spoil. Within two weeks, he observed with exasperation, "we were nearly in as great distress for provisions as ever."

The usually empathetic Hearne was forgetting that in this harsh world, he remained a sojourner. Eventually, he would return not only to the relative comfort of Prince of Wales Fort, but to the ease of life in Europe. The native people with whom he travelled would never escape these harsh conditions and had learned to take their pleasures when they could. Who could say? Tomorrow, they might be dead.

EARLY ON APRIL 24, a large number of people arrived on the south-west side of the lake. These were the wives and children of Dene men who had been hired at Prince of Wales Fort to hunt geese and par-tridges. The families were travelling to the Barren Lands, where the men would join them at the end of goose-hunting season. After three more days at the lake, and together with some of these newcomers, Hearne and Conne-e-quese and the others took down their tents and headed east, back to the Seal River.

At a part of that river called "She-than-nee," they pitched their tents and set fishing nets. Soon they were hungry again, subsisting mainly on cranberries gathered from ridges where the snow melted. The ever-observant Hearne noticed that the Dene who had joined them carried a supply of dried meat, which they secretly shared with Conne-e-quese and his people while offering nothing to himself or the two Homeguard Cree men. He couldn't help wondering if he might have fared better travelling without anyone at all from Prince of Wales Fort. Obviously, despite peace treaties and truces, old antipa-thies remained.

In mid-May, hunters began bagging geese and swans. Then came ducks, gulls, and other birds of passage, all in such numbers that the travellers were able to feast. After a few days, fully restored and with the weather having grown mild, Hearne set out to the northwest with a dozen people, Conne-e-quese having added another wife. Realizing that the melting of the snow signalled the end of sledge hauling, Hearne hired a Dene man to help carry baggage. One of his Cree companions, the highly competent Sossop, shattered his hand when a gun exploded on firing. While serving in the Royal Navy, Hearne had treated more than a few injuries, and now, "as no bones were broken, I bound up the wound, and with the assistance of some of Turlington's drops, yellow basilicon, etc, which I had with me, soon restored the use of his hand; so that in a very short time he seemed to be out of all danger."

Hearne and the others emerged onto the Barren Grounds. Looking out over the treeless, snow-covered tundra rolling away to the horizon, the young Englishman remembered the pastoral, tree-dotted hills around Beaminster and could not help feeling he was approaching the ends of the earth. The bright sun made the snow so soft and heavy that even with snowshoes, walking became difficult. Finally, with stretches of bare ground appearing more and more frequently, and despite the occasional snowdrift, the travellers threw away their worn snowshoes. They continued hauling sledges over frozen rivers, lakes, and ponds until the ice grew too thin. Then, reluctantly, they hoisted their baggage onto their backs.

Hearne carried the Hadley's quadrant and its stand, a valise containing books and papers, a land-compass, a large bag of clothes and toiletries, a few tools (a hatchet, knives, and files), and several other small articles. This awkward load weighed over sixty pounds. In the midday heat, walking became "the most laborious task I had ever encountered; and what considerably increased the hardship, was the badness of the road, and the coarseness of our lodging, on account of the want of proper tents, exposed to the utmost severity of the weather."

Neither Hearne nor the two Cree had travelled any great distance on the Barren Grounds. Nor had anyone back at Prince of Wales Fort done so. The tent Hearne had brought, designed in the treed south, required poles where none could be found. The Englishman felt that Conne-e-quese behaved

both negligently and ungenerously on this occasion; as he never made me, or my Southern Indians, acquainted with the nature of pitching tents on the barren grounds; which had he done, we could easily have procured a set of poles before we left the woods. He took care, however, to procure a set for himself and his wife; and when the [large Cree] tent was divided, though he made shift to get a piece large enough to serve him for a complete little tent, he never asked me or my Southern Indians to put our heads into it.

Here, again, we see a clash of cultures and perceptions. The Dene are proudly self-reliant. Conne-e-quese had assumed that Hearne and his companions would take care of themselves. They were adults, after all, and any child would know enough to acquire tent poles before venturing onto the Barren Grounds. He had agreed to guide Hearne to the Far-Off Metal River; he had not undertaken to hold his hand.

Continually exposed to the elements, the travellers were also usually famished. Sometimes, when hunters did procure food, the seasonal rains would make building a fire impossible and so force people to eat their meat raw. The Dene had long ago adjusted to this, but Hearne and the Cree found raw meat revolting. Even when the hunting was good, the travellers could not carry enough provisions to last more than a couple of days, so getting enough to eat remained a constant challenge.

By the end of June, the geese and ducks had finished migrating, and even partridges and gulls had grown scarce. One morning, after walking seven or eight miles, the travellers came upon three muskox at a lake—large, stinking beasts with broad, curving horns and shaggy brown coats. The expert Dene hunters soon dispatched these animals. But before the women could finish skinning even one of them, rain began hammering down so heavily that, one hundred miles from the nearest trees, and with nothing available but moss, nobody could start a fire.

Hearne describes the meat of the muskox as coarse, tough, and stinking. He and his Cree companions, who had choked down raw caribou and fish, found this almost impossible to eat. Yet the heavy rain, interspersed with snow and sleet, continued long enough that these tentless travellers, who could only huddle beneath deerskins, had helped devour nearly one entire ox before they could build a fire.

Notwithstanding I mustered up all my philosophy on this occasion, yet I must confess that my spirits began to fail me. Indeed our other misfortunes were greatly aggravated by the inclemency of the weather, which was not only cold, but so very wet that for near three days and nights, I had not one dry thread about me. When the fine weather returned, we made a fire, though it was only of moss, as I have already observed; and having got my clothes dry, all things seemed likely to go on in the old channel, though that was indifferent enough; but I endeavored, like a sailor after a storm, to forget past misfortunes.

The old channel meant feast or famine: "sometimes we had too much, seldom just enough, frequently too little, and often none at all."

It meant fasting often for two days and nights. Twice, the travellers had gone hungry for more than three days, and once they had survived seven days on cranberries, leather scraps, and burnt bones. Hearne had seen some of the Dene examine their animal-skin clothing for something to stave off starvation, settling on a piece of rotten deerskin or a pair of old shoes. "Another disagreeable circumstance of long fasting," Hearne writes, "is, the extreme difficulty and pain attending the natural evacuations for the first time; and which is so dreadful, that of it none but those who have experienced can have an adequate idea."

When the sun came out, the travellers dried some muskox meat to make it portable, and then continued north. They reached a river called Catha-wha-chaga, which empties into Yathkyed Lake, or White Snow Lake, and found a number of Dene camped there. Led by a middle-aged man named Keelshies, these native people were heading south to trade furs at the fort. Keelshies agreed to carry a letter, and also to bring a response, promising to meet Hearne later at an appointed place.

The explorer wrote Moses Norton asking him to send powder, shot, tobacco, and knives. The travellers stayed several days at Catha-wha-chaga, where fishing nets produced numerous fifteen-pound trout. Hearne made observations (latitude 63 degrees 4 minutes north) and updated his journal and charts. On the advice of Conne-e-quese, who felt badly about the misunderstanding over tent poles, he traded a knife for a small canoe from a native man travelling in the opposite direction. He also hired a man to carry it.

Through mid-July, the travellers proceeded northwest. They killed several more muskox and prepared the meat, cutting the lean parts into thin slices, drying those in the sun, and then beating them with stones into a fine powder. Hearne, always keenly interested in language, noted that this portable food, clearly a kind of pemmican, was known in most parts of Hudson Bay as *thew-hagon*, though the Dene called it *achees*.

The travellers took up with strangers and successfully hunted deer, Hearne regretting that so many were killed merely for the tongues, marrow, and fat. After spending a few days with these hunters, following the deer where they led, Hearne asked Conne-e-quese when they might proceed farther north. The guide answered that it was too late in the year to reach the Far-Off Metal River. He proposed to continue westward and winter with this larger party, then complete the journey the following spring. "As I could not pretend to contradict him," Hearne writes, "I was entirely reconciled to his proposal."

By the end of July, as more and more Dene arrived in the area, Hearne found himself encamped among seventy tents and six hundred people. Such regional gatherings occurred annually at fixed locations, usually beside a lake or a river where a breeze would blow away the mosquitoes. They offered the men a chance to mingle and gamble and, above all, to take wives from among the women of other bands. At night, with fires blazing, the camp looked like a small town. Some areas grew raucous and rowdy, putting Hearne in mind of The Point in Portsmouth.

In the morning, when people emerged from their tents to pack and drift slowly westward, following the caribou, the vast, treeless area came alive with men, women, children, and barking dogs. Beyond the tents, whichever way he looked, Hearne saw the dark tundra rolling away to the horizon, treeless and empty but for boulders, low-lying moss, and shrub-like *wish-a-capucca*, tough plants from which people made tea. The deer had become so numerous that hunters killed too many, in Hearne's view, leaving their carcasses for wolves and foxes.

The travellers, Hearne among them, crossed the Dubawnt River—the first of several unfordable waterways—in their tiny, two-person canoes. These were so light and unstable that when crossing a river, one person would lie down in the bottom while the other sat on his heels and paddled. Some of the native men had carried these canoes two hundred miles. But early in August, Hearne saw that the man he had hired to carry his canoe was struggling under the load. He transferred the craft to a stronger individual, which left the first fellow carrying nothing but gunpowder and personal effects.

An excellent hunter, Hearne decided to contribute to the deer hunt. To lighten his load while doing so, he asked the lightly burdened man to carry his quadrant and stand, which were cumbersome. Early the next morning, Hearne set out with the Cree and a couple of Dene. After hiking eight or nine miles, the hunters climbed a hill, looked out, and discovered a great herd of deer feeding in a valley. They erected a flag to mark the spot as a campsite, and then pursued the deer, with great success.

That evening, when he arrived back at the new campsite, Hearne learned that some of the Dene had gone off in an entirely different direction—among them the fellow to whom he had entrusted his powder, quadrant and stand. Without that quadrant he would be unable to take observations and make maps. Continuing his journey would be pointless. And the idea of being without powder, which he needed to acquire food and clothing, alarmed both Hearne and the two Cree men.

Hearne had begun to suspect that his Dene fellow travellers, many of them strangers who knew nothing of the arrangements made at Prince of Wales Fort, regarded himself and the Cree as inept hangers-on and wished they would just go away—the sooner, the better. They had been encouraging their departure by deliberate rudeness, which at first Hearne had apprehended as a lack of consideration:

So inconsiderate were those people, that wherever they met me, they always expected that I had a great assortment of goods to relieve their necessities; as if I had brought the Company's warehouse with me. Some of them wanted guns; all wanted ammunition, iron-work, and tobacco; many were solicitous for medicine; and others pressed me for different articles of clothing: but when they found I had nothing to spare, except a few nick-knacks and gewgaws, they made no scruple of pronouncing me a poor servant, [not at all] like the Governor at the Factory, whom, they said, they never saw, but he gave them something useful.

Hearne realized that if he were reduced to depending on this large group of strangers, he would be in trouble. He lay down to rest but tossed and turned all night, unable to sleep. In his *Journey*, which he revised years later in London, the explorer declares that he found himself remembering the "beautiful lines" of a poem by Edward Young:

TIRED Nature's sweet restorer, balmy Sleep!
He, like the world, his ready visit pays
Where Fortune smiles; the wretched he forsakes;
Swift on his downy pinion flies from woe,
And lights on lids unsullied with a tear.

The awkwardness of this interpolation, coupled with the scarcely credible assertion that he lay awake recalling this poem, betrays Hearne's desire to prove himself an educated man—a yearning that, when he revised his manuscript, would overcome him more than once. No sophisticated writer, even of the eighteenth century, would have introduced such anomalous material into the narrative; no competent editor would have allowed it to stand.

At daybreak, Hearne and the two Cree set out to retrieve the missing quadrant. Driven by a sense of urgency, they retraced their path of the previous day and spent hours following one branching track or another. Finally, Hearne proposed that they return to the place where he had given the fellow his quadrant. From there, they followed a path to a small river—"and there, to our great joy, we found the quadrant and the bag of powder lying on the top of a high stone."

The powder bag had been lightened, but at least Hearne and his companions would be able to survive. They hiked the eight or nine miles back to the campsite of the previous night, where they found their baggage safe—but the Dene departed. In the growing darkness, they could see campfires in the distance. They adjusted their bundles and resumed hiking, arriving at the new campsite after ten o'clock. For the first time that day, they ate.

On August 12, 1770, Hearne spent the morning taking observations with his quadrant. The weather was fine and the visibility excellent. Hearne determined his latitude to be 63 degrees 10 minutes north. In longitude, he was 10 degrees 40 minutes west of Prince of Wales Fort. Shortly after noon, when he broke off to eat lunch, Hearne left the quadrant in place: "I let the quadrant stand, in order to obtain the latitude more exactly by two altitudes; but, to my great mortification, while I was eating my dinner, a sudden gust of wind blew it down; and as the ground where it stood was very stony, the bubble, the sight-vane, and vernier, were entirely broke to pieces, which rendered the instrument useless."

With a gust of wind, his worst nightmare had become a reality. Shocked, disbelieving, Hearne stood examining the shattered glass. Without a quadrant, he could take no observations, establish no positions. If he discovered a copper mine or a Northwest Passage, he would be unable to establish its location. Standing in the sunshine, oblivious to the mosquitoes and blackflies, a broken-hearted Hearne realized that, having travelled for six months, he had reached the end of this particular journey. Without a quadrant, he had no choice but to retrace his steps. He gazed southwest across the Barren Grounds. Six hundred miles away lay Prince of Wales Fort. He would have to walk much farther than that, he knew, following caribou and other game through some of the most difficult country in the world, to acquire a new quadrant and begin again.

THE DAY AFTER Hearne broke his quadrant, two dozen strangers arrived at the camp from farther north. Before long, they reminded the Englishman of two things he already knew. First, here in the Barrens, the only law was the survival of the fittest. Second, the Dene were a diverse people, and one small band was not like another. Soon after the strangers arrived, six of the toughest men among them visited Hearne in his tent, which comprised three walking sticks and a blanket. The ringleader sat down to his left and asked to borrow his *skipertogan*—the small, richly ornamented bag in which he kept his pipe and tobacco, as well as a flint and touchwood for making a fire. Later the explorer would observe, "Nothing can exceed the cool deliberation of those villains."

After smoking two or three pipes, the leader asked for several items Hearne did not have, among them a pack of playing cards. One of the men picked up the explorer's bag and asked if it was his. Before Hearne could reply, the man dumped the contents onto the ground, explaining that since he was returning to the fort, the Englishman would no longer need these supplies. The first man took one item, the second another, until at last nothing remained but the empty bag, which they graciously allowed him to keep.

Showing customary sang-froid, Hearne observed that although he would soon be leaving, he would still need a knife to cut his food, an awl to repair his shoes, and a needle to mend his clothes. The men gave him back these items, making certain he understood this to be a great favour. Then, "finding them possessed of so much generosity, I ventured to solicit them for my razors; but thinking that one would be sufficient to shave me during my passage home, they made no scruple to keep the other; luckily, they chose the worst. To complete their generosity, they permitted me to take as much soap as I thought would be sufficient to wash and shave me during the remainder of my journey to the factory."

These new arrivals treated the two Cree men to a similar visit. Here they were more cautious, Hearne tells us, because they did not wish to start a war between nations. But when the visit was over, the Cree retained nothing but their guns, some ammunition, an old hatchet, an ice-chisel, and a file.

It might be thought strange, Hearne observes, that his Dene guide should allow this boldfaced thieving. Having indicated that Conne-e-quese was an older band leader, knowledgeable but not fierce, he now explains that, in comparison with other warrior captains, he was "a man of little note." Indeed, "he was so far from being able to protect us, that he was obliged to submit to nearly the same outrage himself. On this occasion he assumed a great air of generosity; but the fact was, he gave freely what it was not in his power to protect."

On August 19, 1770, considerably poorer than he had been, Samuel Hearne started south with Conne-e-quese, the two Homeguard Cree men, and a few Dene who were bound for Prince of Wales Fort with furs. Just before the explorer departed, the man who had brazenly stolen his gun returned it, having realized that he had no ammunition.

The weather was fine, the deer plentiful, and as he was carrying only his broken quadrant and books, Hearne enjoyed this part of the journey. As he travelled, he smoked the calumet, or peace pipe, with passing strangers, some of whom, carrying furs to trade at the fort, joined their party.

Hearne and the two Cree men had taken care to collect ten or twelve deerskins to make into winter clothes. After carrying these for several weeks, and as the weather turned cold and the snow began to fly, the explorer tried to hire Dene women to dress the skins and sew them into suits. None would do it. Nor would the men trade clothing made from inferior furs for his superior furs, prompting Hearne to deplore their lack of humanity: "though they seem to have a great affection for their wives and children, yet they will laugh at and ridicule the distress of every other person who is not immediately related to them."

As far as the Dene were concerned, the Englishman and the Cree needed to be taught a lesson. They were ridiculous, venturing into the Barren Grounds without women. Why should the Dene warriors order their wives to do the work of these strangers? They could see no compelling reason. Conne-e-quese, who knew better, had withdrawn from active leadership. Having brought along one of his wives, he sported a warm fur suit and enjoyed the nightly warmth of a deerskin tent. But "the old fellow" had lost face when he was robbed, and he felt so ashamed before his nominal charges that he paid them scant attention.

The cold grew intense and the three outsiders suffered from their lack of fur clothing. When the first snows had covered the ground to a depth of six inches, Conne-e-quese and the other Dene donned

This caribou-skin model of a Gwich'in Dene hunter wears a warm, winter suit of the kind that Hearne yearned to don as winter came on and temperatures plummeted.

snowshoes—crafted, of course, by their wives—and trekked onward, at first indifferent, and then scornful, to see the two Cree and the muscular Hearne fall behind, floundering in their moccasins, unable to keep pace. These strangers knew less than young children. What were they doing here?

The future was looking grim when, from out of the blowing snow, leading a dozen or so Chipewyan, an authoritative leader appeared. At nearly six feet in height, considerably taller than most Dene, this singular figure—"one of the finest and best proportioned men I ever saw"— was able to look Hearne almost directly in the eye. The explorer, unaware that he himself cut a ludicrous figure with his ritualistic daily shaving, observed that the stranger did not follow "that ridiculous custom of marking the cheeks with three or four black lines."

Speaking fluent Cree and also a bit of English in addition to his native Athapaskan, this charismatic stranger expressed surprise at meeting a white man in the Barrens. He asked Hearne how he had fallen into such straits. The young explorer could hardly believe his ears. Could this be the native leader he had been originally instructed to find? The one who had not only visited the Far-Off Metal River but had brought back copper from its mines? Could this be Matonabbee?

AMONG NORTHERN EXPLORERS of the eighteenth century, none came closer to exemplifying Jean-Jacques Rousseau's ideal traveller than Samuel Hearne. And this is nowhere more evident than in the profoundly sympathetic yet unflinching word-portrait he would paint of Matonabbee, the peerless Dene leader who now entered his life.

No novelist could have introduced Matonabbee into Hearne's story more dramatically than real life did. The native leader might have arrived before the young explorer had broken his quadrant, or else shortly afterward, along with the brazen thieves. He might have turned up back at Prince of Wales Fort—assuming that Hearne could have made it.

But Matonabbee turned up at exactly the right moment. Perceiving that Hearne was shivering with cold, he immediately supplied him with a warm otter-fur suit. Then, having remembered meeting the two Homeguard Cree men during sojourns at the fort, he ordered his wives to dress their furs and make them suits, too. Acquiring snowshoes here in this rocky, treeless Barrens would prove a greater challenge. But Matonabbee knew of a small river that lay just a few days away, where sparse trees would supply the requisite wood and webbing. He would send women with them to make snowshoes. Then he would slow his pace in travelling toward the fort so that, once they had donned snowshoes, Hearne and the others could catch up.

Before branching off to find the woods, Hearne spent a few days travelling southeast with his new friend. The hunting was excellent, and Matonabbee organized a southern-style feast for the explorer and his companions, an evening that culminated in singing and dancing.

The following day, Matonabbee invited Hearne into his tent. The two men sat cross-legged, talking in Athapaskan while smoking a calumet. Matonabbee asked Hearne if he still wished to travel in search of the copper mine. The younger man responded emphatically: yes! He remained determined to complete the quest and required only a competent guide.

Matonabbee declared that Hearne's difficulties arose not because of the incompetence of his guides, but because of the design of the expedition. Specifically, he noted the absence of women. Women were made for labour, Matonabbee said. One woman could carry or haul as much as any two men. They required little food. They pitched tents, dressed skins, and mended clothing: "There is no such thing as travelling any distance in this country, or for any length of time, without their assistance."

"I could not agree more," Hearne responded. "With a woman to cook, dress furs, and make snowshoes, this journey would have been far different."

Matonabbee took a pull on the pipe, then exhaled and said, "You would take a wife? You would travel as one of the people?"

"Of course," Hearne said. "Beyond that, I would travel alone. No Homeguard."

"You have found your guide," Matonabbee said. "If the governor approves, I will take you to the Far-Off Metal River."

*   *   *

MOSES NORTON emerges from the pages of *A Journey to the Northern Ocean* as one of the most despicable figures in fur-trade history. But Hearne did not discover the darkest truths about the governor until the late 1770s, and he did not put it on record until later, when he appended long footnotes to early drafts of his manuscript. In November 1770, when he arrived back at the fort after his second failed attempt to reach the Far-Off Metal River, Hearne did not yet know enough to detest the governor.

The return journey had not been easy. Late in October, while Matonabbee proceeded south toward Prince of Wales Fort, Hearne had struck off eastward with his Cree companions and three Dene women. After two days, these six reached the sparse woods Matonabbee had remembered. They worked as quickly as possible, but still spent four days making snowshoe frames and small sledges. On the first of November, properly fitted out for wintertime travel, Hearne and the others resumed their southward journey. After five days, they caught up with Matonabbee. During the next two weeks, while trekking southeast, Hearne learned more about this native leader, and later he filled in many other blanks.

Eight or nine years older than Hearne, Matonabbee had been born at Churchill to a Dene hunter and a "slave woman" captured in a raid. His father died when Matonabbee was very young, and Governor Richard Norton—the father of Moses, who was then sixteen or seventeen—had adopted the boy as his son. Richard Norton retired to England in 1741, however, and his successor returned the four-year-old child to his Dene relatives.

In 1752, yet another governor, Ferdinand Jacobs, hired Matonabbee into Churchill's hunting service, where he worked with Moses Norton. During those years, Matonabbee mastered the Cree language, learned some English, and gained some knowledge of the Christian faith. Indeed, he could "tell a better story of our Saviour's birth and life than one half of those who call themselves Christians." He didn't believe a word of the gospel, but pronounced Christianity "too deep and intricate for his comprehension." Later, Hearne would summarize his attitude:

He could by no means be impressed with a belief of any part of our religion, nor of the religion of the Southern Indians, who have as firm a belief in a future state as any people under the Sun. He had so much natural good sense and liberality of sentiment, however, as not to think that he had a right to ridicule any particular sect on account of their religious opinions. On the contrary, he declared, that he held them all equally in esteem, but was determined, as he came into the world, so he would go out of it, without professing any religion at all. Notwithstanding his aversion from religion, I have met with few Christians who possessed more good moral qualities, or fewer bad ones.

Governor Jacobs recognized Matonabbee's potential from the first. With a view to increasing trade, he hired the young man to serve as a mediator, and to make peace between the Dene and the Athapuscow, the Cree who lived far to the west around Lake Athabasca.

During his first visit to these Athabasca Cree, Matonabbee discovered the Dene leader Keelshies living as a prisoner among them. Keelshies had been captured while roaming Cree lands with his family and friends, and their fate was yet to be decided. Although young enough to be the son of Keelshies, Matonabbee negotiated the release of him and his male friends, though not of his goods and six wives.

Accompanied by one wife and a servant boy, Matonabbee proceeded still farther into Athabasca country. He arrived at a camp where five tents housed sixteen men, plus wives, children, and servants. These people welcomed him heartily, accepted his tokens of peace and reconciliation, and proposed to hold a rotating evening feast during which he would visit and be entertained at each tent in succession. At the final tent, they would murder him.

He was, however, so perfect a master of the Southern Indian language [Cree], that he soon discovered their design, and told them, he was not come in a hostile manner, but if they attempted any thing of the kind he was determined to sell his life as dear as possible. On hearing this, some of them ordered that his servant, gun, and snowshoes (for it was winter) should be brought into the tent and secured; but he sprang from his seat, seized his gun and snowshoes, and went out of the tent, telling them, if they had an intention to molest him, that was the proper place where he could see his enemy, and be under no

Samuel Hearne.

MATONABBEE.
c 1737 · d 1782 ·

PRINCE OF WALES'S FORT c 1777

RUTH JEPSON

This portrait of Matonabbee (c. 1737–1782) by Ruth Jepson celebrates the great Dene leader as belonging at the heart of Samuel Hearne's epic journey. Without Matonabbee, certainly, the Englishman would never have reached the mouth of the Coppermine River—and the history of northern exploration would be radically different.

apprehensions of being shot cowardly through the back. "I am sure (said he) of killing two or three of you, and if you choose to purchase my life at that price, now is the time; but if otherwise, let me depart without any further molestation." They then told him that he was at liberty to go, on condition of leaving his servant; but to this he would not consent. He then rushed into the tent and took his servant by force from two men; when finding there was no appearance of further danger, he set out on his return to frontiers of his own country, and from thence to the Factory.

The following year, Matonabbee again travelled west into Athabasca country, accompanied this time by a large party of Dene warriors. Backed by this force, he criss-crossed the area and talked peace with the principal band leaders. In the summer, when his party dispersed, he again faced down a large group of men bent on his destruction. Matonabbee persevered, and eventually, "by a uniform display of his pacific disposition and by rendering a long train of good offices to those Indians, in return for their treachery and perfidy," he single-handedly achieved not only a lasting peace but a mutually profitable trading relationship.

A FEW DAYS' JOURNEY from Prince of Wales Fort, with game growing scarce as a result of overhunting, Samuel Hearne set out at a rapid pace with an advance party of one Cree and three Dene. Almost immediately, he ran into a violent gale. Fierce winds and blowing snow reduced the men to huddling among large rocks, unable even to start a fire. Late that evening, when Hearne emerged from the tent to check on a dog who had been hauling a heavy sledge, he found this valuable creature frozen to death. Next day, when the weather cleared, he himself had to haul the sledge.

Finally, on the freezing cold but sunny afternoon of November 25, 1770, Samuel Hearne once again walked through the high front gate of Prince of Wales Fort. He had been away for eight months and twenty-two days on what he felt to be "a fruitless, or at least an unsuccessful, journey."

In summarizing the trek for Governor Moses Norton, Hearne

focused on the positive. He had found Matonabbee, who was even now approaching the fort, and determined that this peerless native leader was willing to serve as guide for yet another northern expedition. As the governor digested this information, Hearne went further, volunteering to travel with Matonabbee. Norton accepted, Hearne would write, "as my abilities and approved courage, in persevering under difficulties, were thought noways inferior to the task."

Soon after Matonabbee arrived, the three men met in the governor's quarters. There, "with a freedom of speech and correctness of language not commonly met with among Indians," the native leader laid out the reasons for the two previous failures, notably the absence of women. He also outlined the plan he would follow in travelling to the Far-Off Metal River, and presented a rough timetable.

As Matonabbee spoke, Hearne watched with delighted amazement. The native leader declined all offers of spirits and did not drink to excess—and yet showed a discerning fondness for Spanish wines!

His features were regular and agreeable, and yet so strongly marked and expressive that they formed a complete index of his mind; which, as he never intended to deceive or dissemble, he never wished to conceal. In conversation he was easy, lively, and agreeable, but exceedingly modest; and at table, the nobleness and elegance of his manners might have been admired by the first personages in the world; for to the vivacity of a Frenchman, and the sincerity of an Englishman, he added the gravity and nobleness of a Turk; all so happily blended, as to render his company and conversation universally pleasing to those who understood either the Northern or Southern Indian languages, the only languages in which he could converse.

Moses Norton, now fifty, was twice as old as Hearne and fifteen or sixteen years older than Matonabbee. Since 1762, when he had become governor of Prince of Wales Fort, Norton had employed every means at his disposal to prevent HBC men from taking native wives. He was forever urging "virtue, morality, and continence on others; always painting, in the most odious colors, the jealous and revengeful disposition of the Indians, when any attempt was made to violate the chastity of their wives or daughters."

By 1770, Samuel Hearne knew enough to dismiss Norton's

harangues as sheer hypocrisy. Nor was he surprised when the governor again proposed that he take along some of Norton's relatives, with a view to gaining credit for himself. Having found the Cree to be no help at all among the Dene, and almost as much of a worry as any HBC man, Hearne "absolutely refused them; and by so doing, offended Mr. Norton to such a degree, that neither time nor absence could ever afterwards eradicate his dislike of me; so that at my return he used every means in his power to treat me ill, and to render my life unhappy."

Still, as Hearne observed, "whatever our private animosities might have been, [Norton] did not suffer them to interfere with public business; and I was fitted out with ammunition, and every other article which Matonabbee thought could be wanted." Norton supplied Hearne with an antiquated quadrant, however, one far inferior to the one he had broken, justifying this by observing that "having no other instrument on the same construction with the quadrant you had the misfortune to break, we have furnished you with an Elton's quadrant, being the most proper instrument we can now procure for making observations on the land."

In fact, Norton had brought from England *two* of the newer, more portable Hadley's quadrants. The second one was then sitting idle on an HBC sloop and could certainly have gone to Hearne, who had been ready, virtually from the day he entered the fort, to depart again with Matonabbee. Finally, on December 7, 1770, Governor Moses Norton handed him his written orders. That afternoon, not two weeks after he had arrived, Hearne left again for the distant northwest, accompanied by Matonabbee and a handful of Dene.

This time he would reach the Far-Off Metal River or die trying.

7

MASSACRE
AT BLOODY FALLS

IN PREPARING his *Journey* for publication, Samuel Hearne would spend years working on revisions in both Rupert's Land and London, where eventually he gained access to the Hudson's Bay Company archives. He worked from his original field notes and early drafts. Except for two long final chapters, in which he wrote about the "Northern Indians," or Dene, and about the animals and plants of the north, he told the story of his remarkable three-year quest in roughly chronological order.

This painting by A.H. Hider, called Prince of Wales Fort, 1734, *communicates much about the world into which Hearne plunged—the snowshoes, the musket, the powder horn, the dog at work, the treeless horizon. Smoke rises from the fort, which flies a Union Jack.*

While revising, Hearne added many passages of context, clarification, and reflection—passages detailed, insightful, and evocative enough to turn his book into the first recognized classic of northern exploration literature. As well, he added dozens of extended footnotes, which would have been integrated into a more polished text. Scholars have been able to date some of the later additions by comparing Hearne's published *Journey* with a report he sent to HBC headquarters in London in 1772, a narrative held at the British Library and known as the Stowe manuscript.

This manuscript begins with Hearne's third departure, when in December 1770 the young adventurer left Prince of Wales Fort with Matonabbee. During the ensuing weeks and months, Hearne became immersed in the survivalist way of life of his nomadic fellow travellers, who roamed the Barren Lands situated between the Western Cree and the Inuit. As the scholar Victor Hopwood observes, the book Hearne eventually wrote about his expedition suggests with near certainty "that he was adopted into the tribe of his adviser, Matonabbee, and, according to the custom of the Chipewyans, had at least one wife to make his explorations possible."

With his fellow travellers, Hearne lived the cycle of feast and famine, frequently trekking two or three days while tasting nothing but tobacco and snow water. Then the party would kill a few deer and gorge themselves, so that on one occasion Matonabbee ate so much that he fell ill and had to be hauled on a sledge.

Hearne paints a vivid picture of the landscape and of travelling through shrubby woods, mainly stunted pines, dwarf junipers, and small willows and poplars. He describes following the deer, marching through ponds and swamps and among rocks, and stopping for several days at a time where the hunting was good. At a small lake containing so many islands that it resembled "a jumble of serpentine rivers and creeks," Matonabbee and his men rejoined a couple of dozen women and children who had been waiting for them.

Only once does Hearne mention loneliness. Writing of travelling hungry at Christmas, and speaking not of England but of all Europe, whose port cities he knew well from his days as a sailor, he observes, "when I recollected the merry season which was then passing, and reflected on the immense quantities, and great variety of delicacies which were then expending in every part of Christendom, and that with a profusion bordering on waste, I could not refrain from wishing myself again in Europe, if it had been only to have had an opportunity of alleviating the extreme hunger which I suffered with the refuse of the table of any one of my acquaintance."

Hearne writes admiringly of the stoicism of the Chipewyan. Early in the journey, the men returned to a cache of provisions they had carefully secured out of reach of animals while travelling to Churchill, only to discover that some of their countrymen, having left the fort before them, had plundered the site, taking not only all the food but many useful tools. The band bore this loss "with the greatest fortitude," Hearne writes, "and I did not hear one of them breathe the least hint of revenge in case they should ever discover the offenders."

Even when hungry, Hearne notes, the Dene kept a sense of humour. After three or four days of imposed fasting, the men would remain "merry and jocose on the subject . . . and would ask each other in the plainest terms, and in the merriest mood, if they had any inclination for an intrigue with a strange woman." By now, clearly, Hearne understood the Athapaskan language well enough to appreciate jokes. The levity lifted his spirits, which would quickly have sunk "had the Indians behaved in a contrary manner, and expressed any apprehension of starving."

Hearne also responded to the earthiness of the people. Early in February, during a period of intense cold, the travellers had to trek fourteen miles across "Cossed Whoie," or Partridge Lake, utterly without shelter, and with arctic winds driving temperatures down to minus 40 or 50 degrees Fahrenheit.

Several of the women were much frozen, but none of them more disagreeably so than one of Matonabbee's wives, whose thighs and buttocks were in a manner incrusted with frost; and when thawed, several blisters arose, nearly as large as sheep's bladders. The pain the poor woman suffered on this occasion was greatly aggravated by the laughter and jeering of her companions, who said that she was rightly served for belting her clothes so high. I must acknowledge that I was not in the number of those who pitied her, as I thought she took too much pains to shew a clean heel and good leg; her garters being always in sight, which, though by no means considered here as bordering on indecency, is by far too airy to withstand the rigorous cold of a severe winter in a high northern latitude. I doubt not that the laughter of her companions was excited by similar ideas.

Proceeding westward, walking usually from morning until night, the travellers followed the edge of the woods, where fuel and food could be had, while the treeless, rocky barrens remained clearly visible to the north. They encountered a large group of Dene living beyond the Catha-wha-chaga River, where deer were plentiful. Hearne jotted a lot of notes, which he later drew on to describe, in characteristic detail, the making of a pound to trap animals:

The pound is built by making a strong fence with brushy trees, without observing any degree of regularity, and the work is continued to any extent, according to the pleasure of the builders. I have seen some that were not less than a mile round, and am informed that there are others still more extensive. The door, or entrance of the pound, is not larger than a common gate, and the inside is so crowded with small counter-hedges as very much to resemble a maze; in every opening of which they set a snare, made with thongs of parchment deer-skins well twisted together, which are amazingly strong. One end of the snare is usually made fast to a growing pole; but if no one of a sufficient size can be found near the place where the snare is set, a loose pole is substituted in its room.

Hearne also describes the hunt itself, with men, women, and children chasing the hapless deer into the pound, then blocking up the entrance. "This method of hunting, if it deserves the name," he writes, "is sometimes so successful, that many families subsist by it without having occasion to move their tents above once or twice during the course of a whole winter." He suggests that this method of surviving a harsh winter is well adapted to supporting the aged and infirm but encourages indolence in the young and active. Those who live this life procure no furs for the HBC. On the other hand, he reflects—almost subversively— what do the industrious native traders gain through working furiously and constantly running the risk of starving to death?

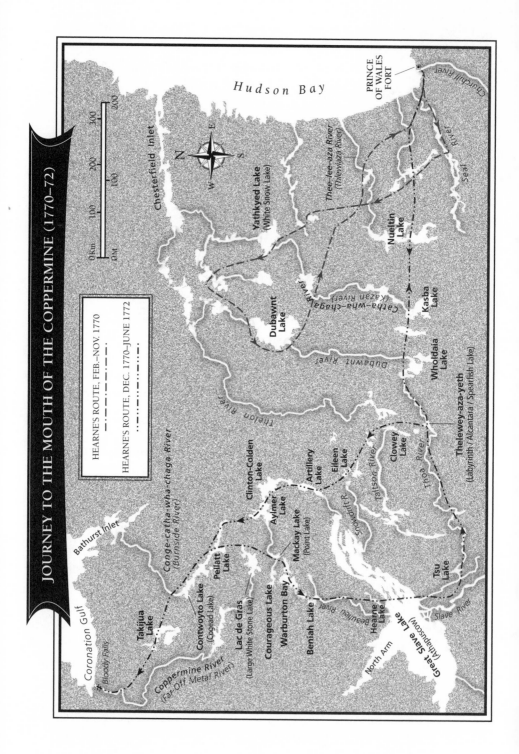

JOURNEY TO THE MOUTH OF THE COPPERMINE (1770–72)

HEARNE'S ROUTE, FEB.–NOV. 1770

HEARNE'S ROUTE, DEC. 1770–JUNE 1772

Hudson Bay

PRINCE OF WALES FORT

Churchill River

Seal River

Chesterfield Inlet

Yathkyed Lake
(White Snow Lake)

Thee-lee-aza River
(Thlewiaza River)

Nueltin Lake

Dubawnt Lake

Catha-wha-chaga River
(Kazan River)

Kasba Lake

Wholdaia Lake

Thelewey-aza-yeth
(Labyrinth / Alcantara / Spearfish Lake)

Dubawnt River

Thelon River

Thoa River

Clowey Lake

Taltson River

Eileen Lake

Artillery Lake

Clinton-Colden Lake

Aylmer Lake

Bathurst Inlet

Conge-catha-wha-chaga River
(Burnside River)

Pellatt Lake

Takijua Lake

Contwoyto Lake
(Cogead Lake)

Lac de Gras

Coronation Gulf

Bloody Falls

Coppermine River
(Far-Off Metal River)

Large White Stone Lake

Courageous Lake

Warburton Bay

Mackay Lake
(Point Lake)

Snowdrift R.

Beniah Lake

Beaulieu River

Hearne Lake

North Arm

Great Slave Lake
(Athapuscow)

Slave River

Tsu Lake

N

0 Km 100 200 300
0 M 100 200

The real wants of these people are few, and easily supplied; a hatchet, an ice-chisel, a file, and a knife, are all that is required to enable them, with a little industry, to procure a comfortable livelihood; and those who endeavour to possess more, are always the most unhappy, and may, in fact, be said to be only slaves and carriers to the rest, whose ambition never leads them to any thing beyond the means of procuring food and clothing.... It is undoubtedly the duty of every one of the Company's servants to encourage a spirit of industry among the natives ... and I can truly say that this has ever been the grand object of my attention. But I must at the same time confess, that such conduct is by no means for the real benefit of the poor Indians; it being well-known that those who have the least intercourse with the factories are by far the happiest.

As their whole aim is to procure a comfortable subsistence, they take the most prudent methods to accomplish it; and by always following the lead of the deer, are seldom exposed to the gripping hand of famine, so frequently felt by those who are called the annual traders.

ANY MAP of Hearne's travels is an approximation based on confusing and sometimes contradictory data. But early in April, roughly six hundred miles west of Prince of Wales Fort, the travellers reached Thelewey-aza-yeth, which means Little Fish Hill. The name derives, Hearne suggests, from "a high hill which stands on a long point near the west end of the Lake." Geographers and fur-trade historians have been debating the identity of this body of water since the 1830s, when Sir John Richardson suggested that Thelewey-aza-yeth lay some-where south of Artillery Lake. Subsequent investigators proposed Alcantara Lake and then Labyrinth Lake, but the prevailing view, put forward in 1999 by W.A. Fuller, is that Hearne is referring to present-day Spearfish Lake.

During the next ten days, while preparing to strike northward, the men hunted deer and the women dried, pounded, and conserved meat for the journey ahead. By now the party had swollen to more than sev-enty, children included. Some of the men prepared tent poles, cutting small birches into staves. Extras they bundled together; dogs would haul these through the summer, and eventually the men would use them to frame canoes and snowshoes.

At Thelewey-aza-yeth, from a giant stranger, Matonabbee purchased a seventh wife—in a transaction that would haunt him. He preferred strong, masculine women to smaller, more delicate ones because the former could carry or haul heavier loads. Most of his wives, Hearne wrote, would have made good grenadiers. In this rough country, "the softer endearments of a conjugal life are only considered as a secondary object"—and he suggests that this is probably wise.

Hearne devotes a great many pages to exploring the status of women in this survivalist warrior culture. Females could be bought or sold, or else won or lost in a wrestling match:

The rank they hold in the opinion of the men cannot be better expressed or explained, than by observing the method of treating or serving them at meals, which would appear very humiliating, to an European woman, though custom makes it sit light on those whose lot it is to bear it. It is necessary to observe, that when the men kill any large beast, the women are always sent to bring it to the tent: when it is brought there, every operation it undergoes, such as splitting, drying, pounding, etc. is performed by the women. When any thing is to be prepared for eating, it is the women who cook it; and when it is done, the wives and daughters of the greatest captains in the country are never served, till all the males, even those who are in the capacity of servant, have eaten what they think proper; and in times of scarcity it is frequently their lot to be left without a single morsel. It is, however, natural to think they take the liberty of helping themselves in secret; but this must be done with great prudence, as capital embezzlements of provisions in such times are looked on as affairs of real consequence, and frequently subject them to a very severe beating.

Hearne observes that, like beauty, a woman's temperament was of little consequence, if only because the most stubborn females would be brutally beaten into compliance. One woman might obey quite cheerfully, another only through fear—but both understood that they must do whatever their lord and master commanded.

Toward the end of April, when the travellers were ready to depart from Thelewey-aza-yeth, one woman went into labour. For two days, the party waited.

The instant, however, the poor woman was delivered, which was not until she had suffered all the pains usually felt on those occasions for nearly fifty-two hours, the signal was made for moving when the poor creature took her infant on her back and set out with the rest of the company; and though another person had the humanity to haul her sledge for her (for one day only), she was obliged to carry a considerable load beside her little charge, and was frequently obliged to wade knee-deep in water and wet snow. Her very looks, exclusive of her moans, were a sufficient proof of the great pains she endured, insomuch that although she was a person I greatly disliked, her distress at this time so overcame my prejudice, that I never felt more for any of her sex in my life; indeed her sighs pierced me to the soul, and rendered me very miserable, as it was not in my power to relieve her.

Some scholars have attempted to repudiate Hearne's portrayal of the status of eighteenth-century Chipewyan females by pointing out that contemporary Dene culture treats women in a far more sympathetic manner. Hearne's anecdotes and depictions bristle with detail, however, and are also corroborated by virtually every one of his contemporaries who addressed the subject. The most likely explanation is that, just as the Royal Navy has transformed itself since the 1760s and no longer flogs anyone through the fleet or strings miscreants from the nearest yardarm, so too have the Dene changed considerably over the past two centuries.

On May 3, 1771, Hearne, Matonabbee, and the others arrived at a place he called "Clowey Lake," some eighty-five miles north of Thelewey-aza-yeth, on the edge of the Barren Grounds. Here, travellers following the deer north and west would traditionally build their canoes. Matonabbee had sent two men ahead to begin this work, which required warm, dry weather. Slowed by rain, the advance party had accomplished little—and rain continued to fall.

Over the next few days, more than two hundred native people arrived at Clowey from various directions. Surrounded by so many strangers, as previously with Conne-e-quese, Hearne worried about being robbed. But this time, because he was under the protection of Matonabbee, a figure of some prestige, nobody accosted him. As a fur-trader sent by the HBC, he faced only the usual requests for tobacco, gunpowder, and shot. Matonnabbee responded to many of these, drawing on his own extensive supplies.

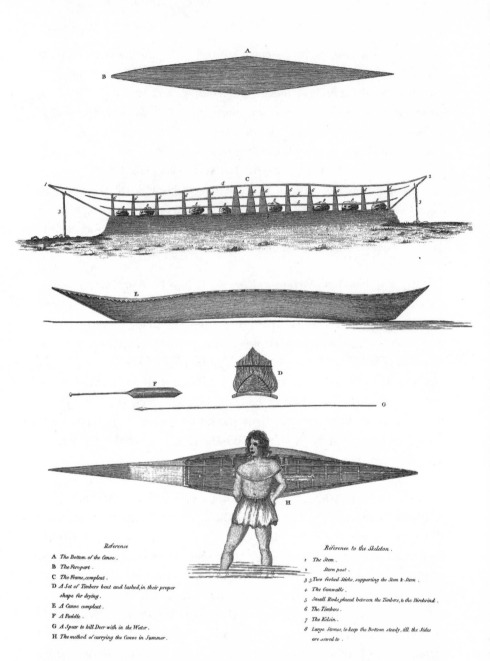

Reference

A The Bottom of the Canoe.
B The Fore-part.
C The Frame, compleat.
D A Set of Timbers bent and lashed, in their proper shape for drying.
E A Canoe compleat.
F A Paddle.
G A Spear to kill Deer with in the Water.
H The method of carrying the Canoe in Summer.

Reference to the Skeleton.

1 The Stem.
2 Stern post.
3 3 Two forked Sticks, supporting the Stem & Stern.
4 The Gunwalls.
5 Small Rods, placed between the Timbers, & the Birchrind.
6 The Timbers.
7 The Kelson.
8 Large Stones, to keep the Bottom steady, till the Sides are sewed to.

This page of "Indian Implements," which is devoted to the canoe, appears in Hearne's book as Plate III. The explorer's attention to detail is evident not only in his drawings, but in a footnote describing precisely how the Dene constructed canoes: "Fig. D. is an endview of a set of timbers, bent and lashed in their proper shape, and left to dry."

But now came the first of several unhappy incidents that, taken together, would threaten to put a premature end to Hearne's journey. While waiting for the canoes to be built, and having relatively little to do, Matonabbee noticed a young woman who was utterly unlike any of his seven wives. She was attractive, of moderate size and fair complexion. Also, Hearne tells us, "she apparently possessed a mild temper, and very engaging manners."

Matonabbee did what any powerful Chipewyan man would do: he called out her husband and demanded to wrestle for her. At Clowey Lake, Hearne tells us, scarcely a day went by without some such contest arising. A small or weak man, unless he was a good hunter and well liked, would rarely be allowed to keep an attractive wife. Indeed, some of the toughest men made a livelihood by demanding to wrestle for the wives of others before finally agreeing to be bought off with furs, tools, and utensils.

For Hearne, who had witnessed European ferocity as a young sailor, these wrestling matches were relatively mild affairs—they could scarcely even be called fighting. They consisted almost entirely of two men hauling each other around by the hair until one tumbled to the ground or cried out that he'd had enough. The men rarely struck or kicked one another, though it was not uncommon for one to cut off his hair and grease his ears immediately before he emerged from his tent to wrestle. Hearne observed that "it is sometimes truly laughable, to see one of the parties strutting about with an air of great importance, and calling out, 'Where is he? Why does he not come out?' when the other will bolt out with a clean shorned head and greased ears, rush on his antagonist, seize him by the hair, and though perhaps a much weaker man, soon drag him to the ground, while the stronger is not able to lay hold on him."

So ritualized was this contest that nobody would interfere except to shout advice. Hearne would have found these wrestling matches entertaining but for the women involved:

And it was often very unpleasant to me, to see the object of the contest sitting in pensive silence watching her fate, while her husband and his rival were contending for the prize. I have indeed not only felt pity for those poor wretched victims, but the utmost indignation, when I have seen them won, perhaps, by a man whom they mortally hated. On those occasions their grief and reluctance to follow their new lord has been so great, that the business has often ended in the greatest brutality; for, in the struggle, I have seen the poor girls stripped quite naked, and carried by main force to their new lodgings. At other times it was pleasant enough to see a fine girl led off the field from a husband she disliked, with a tear in one eye and a finger on the other: for custom, or delicacy if you please, has taught them to think it necessary to whimper a little, let the change be ever so much to their inclination.

For an attractive young woman who wished to remain with a particular husband, the only protection was motherhood, because children stayed with the women, and few men wished to provide for the offspring of others.

Matonabbee challenged the husband of the woman he desired and refused to be bribed. He defeated the younger man at wrestling and carried off his new wife. This might well have been the occasion when the woman put up such a furious fight she was stripped naked. Scrupulous about relating events of significance, Hearne might have felt that nothing would be gained by naming his friend—especially since he was about to describe a later incident "which by no means does honour to Matonabbee."

[I]t is no less a crime than that of having actually stabbed the husband of the above-mentioned girl in three places; and had it not been for timely assistance, [Matonabbee] would certainly have murdered him, for no other reason than because the poor man had spoken disrespectfully of him for having taken his wife away by force. The cool deliberation with which Matonabbee committed this bloody action, convinced me it had been a long premeditated design; for he no sooner heard of the man's arrival, than he opened one of his wives' bundles, and, with the greatest composure, took out a new long box-handled knife, went into the man's tent, and, without any preface whatever, took him by the collar, and began to execute his horrid design. The poor man anticipating his danger, fell on his face, and called for assistance; but before any could be had he received three wounds in the back. Fortunately for him, they all happened on the shoulder-blade, so that his life was spared. When Matonabbee returned to his tent, after committing this horrid deed, he sat down as composedly as if nothing had happened, called for water to wash his bloody hands and knife, smoked his pipe as usual, seemed to be perfectly at ease, and asked if I did not think he had done right.

Later in his book, comparing the Chipewyan with other native groups, Hearne insists that except for the wrestling matches, the "Northern Indians" were the mildest in Rupert's Land. Among them, murder was almost unknown. A murderer would be shunned, "obliged to wander up and down, forlorn and forsaken even by his own relations and former friends.... And he never leaves any place but the whole company say, 'There goes the murderer!'"

YEARS LATER, enriching his original account of the trek to the Far-Off Metal River with passages of rumination and reflection, Hearne would interrupt his narrative to defend wife-swapping and polygamy as effective adaptive mechanisms in these fierce northern climes. He observed that Dene men would exchange a night's lodging with each other's wives, and that, far from being regarded as criminal, such activity would seal a friendship. If either man died, the other would consider himself bound to support the children of his dead friend: "Those people are so far from viewing this engagement as a mere ceremony, like most of our Christian god-fathers and god-mothers, who, notwithstanding their vows are made in the most solemn manner, and in the presence of both God and man, scarcely ever afterward remember what they have promised, that there is not an instance of a Northern Indian having once neglected the duty which he is supposed to have taken upon himself to perform."

According to Hearne, the Dene also practised a superior brand of polygamy. They might take two or three sisters as wives, but unlike some peoples, they would never allow a brother to visit with his own sister or niece. Polygamy, yes; incest, no. Hearne's observations would have gladdened the heart not just of Voltaire, but of the more anthropologically minded Rousseau.

On May 20, 1771, travelling now with two hundred men, women, and children, Hearne and Matonabbee started north, canoeing and portaging where necessary. Scarcely one week out of Clowey Lake, two young women disappeared in the night, obviously bent on rejoining their previous husbands—and one of them was the woman Matonabbee had taken by force. She had never accepted her new situation, Hearne wrote, "and chose rather to be the sole wife of a sprightly young fellow of no note (although very capable of maintaining her), than to have the seventh or eighth share of the affection of the greatest man in the country."

To Hearne's surprise, Matonabbee was devastated by the loss of this wife, "entirely disconcerted and quite inconsolable." The following day, before he'd had a chance to recover, Hearne's friend suffered yet another blow. Six weeks before, at Thelewey-aza-yeth, Matonabbee had bought a seventh wife from an especially powerful warrior, a man who stood six foot four. And he was well pleased with the woman, who was both personable and extremely competent. Now, the aggressive warrior announced that he wanted this woman back. Matonabbee could either wrestle the giant for her or relinquish much of value, including ammunition, tools, a kettle, and some ironwork.

Physically powerful and athletic as he was, Matonabbee knew he could not defeat the fierce giant who challenged him. Also, having just lost his most attractive wife, he could hardly bear to lose his most competent. With Hearne counselling him against bloodshed, Matonabbee settled the argument the only other way he could: by giving the extortionist most of the goods he demanded, with as much grace as he could muster. Outraged and mortified, Matonabbee—"who at that time thought himself as great a man as then lived"—felt this affront so keenly, especially as it was offered in Hearne's presence, that he announced he would proceed no farther. He told Hearne that these people were not worthy of a great leader, and he would travel with them no more. He would turn west and rejoin the Athabasca Cree, who, though they belonged to another language group, had never treated him with anything approaching such disrespect.

No, he would not resume the northward journey. No, despite the agreement he had made at Prince of Wales Fort, he would not guide Hearne to the copper deposits. Instead, he would lead the Englishman westward and then send him back to the fort, guaranteeing his safe passage with native fur-traders travelling in that direction. His mind was made up, his decision final. He would discuss it no more.

Samuel Hearne withdrew to his campsite and stood looking out over the Barren Grounds. For six months, he had endured pain, toil, and hunger. Now what? Was he going to watch his third expedition end as the first two had ended—in abject failure? Hearne waited a couple of hours, allowing Matonabbee to cool down. Then, having thoroughly considered the situation, he again approached the native leader: "I used every argument of which I was master in favour of proceeding on the journey; assuring him not only of the future esteem of the present governor of Prince of Wales Fort, but also of that of all his successors as long as he lived; and that even the HBC themselves would be ready to acknowledge his assiduity and perseverance in conducting a business which had so much the appearance of proving advantageous to them."

After much discussion along these lines, and after Hearne had pleaded with sufficient respect and deference—this act of humility necessary because the Englishman had witnessed the shaming—Matonabbee relented. Late that afternoon, he gave the order to strike camp.

As AGAIN he started north, hauling supplies on a deerskin slung between two poles, the sole European among a couple of hundred Dene, Samuel Hearne felt relieved but far from jubilant. Back at Clowey Lake, where the travellers had built canoes, he had realized that trouble was brewing. But he had only two choices: he could deal with it, or he could abandon his quest—and that was no choice at all. At Clowey, Hearne had noticed that people were building more than canoes. The men hacked out three-quarter-inch boards and constructed "targets," or shields, measuring two feet by three. From Matonabbee, Hearne learned that these shields would ward off the arrows of the Inuit they would encounter at the Far-Off Metal River. He realized then that most of his companions were travelling northwest "with no other intent than to murder the Esquimaux" from those environs.

During the past couple of years, while sailing up and down the west coast of Hudson Bay, Hearne had met numerous Inuit people. He had mastered the rudiments of their language, and he knew most of them to be peaceful and good hearted. At Clowey Lake, he had said as much, and had urged his companions to approach those people in peace, as possible trading partners, and not with a view to waging war. The Dene had reacted with derisive fury, accusing Hearne of cowardice: perhaps he was afraid to fight the Inuit?

As I knew my personal safety depended to a great measure on the favourable opinion they entertained of me in this respect, I was obliged to change my tone, and replied that I did not care if they rendered the name and race of the Esquimaux extinct; adding at the same time, that though I was no enemy to the Esquimaux, and did not see the necessity of attacking them without cause, yet if I should find it necessary to do it, for the protection of any one of my company, my own safety out of the question, so far from being afraid of a poor, defenceless Esquimaux, whom I despised more than feared, nothing should be wanting on my part to protect all who were with me.

This declaration was received with great satisfaction; and I never afterwards ventured to interfere with any of their war-plans. Indeed, when I came to consider seriously, I saw that it was the highest folly for an individual like me, and in my situation, to attempt to turn the current of a national prejudice which had subsisted between these two nations from the earliest periods, or at least as long as they had been acquainted with the existence of each other.

Contemporary archaeologists have devoted considerable attention to the area around the mouth of what is now called the Coppermine River—an area that, because it is rich in fish, fowl, and mammals, has been contested for over three thousand years.

Scientists have found evidence that the Paleoeskimo, the Dorset people believed to be progenitors of the Inuit, visited almost 3,500 years ago, and that ancestral Dene frequented the area for 1,000 years, starting around 500 B.C. In surmising that despite his best intentions, he was moving ineluctably toward a violent confrontation, Hearne had ancient history on his side.

Toward the end of May, Keelshies joined the travellers. A week or so before, Matonabbee had learned that this wily old Dene leader was encamped not far away. The previous year, this same Keelshies had undertaken to carry a letter from Hearne to Prince of Wales Fort and then to return with a quantity of supplies. Matonabbee dispatched two young men to fetch him.

To Hearne, Keelshies delivered a packet of letters from England, including missives from his mother and sister. These carried news of their domestic life in Peckham, of friends and acquaintances in Beaminster, and of notable events in England and Europe and beyond. In London, engineers had constructed yet another way to cross the Thames—Old Blackfriars Bridge. In Africa, the Scottish explorer James Bruce had discovered the source of the Blue Nile. And an English "quack" named John Hill had introduced methods of obtaining specimens for microscopic study. From a boulder in the Barren Lands, the rest of the world seemed terribly far away.

Hearne would reread the letters in a quiet moment. From Prince of Wales Fort, Keelshies had also brought a two-quart keg of French brandy, and this he produced with a flourish. Hearne had asked Governor Norton to supply powder, shot, tobacco, and knives, but these supplies, apparently, Keelshies had expended. During the past winter, he had lost several close relatives. According to custom, he had thrown away all his possessions, including ammunition, and so,

Above the treeline, in the Barren Lands of the subarctic, travellers can walk for days without encountering greenery. When Hearne and his companions arrived at a river and discovered a few small trees, they noted the event for future reference. Matonabbee gave evidence of having done exactly that when he first met the Englishman and told him where to seek wood for snowshoes.

to support his family, had been obliged to use the goods intended for Hearne.

As he related this, Keelshies wept, claiming that he felt sorry for having dispersed the supplies. Hearne believed that he cried at the memory of his dead loved ones. In recompense for the missing ammunition, Keelshies produced four dressed moosehides. Normally these would fetch far less than the missing goods, but Hearne accepted them gladly: he had plenty of powder and shot but desperately needed shoe leather.

Before long, Matonabbee decided to reduce the number of travellers by splitting off most of the women and all the children. Together with a few men, these people would proceed north at a slower pace, and would wait at an appointed place for the warriors to return from the Far-Off Metal River. The native leader selected two of his wives, both young and childless, to accompany Samuel Hearne and himself. To lighten their loads, the men took a minimal amount of ammunition. The other warriors made similar choices. On the first of June, about sixty men set out northward, while fifty others stayed behind with the women and children. Having prepared shields and talked of war, these men now decided that the distance was too great, the potential gains too few.

On departure, the women and children left behind "set up a most woeful cry, and continued to yell most piteously as long as we were within hearing." The departing warriors ignored this howling and, with Hearne among them, walked away, laughing and apparently merry.

During the next sixteen days, the men trekked north through rain, sleet, and driving snow, covering 180 miles in sixteen days. At this latitude, 65 degrees north, they were still able at this season to walk across frozen creeks, rivers, and lakes. They could also hunt and travel at any time of the day or night because the sun spent so little time below the horizon. The deer were plentiful, and the hunters killed so many for fat, marrow, and tongues that Hearne protested, arguing that killing so many deer in one part of the country would lead to scarcity elsewhere. The Chipewyan replied that they preferred to live on the best parts of the animals; they hunted always with humility, and showed respect to animal spirits, who alone decided questions of plenty.

Continuing northward, hiking between ten and thirty miles each day, stopping only to hunt and eat, the travellers moved whenever rain and fog lifted. In the earliest of the extant journals, the Stowe manuscript, Hearne wrote, "By the time we arrived at the little river, it was about two in the morning, but in these high latitudes and time of the year the Sun is always seen, so that it makes little difference in regard to the night." In the later version, he refined this, observing that the bright, clear sun "did not set all that night, which was a convincing proof, without any observation, that we were then considerably to the North of the Arctic Polar Circle."

Now the ice melted, and the travellers, sixty men and seventy or eighty women, had to take turns using the few small canoes to cross the rivers and lakes. In late June, they spent a day crossing the Conge-catha-wha-chaga (Burnside) River to its north side, and there encountered a small party of "Copper Indians," or Yellowknife Dene, from farther west. These strangers, closely related to the Chipewyan with whom Hearne was travelling, welcomed the new arrivals with a feast, treating the principal men, including Matonabbee and Hearne, to the finest delicacies.

The Yellowknife, apprised of the party's warlike intentions, not only approved but desired to help. While smoking the calumet with the leaders, Hearne determined that these native people would like nothing better than to have a European settlement in the area, and could see no impediment. They admitted that having travelled to the mouth of the great river, they had never yet seen it clear of ice, but they did not believe this would impede ships from using it. These Dene proved so hospitable that Hearne regretted having few articles to distribute among them.

As I was the first [European] whom they had ever seen, and in all probability might be the last, it was curious to see how they flocked about me, and expressed as much desire to examine me from top to toe, as an European naturalist would a non-descript animal. They, however, found and pronounced me to be a perfect human being, except in the colour of my hair and eyes: the former, they said, was like the stained hair of a buffalo's tail, and the latter, being light, were like those of a gull. The whiteness of my skin also was, in their opinion, no ornament, as they said it resembled meat which had been sodden in water till all the blood was extracted. On the whole, I was viewed as so great a curiosity in this part of the world, that during my stay there, whenever I combed my head, some or other of them never failed to ask for the hairs that came off, which they carefully wrapped up, saying, "When I see you again, you shall again see your hair."

Matonabbee decided to leave all the remaining women at Conge-catha-wha-chaga, where deer were plentiful. Before departing, the men would kill as many deer as would be needed during their extended absence. From this spot, as well, Matonabbee sent his brother and a few Yellowknife men to the great river to announce their arrival to local native people, and to inform them that Hearne was scouting locations for a trading post. The explorer sent along tobacco and other gifts.

During the next few days, Hearne grew concerned at the way his fellow travellers began treating the Yellowknife. Several of his "crew" carried off young women. They found these women unusually desirable, and he puzzled over this because "they are in reality the same people in every respect; and their language differs not so much as the dialects of some of the nearest counties in England do from each other."

The warriors also seized furs and skins that had been dressed to make clothing, as well as bows and arrows. Hearne worried because deer hunters needed these to survive. Here in the Barrens, hundreds of miles from any forest, the Yellowknife could hardly expect to find raw materials to make more bows. He protested the thievery to Matonabbee, who attempted to stop his countrymen from taking furs, clothing, and arms without at least making some return. But despite Hearne's pleas, the native leader didn't even try to prevent his men from taking women. This was a warrior culture, and any such attempt would have served only to undermine his prestige.

At Conge-catha-wha-chaga, north of Contwoyto Lake, Hearne managed to take two observations. He determined his latitude to be 68 degrees 46 minutes north, and his longitude to be just over 24 degrees west of Prince of Wales Fort, or 118 degrees 15 minutes west of London. As the crow flies, the party was roughly 700 miles northwest of Churchill, although they had travelled easily twice that distance.

On July 1, 1771, having procured enough food to sustain the women, and guided by Yellowknife who knew the territory, the warriors headed north and west toward the great river. The first day out, a snowfall forced them to seek shelter beneath overhanging rocks and in the crevices of cliff faces. Continuing snow, sleet, and rain reduced them to travelling ten to twelve miles a day.

At the aptly named Stony Mountains, several warriors declared the journey more trouble than it was worth and turned back. The others, guided by Yellowknife who knew the best way through the rubble, "made a tolerable shift to get on, though not without being obliged frequently to crawl on our hands and knees." The freakish weather grew worse, with snow and sleet preventing progress for as long as a day. The men did not have among them a single dry garment. They were sheltering in crevices and caves, the best of which were dank and dripping with water. After one particularly wet and miserable night, unable even to light a fire, fifteen more Chipewyan men turned back.

Then, out of the northwest, came a gale carrying so much snow that the oldest native man in the party declared he had never seen anything like it—not even in winter. Hearne wrote that "the flakes of snow were so large as to surpass all credibility, and fell in such vast quantities, that though the shower only lasted nine hours, we were in danger of being smothered in our caves."

At last, the weather broke. A breeze, a light rain, and sunshine melted the new-fallen snow. The men began making eighteen to twenty miles a day. They came upon herds of buffalo or muskox, killed as many as they needed, and cut up the skins to serve as soles for shoes. Beside a small creek, they found a few stunted willows. Here they camped and, for the first time since leaving the women, managed to make a fire and cook a decent meal. As evening came on, the mosquitoes attacked in thick clouds; almost insufferable, they made sleep impossible.

The weather grew hotter, more sultry. The leading travellers met up with a group of Yellowknife led by a man called Oule-eye. Hearne and Matonabbee smoked the calumet of peace with him. But although this particular band carried considerable food, they offered the newcomers not a morsel. Hearne judged that "if they had been permitted,

[they] would have taken the last garment from off my back, and robbed me of every article I possessed."

When the rest of their own large party caught up, Matonabbee and his men took what they chose from these strangers—on this occasion, to Hearne's satisfaction. The warriors moved on. Arriving at a small river, Hearne climbed to the top of a chain of hills and deduced that it flowed into the Far-Off Metal River. The men killed several fine buck, built a fire, and enjoyed their best meal in months, highlighted by a dish called *beatee*, which Hearne described as cooked in a pouch and resembling a Scottish haggis.

On July 14, 1771, after a final, forced march of nine or ten miles along the tributary, Hearne and his fellow travellers reached their destination. Standing on one bank of what is now known as the Coppermine River, he was not surprised to see that it scarcely resembled the glorious waterway of legend. Not two hundred yards across, filled with rocks and shoals, marked by three sets of rapids that he could see, with doubtless many more to the north, this river would never accommodate European ships. Indeed, it would challenge canoes.

Was even a trading post possible? A few trees clung to the banks, but on the surrounding hills, for every crooked and dwarfish tree that poked skyward, ten charred sticks lay on the ground, the result of fire. No trading post would ever grace this spot. Hearne scrawled in his journal, then turned to his immediate task: to survey the Coppermine. He left the river to check his instruments.

The next day, travelling with about sixty men, he reached the Far-Off Metal River forty miles south of the coast, and began his survey. He covered eight or ten miles before a heavy rain came on, destroying visibility and forcing him to stop.

Resuming his trek the following morning, he travelled another ten miles along the crooked river. He observed that it varied considerably, broadening to widths approaching five hundred yards, but that everywhere it contained rocks, shoals, and rapids.

Along the banks, Hearne identified stunted pines, dwarf willows, plenty of *wishacumpuckey*, which the English used for tea, and also some *jackashypuck*, which the natives used for tobacco. He spotted cranberry and heathberry bushes, though none bore fruit. As he continued north, the sparse woods grew thinner. Finally, they petered out entirely, and the river wound north through rocky, barren hills and through marshes fed by streams of melting snow.

Hearne remarked that although deer were plentiful, his fellow travellers were splitting, drying, and carrying quantities of meat. Matonabbee explained that they would need these as they approached the sea, when they would shoot no guns and light no fires, as those activities would alert enemies and allow them to escape.

Alone with the Dene leader, standing on the banks of the Coppermine River, Hearne again expressed misgivings. He could not understand the need to attack any Inuit discovered in this vicinity. He reminded Matonabbee of his previous visit to the area, when with Idotliazee he had been welcomed by the Inuit. "You came and went in peace. And did you not leave presents and promise friendship?"

Matonabbee could only shake his head in frustration. Could not Hearne see that this march had acquired a momentum of its own? If Matonabbee did not direct an attack, another band leader would step forward and do so. Surely that was obvious? On arriving at the Coppermine, Matonabbee had sent three scouts north toward the Arctic sea. Now, derisively, he said, "Perhaps the scouts will find no enemies."

WHY WERE Hearne's fellow travellers bent on attacking Inuit? Why had these various Dene bands, some of them Chipewyan, others Dogrib and Yellowknife, trekked through ferociously difficult terrain to commit an act of aggression that could yield little material gain? Certainly, Hearne could not comprehend it. And scholars have been debating the question for centuries.

Some have argued that the Dene and the Inuit were traditional enemies, and that both sides had committed atrocities. Decades before, at the invitation of William Stuart, ten young Dene men had travelled east to York Fort to train as fur-trade ambassadors. Governor James Knight, realizing that these ten might be murdered by hostile Cree, had sent them north to winter at Churchill—where they were massacred by a large party of Inuit.

Other scholars have contended that nowhere in the north did

regional groups conduct full-scale war. Aggression was invariably local, with one band of men seeking to acquire the wives of another group or else exacting revenge for a previous transgression. Some have suggested that the Dene might have been motivated to revenge a specific act committed by the "Copper Inuit" of the area, but this is unlikely, if only because the attentive Hearne, fluent in Athapaskan, would have learned of and reported it.

Even allowing for a long history of mutual antipathy, the most plausible explanation is psychological. Like most native peoples, the Dene believed that the natural and the supernatural were intertwined and inseparable, two aspects of the same whole—a perspective reminiscent of the yin-yang world view advanced in ancient China. The Dene rejected the notion that events happen randomly, believing instead that they arise synchronistically, as part of a meaningful universe in which powerful spirits play a role.

Decades before, James Knight had noted that "the Devil must have so many deaths every year, and if [native groups] can but kill their enemies, they [would then] be spared themselves." One of Hearne's contemporaries, writing of some Western Cree, had observed that "if any person dies with sickness or is killed amongst them, then they must go to war with the other natives . . . and kill as many as they can of them, and then they say that they are even with them for the death of their friend or friends."

Little more than a year after Hearne talked with Matonabbee on the banks of the Coppermine, Matthew Cocking would describe how a hospitable group of native people to the southwest responded to a period of hardship: "They inform us that many of their countrymen are sickly, and buffalo very scarce that way, so as they are greatly distressed for want of food. On this account, they say, the War Pipe has been smoked and several are intended to go to war. They have brought a present of tobacco to be smoked by their friends here, with a desire that they will accompany them in this expedition."

Accordingly, the Dene on the Coppermine felt driven to commit an act of aggression neither by racial hatred nor by a desire for specific vengeance, but rather to protect themselves from illness or death that might otherwise arise through disease or apparent accident. Fur-trade scholar Barbara Belyea has argued that, essentially, an "enemy" was a scapegoat: "That death from hunger or disease could be compensated by war obeys a logic that escapes us, and that may have puzzled the winterers [like Hearne] as well. They were curious enough to question their companions and diligent enough to note down the responses. The reasons they recorded did not include the inveterate enmity of large, culturally distinguished groups. War, at least on the attacking side, concerned warriors more than general populations."

Some of the Dene travelling with Hearne, especially the younger men, were undoubtedly bent on proving their manhood. Collectively, the warriors were acting to protect themselves and their families by propitiating the forces of death and destruction. In turning on a group of people they scarcely knew, the attackers were following yet another established practice: that of leap-frogging immediate neighbours. The Western Cree of the plains and parklands did not attack neighbouring Blackfoot groups, but would instead join them in raiding more distant tribes. The Cree of the Athabasca region tolerated the nearby Chipewyan, but raided Dene groups living farther down the Mackenzie River.

This explains Matonabbee's exasperation: why could Hearne not see that the universe demanded an act of war? And that any Inuit discovered at this distance from home would serve perfectly to propitiate the spirits communicating that demand?

Not long after Hearne registered his disapproval on the banks of the Coppermine, Matonabbee's three scouts returned with news that thrilled the entire camp. A dozen miles north, near the foot of a great waterfall, they had discovered five Inuit tents on the west side of the river—at a site that was perfect for an ambush. Instantly abandoning any thought of Hearne's survey, Matonabbee and his lieutenants began developing a plan of attack. Here, where the Coppermine ran smooth, they would cross to the west side. Carrying guns, spears, and shields, they would quietly proceed north. On arriving at the camp, they would wait until nightfall. While the Inuit slept all unsuspecting, they would steal upon them and murder them in their tents.

On learning this plan, Hearne tried one last, desperate gambit: "The governor will not be pleased. What about the survey? We came to do a job."

"First, we war," Matonabbee said. "Later, we survey."

The warriors dispersed. Using natural dyes, they painted their shields red or black and sometimes both, adding images of powerful birds or beasts of prey, or else of imaginary beings. A gifted natural artist, Hearne remained unimpressed, describing the images as blotches bearing little resemblance to "any thing that is on the earth, or in the water under the earth"—so echoing the Bible for perhaps the only time. Each warrior drew the figure on which he would most rely in the coming battle. With this "piece of superstition" completed, the men crossed the Coppermine and followed it north. They communicated in whispers and avoided the tops of hills, where they might be spotted, wading where necessary through swamps knee-deep in marly clay.

Hearne was struck by the single-mindedness of the party. Normally an undisciplined rabble, they "acted on this horrid occasion with the utmost uniformity of sentiment." Guided by an old Yellowknife man who had spent his life in the area, the men followed where Matonabbee led. Hearne also remarked a new spirit of generosity. Suddenly, the warriors were willing and even happy to share, and to lend knives, arrows, or ammunition to anyone who might need them.

These fifty or sixty well-armed men, Hearne realized, would vastly outnumber any group that occupied only five tents. But where a devout Christian might have prayed for the intervention of the Lord, Hearne feared that the Inuit would be massacred "unless Providence should work a miracle for their deliverance."

Under cover of rocks and hills and the roar of the greatest rapids on the Coppermine, the warriors drew within two hundred yards of the Inuit camp, then stopped, waited, and watched. Matonabbee urged Hearne to remain at this spot until the battle was over, contending that otherwise he might get killed by a stray arrow—and this the English would never forgive.

Hearne flatly refused, arguing that if an Inuk escaped, he might run this way and attempt to murder him in passing. No: he preferred to move forward with everyone else—though he would not take part in any assault and would raise no arm except in self-defence. Matonabbee and his lieutenants expressed satisfaction with this speech. One warrior handed Hearne a spear, another a broad bayonet. The HBC officer still carried no shield, but he was satisfied to proceed without that encumbrance.

Bright sunshine gave way to twilight. The Inuit built fires, ate dinner, and eventually withdrew into their tents. A couple of hundred yards away, the warriors waited. They painted their faces—some all black, some all red, some a mixture of the two. To make themselves faster and harder to grasp, they pulled off their stockings and cut short the sleeves of their jackets. The mosquitoes were "so numerous as to pass all credibility," yet some men went further, removing shirts and stripping down to breechcloths and shoes. Judging that these preparations might be prudent, Hearne removed his stockings and cap and tied up his long blond hair.

The warriors waited until one o'clock in the morning, when the Inuit would be fast asleep. Finally, Matonabbee gave the signal to advance. The warriors rushed from their hiding places in the hills. Hearne stumbled forward and stood watching as they fell on the Inuit in their tents. His description of what happened next is the most controversial passage in northern exploration literature:

In a few seconds the horrible scene commenced; it was shocking beyond description; the poor unhappy victims were surprised in the midst of their sleep, and had neither time nor power to make any resistance; men, women, and children, in all upward of twenty, ran out of their tents stark naked, and endeavoured to make their escape; but the Indians having possession of all the landside, to no place could they fly for shelter. One alternative only remained, that of jumping into the river; but, as none of them attempted it, they all fell a sacrifice to Indian barbarity.

The shrieks and groans of the poor expiring wretches were truly dreadful; and my horror was much increased at seeing a young girl, seemingly about eighteen years of age, killed so near me, that when the first spear was stuck into her side she fell down at my feet, and twisted round my legs, so that it was with difficulty that I could disengage myself from her dying grasps. As two Indian men pursued this unfortunate victim, I solicited very hard for her life; but the murderers made no reply till they had struck her to the ground. They then looked me sternly in the face, and began to ridicule me, by asking if I wanted an Esquimaux wife; and paid not the smallest regard to the shrieks and agony of the poor wretch, who was twining round their spears like an eel!

Indeed, after receiving much abusive language from them on the occasion, I was at length obliged to desire that they would be more expeditious in dispatching their victim out of her misery, otherwise I should be obliged, out of pity, to assist in the friendly office of putting an end to the existence of a fellow-creature who was so cruelly wounded. On this request being made, one of the Indians hastily drew his spear from the place where it was first lodged, and pierced it through her breast near the heart. The love of life, however, in this most miserable state, was so predominant, that though this might justly be called the most merciful act that could be done for the poor creature, it seemed to be unwelcome, for though much exhausted by the pain and loss of blood, she made several efforts to ward off the friendly blow.

My situation and the terror of my mind at beholding this butchery, cannot easily be conceived, much less described; though I summed up all the fortitude I was master of on the occasion, it was with difficulty that I could refrain from tears; and I am confident that my features must have feelingly expressed how sincerely I was affected at the barbarous scene I then witnessed; even at this hour I cannot reflect on the transactions of that horrid day without shedding tears.

As a boy, the Englishman had witnessed barbarity and violence while fighting in the Seven Years War. Yet he remained unprepared for what followed:

The brutish manner in which these savages used the bodies they had so cruelly bereaved of life was so shocking that it would be indecent to describe it; particularly their curiosity in examining, and the remarks they made, on the formation of the women; which, they pretended to say, differed materially from that of their own. For my own part I must acknowledge, that however favourable the opportunity for determining that point might have been, yet my thoughts at the time were too much agitated to admit of any such remarks; and I firmly believe, that had there actually been as much difference between them as there is said to be between the Hottentots and those of Europe, it would not have been in my power to have marked the distinction. I have reason to think, however, that there is no ground for the assertion; and really believe that the declaration of the Indians on this occasion was utterly void of truth, and proceeded only from the implacable hatred they bore to the whole tribe of people of whom I am speaking.

Hearne had forgotten that, in the heat of battle, warriors often lose control. He staggered upriver to stand looking at the thundering rapids.

George Back of the Royal Navy painted A Part of Massacre Rapid (*Bloody Falls*) *after retracing a segment of Hearne's journey fifty years later. Back wrote: "The havoc that was there made was but too clearly verified—from the fractured skulls—and whitened bones of those poor sufferers—which yet remained visible."*

"Bloody Fall," he thought. "That's what I shall call this place."

Yet even as he formulated this thought, articulating a name that would later be pluralized into Bloody Falls, Hearne realized that even a damning name would not do justice to this terrible day. He would have to bear more complete witness. At some level, too, as the horror continued to unfold behind him, he realized that this day could never be understood in isolation—that, somehow, he would have to communicate the whole story around it. With that recognition, he became more than an ex-sailor, more even than an intrepid explorer. In that instant, Samuel Hearne became a man with a story to tell.

But now, having completed the initial slaughter, his companions spotted seven more tents. These were pitched on the east side of the river, beneath an overhanging cliff that had hidden them from view. Two dozen Inuit had emerged from those tents to stand, shocked and horrified, on that far bank.

Here below the falls, the river was eighty yards wide and fast-flowing—impossible to cross without a canoe. The warriors had left their canoes and baggage upstream. Now, from the west side of the river, they began firing their guns, shooting at Inuit who stood armed with bows and arrows. Hearne realized that these people had never seen guns, because when bullets struck the earth around them, they hurried in groups to study the dust and then to examine the lead balls they found flattened against rocks.

Finally, when one man took a bullet in the calf, the Inuit realized that even at such a great distance, they remained in danger. They piled into their kayaks and canoes and paddled downstream to a shoal, where they debarked and stood knee-deep in the cold, rushing water.

With those Inuit out of reach, the marauders turned to plundering the five tents of utensils, tools, hatchets, bayonets, and knives. Then they clustered on a high hill, where the surviving Inuit could not help but see them. They raised their spears in the air and shouted their victory, clashing their spears and derisively calling out an Inuit greeting—*"Tima! Tima!"*—which translates roughly as "What cheer?"

Tiring of this, they decided to retrieve their canoes, cross the Coppermine, and plunder the seven tents on the east side. To this end, they started back up the river. At the foot of the waterfall, to their amazement, they discovered an old woman previously hidden from view by boulders. Oblivious to everything that had transpired a few hundred yards away, she was fishing, using a light, spiked pole to kill salmon. She would thrust this implement into the water at the foot of the rapids and jerk it upward, spearing two, three, even four fish at a time.

The old woman did not hear them approach—either because of the roar of the falls or because she was hard of hearing. Certainly, her eyesight was poor, because she did not realize that the newcomers were enemies and that they meant to harm her until they had drawn near. Realizing her danger at last, she tried to flee, but "the wretches of my crew transfixed her to the ground in a few seconds, and butchered her in the most savage manner. There was scarcely a man among them who had not a thrust at her with his spear; and many in doing this, aimed at torture, rather than immediate death, as they not only poked out her eyes, but stabbed her in many parts very remote from those which are vital."

Having butchered the old woman, the marauders proceeded upriver to their baggage. They had only three or four canoes with

A contemporary view of the outflow of Bloody Falls looking north. Photographer Paul vanPeenen notes that the Inuit of whom Samuel Hearne writes "were likely camped on the right. In this photo there are some people from Kugluktuk [Coppermine] on the rocks fishing for Arctic char."

them because those who had turned back at Stony Mountain had taken several canoes. As a result, the men now spent some time ferrying each other across the Coppermine.

Once they had reassembled, they returned north along the east side of the river. They approached the seven tents furtively, hiding behind boulders, and were thrilled to discover that some Inuit had returned to the campsite and were busily tying their goods into bundles. The Dene attacked with ferocity, but the Inuit, not totally unprepared, managed to jump into their kayaks and paddle out of range—all except one. This old man was so intent on retrieving his goods that he waited too long. The invaders fell on him with their spears: "I verily believe not less than twenty had a hand in his death, as his whole body was like a cullender."

The warriors plundered these seven tents as they had the first five, taking the utensils, tools, and weapons. They threw the tents and tent poles into the rushing river. They did the same with great stores of dried salmon, muskox flesh, and other provisions. They smashed the stone kettles into pieces. In short, they did all the damage they could to those they could not murder, who remained standing on the shoal in the river, shocked spectators of this destruction.

Finally, the warriors lit a fire and cooked fresh salmon.

Traumatized by what he had witnessed, initially unable to eat, Samuel Hearne faced a choice: he could complete the quest he had begun two years before, or he could refuse to associate with those who had acted so brutally, strike out on his own, and perish. Hearne chose to survive. Having travelled without sustenance for two days, he sat down at the fire and ate salmon.

A sated Matonabbee, still licking his fingers, said, "Now we will finish your survey."

8

RETURN FROM
THE ARCTIC COAST

AT THIS TIME of year, and in this northerly latitude, the sun never set. When Matonabbee announced that he was ready to resume the survey, it was five o'clock in the morning of July 17, 1771. Samuel Hearne, still shaken, climbed to the top of the nearest hill and looked around. At the Inuit campsites, he had seen whalebone and countless sealskins. Gazing north beyond the rocky, low-lying hills, he could discern what appeared to be the northern ocean, roughly eight miles distant, at the mouth of the Far-Off Metal River. Turning to face the waterfall, below which the river narrowed to twenty yards, Hearne remembered the terrible moment when he had thought, "Bloody Fall." He shook his head to dispel the flood of horrible memories. If he refused to think about what he had seen, perhaps he would forget?

Years later, positioning himself as a dispassionate scientist, he would describe the local Inuit: "The Esquimaux at this river are but low in stature, none exceeding the middle size, and though broad set, are neither well-made nor strong bodied. Their complexion is of a dirty copper colour; some of the women, however, are more fair and ruddy. Their dress much resembles that of the Greenlanders in Davis's Straits." He would detail their weapons, fishing tackle, canoes, circular deerskin tents, furniture, stone kettles, and copper utensils. Among the spoils of the twelve tents at Bloody Falls, he would remember two pieces of iron—utensils, he reflected, which Maton-abbee had probably dispensed as gifts when he had first visited the area. These Inuit, he would conclude, were closely related to those of Hudson Bay, though one custom marked them out as belonging to a different group: the men pulled out the hair on their heads by the roots.

The mouth of the Coppermine River. This is a photographic replication, made on July 19, 2001, of a painting George Back created one hundred and eighty years before, on July 19, 1821. Its ultimate significance is that, fifty years (and two days) before the latter date, on July 17, 1771, Samuel Hearne became the first European to stand on this spot and look out over Coronation Gulf.

For the next several hours, with Matonabbee and the others, Hearne trekked north along the Coppermine, judging it so full of shoals and rapids that even a boat could scarcely ascend it. An obsessive naturalist, he lost himself in the wildlife, identifying gulls, black-heads, loons, old wives, ha-ha-wies, dunter geese, arctic gulls, and willicks. In the ponds adjacent to the river, he saw moulting swans and geese, and in the marshes, curlews and plovers and many hawk's-eyes. As for mammals, he saw evidence of muskox, deer, bears, wolves, wolverines, foxes, and hares.

Arriving finally at the coast with the sun lying low on the horizon, Hearne saw that the Coppermine emptied into the northern ocean over a ridge or bar. He took out his pocket telescope and looked out over what today we call Coronation Gulf. Open water extended three-quarters of a mile from shore, beyond which seals cavorted on hard-packed ice. From where he stood, Hearne could make out some round islands. He tasted the river water and found it to be fresh, not salty. But that, he knew, was only because the tide was out. As a veteran sailor, he judged from the marks on the ice along the riverbanks that at high tide the water rose twelve to fourteen feet. That meant salt water would reach only a little way up the river—certainly not as far as at Churchill, where tides forced salt water five miles upstream. He later recorded,

By the time I had completed this survey, it was about one in the morning of the eighteenth; but in those high latitudes, and at this season of the year, the Sun is always at a good height above the horizon, so that we had not only day light, but sunshine the whole night: a thick fog and drizzling rain then came on, and finding that neither the river nor sea were likely to be of any use, I did not think it worth while to wait for fair weather to determine the latitude exactly by an observation; but by the extraordinary care I took in observing the courses and distances when I walked from Conge-catha-wha-chaga, where I had two good observations, the latitude may be depended upon within twenty miles at the utmost. For the sake of form, however, and after having had some consultation with the Indians, I erected a mark, and took possession of the coast, on behalf of the Hudson's Bay Company.

This detail from Hearne's map of the Coppermine River notes the location of Bloody Falls: "A Fall of 10 ft. Here the Northern Indians killed the Esquimaux." At the mouth of the river, Hearne wrote: "From here I turned back."

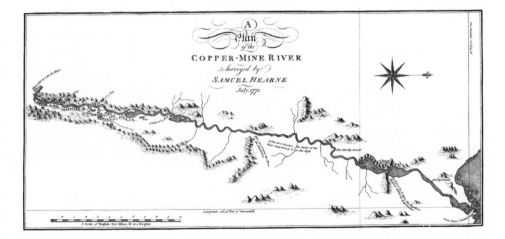

Lacking tools to etch his name into stone, as he had done so memorably at Churchill, the explorer traded tobacco for one of the shields. Into that he cut the particulars of his arrival: "Samuel Hearne ... HBC ... July 17, 1771." This marker he placed in a heap of stones on a hill near the mouth of the river on the south side.

Having asserted this claim to the northern coast of North America, Hearne turned to his final task: investigating the fabled copper mine. As fog and rain came on, Hearne and the Dene walked a dozen miles southeast, guided still by the old Yellowknife man. Sheltering from the drizzle beneath an overhanging rock, they lay down and, for the first time in three days, went to sleep. Five hours later, at six o'clock in the morning, one of the hunters killed an aging muskox. The relentless rain made a fire impossible, so again the men ate the meat raw. Because the beast had been so old, even the Dene found this difficult.

After marching southeast for another eighteen or nineteen miles, Hearne and his companions arrived at the site of the richest copper mine: "This mine, if it deserve that appellation, is no more than an entire jumble of rocks and gravel, which has been rent many ways by an earthquake. Through these ruins there runs a small river; but no part of it, at the time I was there, was more than knee-deep."

The native people who had inspired Hearne's quest, Matonabbee among them, had described this mine as incredibly rich and valuable. They had asserted that if the HBC built a factory on the river, the Company could ballast its ships with copper instead of stones. They had described hills made entirely of copper, and littered with great lumps of that metal.

But their account differed so much from the truth, that I and almost all my companions expended near four hours in search of some of this metal, with such poor success, that among us all, only one piece of any size could be found. This, however, was remarkably good, and weighed above four pounds. I believe the copper has formerly been in much greater plenty; for in many places, both on the surface and in the cavities and crevices of the rocks, the stones are much tinged with verdigris [a green patina or crust of copper sulphate or chloride].

The Dene passed around the single large piece of copper they had found, debating which animal it most resembled. At last they agreed that it looked most like "an Alpine hare couchant; for my part, I must confess that I could not see it had the least resemblance to any thing to which they compared it."

Hearne would carry that piece of copper all the way back to Churchill and ultimately send it to London. Now, hundreds of miles and many months northwest of Prince of Wales Fort, he stood among the rocks and faced the accumulated bitter truth. No Northwest Passage. No navigable river from the Arctic coast. No future HBC trading post. No fabulously wealthy copper mine. For himself, no riches, no fame, no lasting glory.

And yet, even as he stood among the piles of worthless rock, the exhausted Hearne wondered whether out of this remarkable journey he could not salvage something of value. Alone among Europeans, he had crossed the Barren Grounds to the northern ocean. Already he had a terrible story to tell. And this adventure, he knew, was far from over.

PRESENT-DAY mountain climbers tell us that the hardest part of conquering any Everest is not attaining the peak but getting safely down again. In 1771, having reached the mouth of the Far-Off Metal River, Samuel Hearne had achieved his objective. But if for an instant he imagined that his return to Prince of Wales Fort would prove easier than the outward journey, he quickly discovered otherwise.

As the travellers resumed their southeasterly trek, the weather turned ugly. Bright sunshine gave way to fog, cold rain, and heavy snow. The path was rocky and difficult, yet Matonabbee set a blistering pace—and maintained it day after day. On July 22, by Hearne's reckoning, the men covered forty-two miles. The next day, they hiked forty-five more, putting up in the middle of the Stony Mountains. Now the weather turned hot and sultry. The travellers started hiking early in the morning and walked until midnight or later. They slept two or three hours and then resumed walking. Arriving within sight of the hills around the Conge-catha-wha-chaga (Burnside) River, where they had left their wives and children, some of the men vowed not to sleep until they had rejoined their families. The party walked until six the next morning, and then discovered to their dismay that the women had crossed the next river and moved on.

In the distance, to the south, a plume of smoke wound skyward. The travellers rested briefly and then pressed on, crossing the river and arriving, after another long hike, at a recently vacated campsite. Spying yet another pillar of smoke, they made for that, increasing their pace. Still they didn't reach it until almost midnight—when, to their acute disappointment, they discovered that the women had departed the previous morning. Having vowed not to rest, again the men pressed on. At two o'clock in the morning of July 25, near Cogead Lake (Contwoyto), they reached a few of the women's tents.

Hearne arrived limping badly, his feet and legs swollen, his ankles stiff and sore. He had bruised his toenails among the rocks, so that several had turned black, festered, and fallen off. As well, he had chafed the skin off the tops of both feet and from between all his toes. Sand and gravel had irritated the raw skin:

For a whole day before we arrived at the women's tents, I left the print of my feet in blood almost at every step I took. . . . Several of the natives complained of sore feet, but none were injured so badly. This being the first time I had been in such a situation, or seen anybody foot-foundered, I was much alarmed, and under great apprehensions for the consequence. Though I was but little fatigued in body, yet the excruciating pain I suffered when walking had such an effect on my spirits, that if the Indians had continued to travel two or three days longer at that unmerciful rate, I must unavoidably have been left behind; for my feet were in many places quite honey-combed, by the dirt and gravel eating into the raw flesh.

Hearne feared that he might lose his feet. He washed them in warm water, rinsed the swollen parts in wine, and dressed the raw spots with "Turner's certate." The next day, as the travellers rested, the swelling and inflammation abated and the explorer realized that all he needed to do was stay off his feet. This painful foot-foundering, "which before I had considered to be an affair of the greatest consequence," he now dismissed as inconsequential.

After resting for one day, the travellers resumed their march at a slower pace. The weather was pleasant, the ground dry and relatively free of stones. Covering eight or nine miles a day, they arrived at the place where the families had been told to wait. Some were there, but others, including several of Matonabbee's wives, had yet to arrive. Spotting a large smoke column to the east, the native leader sent two young men to investigate. They returned not only with the missing families, but with a moveable village of more than forty tents.

Among the new arrivals was the man Matonabbee had stabbed at Clowey Lake. Now, submissively, this young Chipewyan man led his wife to the leader's tent and withdrew without a word. Hearne watched as the young woman sat and then reclined on one elbow, crying softly. Finally, sobbing, she lay back. *"See'd dinne, see'd dinne,"* she said. "My husband, my husband."

Matonabbee told her that if she had respected him as her husband, she would never have fled into the night. He would not keep her against her will. She was free to stay or to go, as she pleased. With seeming reluctance—"though most assuredly with a light heart," as Hearne put it—the young woman rose and returned to the tent of the husband she loved.

WHILE REJECTING any notion of life after death, eighteenth-century Dene believed fervently in magic. They attempted to heal the seriously ill by using charms and incantations, and whenever a prominent individual died, they believed that some enemy had "conjured" or invoked that death—perhaps one of their own, but probably a Cree or Inuit person. The Dene had conjurors of their own, highly skilled men who reminded Hearne of magicians and "jugglers" (sleight-of-hand artists) he had seen working the streets of London.

To treat injuries, Dene conjurors would blow, spit, and suck on the wound, or else chant over it unintelligibly.

For some inward complaints, such as griping in the intestines, difficulty of making water, etc., it is very common to see those jugglers blowing into the anus, or into the parts adjacent, till their eyes are almost staring out of their heads; and this operation is performed indifferently on all, without regard either to age or sex. The accumulation of so large a quantity of wind is at times apt to occasion some extraordinary emotions, which are not easily suppressed by a sick person; and as there is no vent for it but by the channel through which it was conveyed thither, it sometimes occasions an odd scene between the doctor and his patient; which I once wantonly called an engagement, but for which I was afterwards exceedingly sorry, as it highly offended several of the Indians; particularly the juggler and the sick person, both of whom were men I much esteemed, and, except in that moment of levity, it had ever been no less my inclination than my interest to show them every respect that my situation would admit. . . .

Being naturally not very delicate, they frequently continue their windy process so long, that I have more than once seen the doctor quit his patient with his face and breast in a very disagreeable condition. However laughable this may appear to an European, custom makes it very indecent, in their opinion, to turn any thing of the kind to ridicule.

Let it not be said that Hearne lacked a sense of humour. Farcical episodes notwithstanding, this empathetic observer turned his skeptical intelligence not only on the Dene belief in magic, but on the sometimes remarkable effects of that belief. To this subject he returned repeatedly in *A Journey to the Northern Ocean*. His accounts and observations, once published, would move the poet Samuel Taylor Coleridge to write of "Hearne's deeply interesting anecdotes."

Coleridge would be particularly struck by three incidents, the first of which happened early in August 1771. The new arrivals in the forty tents included one man who was dangerously ill. Having failed to cure him with the usual sucking, blowing, and chanting, the conjurors resorted to "another very extraordinary piece of superstition; which is no less than that of pretending to swallow hatchets, ice-chisels, broad bayonets, knives and the like; out of a superstitious notion that undertaking such desperate feats will have some influence in appeasing death, and procure a respite for their patient."

The man's friends built an elaborate six-foot-square "conjuring house." Having covered it with tent cloth, they laid the sick man inside. Several conjurors arrived, stripped naked, and knelt around the man, sucking and blowing over his body and conversing with invisible spirits. Outside the tent, one of the naked men made an elaborate show of swallowing a broad bayonet: "Though I am not so credulous as to believe that the conjuror absolutely swallowed the bayonet, yet I must acknowledge that in the twinkling of an eye he conveyed it to—God knows where."

After parading around, feigning discomfort in his stomach and bowels, the conjuror regurgitated the weapon. Hearne confessed this to be "a very nice piece of deception, especially as it was performed by a man quite naked." Several native people, convinced that Hearne himself possessed magical powers, sought his opinion of this sleight of hand, and the explorer equivocated, explaining that he had been too far away to see. Clearly, these witnesses believed the conjuror had worked a miracle—and, incredibly, the sick man soon recovered.

Hearne had been raised among people who believed that seventeen centuries before, one man had earned eternal life for believers by being crucified to death. Hearne's refusal to entertain the possibility of miracles, which by definition violated the laws of nature, and his repeated references to "superstitions" reflect the influence and vocabulary of Voltaire. The "magic acts" he witnessed among the Dene virtually compelled the scientific-minded explorer to question religious beliefs—notably, those of his own society.

A few days after the conjuror's performance, the various Chipewyan bands dispersed, heading off toward their own favourite hunting grounds. Reduced to a dozen tents, the travellers resumed their trek—not directly toward Prince of Wales Fort, because such a course could end only in starvation, but rather by following the deer in that general direction. Initially, this meant travelling southwest at a rate of eight or nine miles a day, a pace that suited the tender-footed Hearne. Toward the end of August, travelling along Large White Stone Lake, known today as Lac de Gras, the party killed many deer, whose pelts were now in season.

Hearne marvelled that these creatures did not become scarce, so great were the demands on their numbers. A suit of warm clothing required eight or ten deerskins. For these, the deer had to be killed in August or September, because by mid-October the hair became so long and loose that it would drop off. The native peoples needed skins to dress into leather for shoes and stockings, and also to make *clewla*, or thongs, that could be fashioned into snowshoe webbing. Hearne estimated that an average adult would require twenty deerskins a year for personal domestic use, and that a band would need still more for communal tents and equipment.

By late October, when the rutting season was over, deerskins would be thin and filled with worms and warbles, and so useless for anything but *clewla* and the toes of snowshoes. Many of the native peoples—like the common seamen he had known in the Royal Navy—had found another use for such vermin:

They are always eaten raw and alive, out of the skin; and are said, by those who like them, to be as fine as gooseberries. But the very idea of eating such things, exclusive of their appearance (many of them being as large as the first joint of the little finger), was quite sufficient to give me an unalterable disgust to such a repast; and when I acknowledge that the warbles out of the deers' backs, and the domestic lice, were the only two things I ever saw my companions eat, of which I could not, or did not, partake, I trust I shall not be reckoned over-delicate in my appetite.

Advancing slowly, covering at most twelve miles a day, the travellers made for Point Lake, a large body of water abounding with fish, frequented by animals, and never yet visited by a European. Scholars have debated the identity of this lake, and W.A. Fuller makes a compelling case that it is not the contemporary Point Lake, but rather Mackay Lake. The party spent several days here, enduring wind, rain, and snow while waiting to cross a narrow river, probably the Lockhart. The deep, rushing water prevented them from fording, but hunting was good. When the weather improved, they ferried each other across the river and continued southwest along the other side, arriving at a small scrubby woods—the first stand of trees they had seen, excepting those along the Coppermine, since the previous May.

One of the women had been suffering for some time with a consumption—coughing, fever, and chest pain—and now she became too weak to keep up. Whether the conjurors had already tried and failed in her case or she lacked influence among them Hearne did not know. But her relatives deposited food and water beside her, pointed the way they intended to travel, and, without further ceremony, walked off

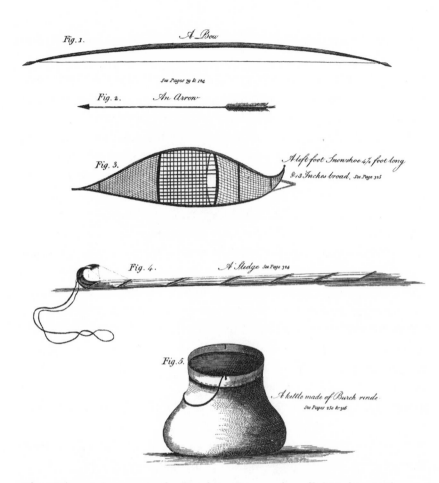

Fig. 1.   A Bow

See Pages 29 & 124

Fig. 2.   An Arrow

Fig. 3.   A left foot Snowshoe 4½ foot long
& 13 Inches broad. *See Page 325*

Fig. 4.   A Sledge *See Page 324*

Fig. 5.   A kettle made of Burch rinde
See Pages 250 & 326

Plate V from A Journey to the Northern Ocean, *also called "Indian Implements,"
again displays the author-explorer's attention to detail. Hearne depicts a bow, an arrow,
"a left foot snowshoe 4½ feet long & 13 inches broad," a sledge or toboggan, and a kettle
made of "birch rinde" or birchbark.*

after the others. Hearne remarked that in this difficult country, where
survival depended on following herds of animals, such hard-hearted-
ness was necessary for self-preservation. Better to leave behind one
person who is beyond recovery than to lose an entire family to starvation. Still, he felt a pang when three times, after having been left
behind, the consumptive woman managed to catch up with the others:
"At length, poor creature, she dropped behind, and no one attempted
to go back in search of her."

September announced the arrival of winter with cold, rain, sleet, and snow. The travellers hunted deer and prepared dried meat against looming scarcity. Before long, the constant precipitation began to rot the tents. By the end of the month, the cold had frozen the ponds and lakes solid and the travellers could cross without danger. But then came heavy, drifting snow and a gale out of the northwest gusting so violently that it blew down several tents, Hearne's among them.

This would have meant nothing but cold and inconvenience except that the tent poles fell on the quadrant. They smashed the wainscot case and broke two bubbles, the index, and several smaller parts, rendering the instrument useless. Dejectedly, Hearne broke the quadrant into pieces and distributed the brasswork to the native people, who turned it into lumps for later shaping into utensils. The explorer once again could take no further readings. He had been reduced to estimating distances using a faulty compass and an unreliable watch.

Hunting now for moose and beaver, the travellers proceeded into Athabasca country. There they found enough wood to make temporary sledges. And when, in November, they arrived at the main treeline, south of which the woods grew thicker, they made snowshoes and sledges that would last the winter. Continuing southwest, they reached Anaw'd Whoie, or Indian Lake, which is today called Hearne Lake. Here, they not only fished successfully but snared twenty or thirty rabbits each night—and so resolved to stay a while.

At Hearne Lake, the conjurors decided to heal another man. The ensuing episode, described at length in *A Journey to the Northern Ocean*, would again intrigue not only Hearne but Coleridge. The sick man was suffering from "the dead palsy" and was paralyzed on one side from the crown of his head to the sole of his foot. He also suffered stomach cramps. Having lost his appetite, he had dwindled to a skeleton and could hardly speak.

The same conjuror who had swallowed the bayonet now proposed to swallow a piece of board the size of a barrel stave. His assistants built a tent and installed the sick man. The healer had got wind of Hearne's skepticism, and when it came time to conduct the ceremony, he called the Englishman forward. The throng opened a lane and Hearne moved from the rear to the front. The naked conjuror made him examine the board, and then began his performance.

He shoved one-third down his throat and paraded around. Then he swallowed a second third and did the same. Finally, he swallowed the whole board, except for a small piece at the end. After walking back and forth three times, he hauled the entire board out of his throat and rushed it into the conjuring tent. The sharp-eyed Hearne watched all this closely yet failed to detect the requisite sleight of hand, as "this feat was performed in a dark and excessively cold night; and although there was a large fire at some distance, which reflected a good light, yet there was great room for collusion: for though the conjuror himself was quite naked, there were several of his fraternity well-clothed, who attended him very close during the time of his attempting to swallow the board, as well as at the time of his hauling it up again."

The previous day, while hunting several miles from camp, Hearne had by chance spotted the conjuror sitting under a bush, busily shaping a small piece of wood to look exactly like the piece at the end of the large board he would apparently swallow. Clearly, after an assistant had concealed the main piece, he would complete the trick by sticking this into his mouth. The bayonet trick, Hearne surmised, worked the same way, yet he had to admire the perseverance and dexterity of those involved.

Several native people, Matonabbee among them, wanted to know what Hearne thought of this latest performance. Not wishing to offend, the explorer turned the discussion to the spirits with whom the conjurors communicated, and learned that the board-swallower's spirit usually took the shape of a cloud: "This I thought very apropos to the present occasion; and I must confess that I never had so thick a cloud thrown before my eyes before or since; and had it not been by accident, that I saw him make a counterpart to the piece of wood said to be swallowed, I should have been still at a loss how to account for so extraordinary a piece of deception, performed by a man who was entirely naked."

As soon as the conjuror had completed his trick, five men and an old woman stripped themselves naked and followed him into the tent. These seven fell to sucking and blowing and singing and dancing around the sick man, and they kept this up, incredibly, without taking food or water, for three days and four nights. When finally they emerged, their mouths were parched black from thirst and their throats were so raw they could hardly speak.

But what amazed Hearne (and later Coleridge) was that the sick man emerged from the conjuring tent with his appetite restored— and with the ability to move the fingers and toes that had been paralyzed. In three weeks, he was walking again, and in six, he was once more able to hunt. The man never did regain his cheerful, lively, and generous personality, Hearne wrote. Instead, he became gloomy, quarrelsome, and covetous. Still, the conjurors had restored the man to mobility. And if their deceptions could be uncovered, their results could not so easily be explained: "Perhaps the implicit confidence placed in [the healers] by the sick may, at times, leave the mind so perfectly at rest, as to cause the disorder to take a favourable turn; and a few successful cases are quite sufficient to establish the doctor's character and reputation. But how this consideration could operate in the case I have just mentioned I am at a loss to say; such, however, was the fact, and I leave it to be accounted for by others."

ON DECEMBER 24, 1771, Samuel Hearne became the first European to see Great Slave Lake, the fifth largest lake in North America, tenth largest in the world. Cold and deep, it remains frozen for eight months of each year, and it was frozen when Hearne arrived. Seeing the trees around the lake and on the low-lying islands through which he walked—mostly pine, but also tall poplars and birches—Hearne felt moved to rough out a sketch of the scene, a drawing that, turned into an engraving, would testify to his artistic talents: *A Winter View in the Athapuscow Lake.*

Camped on the northern edge of the lake, southeast of the present-day city of Yellowknife, the travellers found deer and plenty of fish: pike, trout, perch, barble, tittameg, and methy. From the ice they pulled the largest trout and pike that Hearne had ever seen, including some that weighed thirty-five to forty pounds. On the islands dotting the lake, the native people discovered countless beaver. The days had grown short, but the brightness of the aurora borealis, the so-called northern lights, allowed them to hunt beaver at any time, "for it was frequently so light all night, that I could see to read a very small print."

Samuel Hearne drew the original sketch of A Winter View *in the Athapuscow Lake in 1771. Fur-trade scholar I.S. MacLaren has criticized this "highly stylized rendition of Great Slave Lake [for conveying] the North in the pre-picturesque esthetic of a French formal garden, in which symmetry serves as the paramount structural quality." As an untrained natural artist, Hearne could hardly be expected to challenge the formal conventions of his times; most viewers have found great charm in this historically significant engraving.*

What was Hearne reading? He does not say. But subsequent third-person testimony, as well as the scientific and humanist attitudes he reveals throughout his career, suggest a likely candidate: Voltaire's *Philosophical Dictionary*, originally published seven years before. This much is certain: at Great Slave Lake, the explorer's watch, borrowed from Moses Norton, ran out of time. Since breaking his quadrant, Hearne had been using this rudimentary timepiece to estimate distances, especially in foggy weather or worse, when he could not see the sun. He would employ his compass—also faulty, though he did not realize it—to determine direction. Then he would establish distance by multiplying approximate pace by duration: march three miles an hour for four hours and you cover twelve miles.

Now, deprived not only of his quadrant but of any means at all of accurately estimating distance, Hearne crossed Great Slave Lake and carried on, roughing out his map as best he could. Arriving on the south side of the lake, Hearne found fine, level country that contrasted sharply with the rough, rocky hills to the north. He described the spot clearly enough that more than a century later, geographer Charles Camsell would determine that the party had crossed the lake south of what is now the Taltson River.

Here, Hearne saw numerous moose and buffalo. In *A Journey to the Northern Ocean*, he would include long descriptions of both. His word-pictures of the latter, the wood bison, were the first ever written:

They are of such an amazing strength, that when they fly through the woods from a pursuer, they frequently brush down trees as thick as a man's arm; and be the snow ever so deep, such is their strength and agility that they are enabled to plunge through it faster than the swiftest Indian can run in snow-shoes. To this I have been an eye-witness many times, and once had the vanity to think that I could have kept pace with them; but though I was at that time celebrated for being particularly fleet of foot in snowshoes, I soon found that I was no match for the buffalos, notwithstanding they were then plunging through deep snow, that their bellies made a trench in it as large as if many heavy sacks had been hauled through it.

From the south side of Great Slave Lake, the travellers continued southwest, hoping to encounter locals with whom to trade. Like many of his fellow travellers, Hearne wished to acquire dressed skins to make a new tent and shoes. The men were killing many moose and buffalo, but the cold prevented dressing, an activity that involved soaking the skins in a lather of brains and soft fat or marrow, drying them in the heat of a fire, and hanging them in smoke for several days. The women would then wash the skins in warm water, wring them dry, and rub and stretch them by the heat of another fire.

One day, a hunting party made a remarkable discovery that was to have unfortunate consequences. Coming across a strange snowshoe track, they followed it to a small hut in which they found a resourceful young Dogrib woman who spoke several languages. For the past seven months, she had lived alone, surviving by snaring partridges, rabbits, and squirrels and trapping the occasional beaver or porcupine. She had started a fire using two sulphurous stones, and had kept it alight all winter. She had turned an iron hoop into a knife, and the shank of an arrowhead into an awl. This last she had used to sew and decorate her clothing, which showed "no little variety of ornament" and was, according to Hearne, "very pleasing, though rather romantic in appearance."

The hunters brought the young woman to their camp, where she told her story. She came from a tribe of Dogrib Dene far to the west, a people who made hatchets and chisels from deers' antlers, and knives from stones and bones. Having learned from their neighbours of the existence of metals, they had sent a party east to investigate, this young woman among them. Late one night in the summer of 1770, a band of Athabasca Cree had attacked them. They killed the woman's father, mother, and husband—everyone except herself and three other young women. She had concealed her four- or five-month-old baby in a bundle of clothing. Back at camp, the Cree discovered the infant, and one of the Cree women murdered it on the spot. This "last piece of barbarity," Hearne wrote, alienated the Dogrib woman forever.

The warrior who became her husband treated her well, but she could not reconcile herself to living among people who had killed her loved ones. She escaped the following summer. Making for home, she lost her way, and rather than wander aimlessly through the winter, built the hut in which the hunters had found her. The woman's story, Hearne wrote, "which she delivered in a very affecting manner, only excited laughter" among his fellow travellers, who were not inclined to show any sign of weakness. Their apparent levity notwithstanding, the Chipewyan hunters found the woman extremely attractive, and "the poor girl was actually won and lost at wrestling by near half a score of different men the same evening."

The arrival of the woman also occasioned an incident that reflected poorly on Matonabbee. Initially, he was among those who proposed to wrestle for her, even though he was already keeping seven adult wives and a girl of eleven or twelve. One of his wives made him ashamed to enter the contest, however, by tartly observing that he already had more wives than he could attend: "This piece of satire, however true, proved fatal to the poor girl who dared to make so open a declaration; for the great man, Matonabbee, who would willingly have been thought equal to eight or ten men in every respect, took it as such an affront, that he fell on her with both hands and feet, and bruised her to such a degree, that after lingering some time she died."

This woman had been his favourite. But as a proud leader in a warrior culture, Matonabbee could not overlook such a blatant insult to his manhood: he had no choice but to react. He had not intended to kill the woman he loved best. Afterward, he felt sick about it. His fellow Chipewyan, and Hearne, too, understood that the death had been accidental. But of those in the camp, only the Englishman regarded as questionable even the idea of raising a hand to a woman. Matonabbee carried on, his reputation undiminished.

IN MID-JANUARY, the travellers arrived at the Slave River—Hearne called it the Athapuscow—an impressive waterway lined with mighty pines, poplars, and birches. The mariner in Hearne surmised that these must be among the tallest and stoutest trees in North America: "Some of this wood is large enough to make masts for the largest ships that are built."

The explorer remarked that several rivers emptied into Great Slave Lake on the south, while others flowed out on the north side, to wend through the Barren Lands and on to Hudson Bay: "These rivers, though numberless, are all so full of shoals and stones, as not to be navigable for an Indian canoe to any considerable distance; and if they were, it could be of little or no use to the natives, as none of them lead within several hundred miles of Churchill River."

The travellers, failing to turn up any trace of Athabasca Cree, resolved to hunt buffalo, moose, and beaver and then to make their way east to Prince of Wales Fort in time to trade for goods brought by the autumn ship from England. They followed the river southeast and, near the end of January, struck off eastward "at that part where it begins to tend due south." Fur-trade scholar Richard Glover would later note that the river winds north-northwest from the south-southeast: "The apparent error of Hearne's compass may explain his errors in his observations for latitude."

The woods were filled with animals, and thick enough that the men had to cut a path for the women hauling sledges. Travelling east, the party eventually arrived back at Clowey Lake, where they had built canoes the previous May. Here they encountered a group of Chipewyan who had recently visited Churchill and whose leader delighted Hearne and Matonabbee by presenting each of them with a foot of tobacco. Before continuing westward, the strangers also gave the travellers a two-quart keg of brandy. The abstemious Hearne wrote, "Having been so long without tasting spirituous liquors, I would not partake of the brandy, but left it entirely to the Indians, to whom, as they were numerous, it was scarcely a taste for each."

Hunting beaver, moose, and buffalo with great success, the party proceeded slowly eastward. Early in March, some of the warriors came across strange tracks and followed them to a small band of poor, inoffensive people. These they plundered, seizing not only the few furs they had accumulated, but also one of their young women.

Having travelled among the Chipewyan for over two years, Hearne had adjusted to nearly everything except these acts of cruelty. Close as he was to the natural world, he could not accept that the "survival of the fittest" should apply to human society and that the strong should treat the weak with ruthless contempt: "Every additional act of violence committed by my companions on the poor and distressed served to increase my indignation and dislike; this last act, however, displeased me more than all their former actions, because it was committed on a set of harmless creatures, whose general manner of life renders them the most secluded from society of any of the human race."

Worse was yet to come, though the next several weeks proved relatively uneventful. Despite the tensions, Hearne continued to study the countryside, and later he would interview Matonabbee and others about areas he had not visited. Of the Thelon River valley, for example, he wrote a long description, citing the abundance and varieties of game, including geese, ducks, and swans: "It is also reported, though I doubt the truth of it, that a remarkable species of partridge, as large as English fowls, are found in that part of the country only."

Hearne would insert this celebration of Thelon country awkwardly into his narrative. Yet a present-day authority on the area, David Pelly, observes: "For a man who never saw the place, Hearne was remarkably accurate in his assessment of what was, from a white man's perspective, a vast uncharted territory and a total mystery."

Continuing southeast, Hearne and his fellow travellers fell in with other bands bound for Prince of Wales Fort, their numbers swelling eventually to more than two hundred. Some of the newcomers supplied dressed moosehides for tenting and shoe leather on the understanding that they would receive payment at Churchill.

In March, warmer weather began to thaw the frozen rivers and lakes. Still, the snow would remain hard-packed until mid-afternoon, and the young men used the mornings to run down moose. A good runner could tire most of them in less than a day, because unlike deer, they are tender footed and short winded. Even so, Hearne had known some of the men to chase a moose for two days before cornering the exhausted animal. Then, unable to get too close because of the flashing hooves, they would lash a knife or bayonet to a stick and use that to kill the creature. He writes, "Though I was a swift runner in those days, I never accompanied the Indians in one of those chases, but have heard many of them say, that after a long [chase], the moose, when killed, did not produce more than a quart of blood, the remainder being all settled in the flesh; which, in that state, must be ten times worse tasted, than the spleen or milt of a bacon hog."

Early in April, the travellers spotted swans flying north—harbingers of spring. One week later, they pitched their tents farther along that river near strangers, fellow Dene who were subsisting by snaring deer and who were so poor that they did not own a gun. Ever since the approach to Bloody Falls, when he had protested the looming attack on innocents, Hearne had been at odds with the band's young hotheads, who put him in mind of the worst British seamen. Now, dislike gave way to mutual contempt:

The villains belonging to my crew were so far from administering to [the poor people's] relief, that they robbed them of almost every useful article in their possession; and to complete their cruelty, the men joined themselves in parties of six, eight or ten in a gang, and dragged several of their young women to a little distance from their tents, where they not only ravished them, but otherwise ill-treated them, and that in so barbarous a manner as to endanger the lives of one or two of them. Humanity on this, as well as on several other similar occasions during my residence among those wretches, prompted me to upbraid them with their barbarity; but so far were my remonstrances from having the desired effect, that they afterwards made no scruple of telling me in the plainest terms, that if any female relation of mine had been there, she should have been served in the same manner.

In May, the travellers learned that another large group of Dene, also carrying furs to Prince of Wales Fort, had camped not far away. Matonabbee sent a messenger inviting those people to join him, which they did. This melding of parties, Hearne observes, had become standard practice—a way of fooling English traders into believing that band leaders were more powerful than they were. Most HBC men thought "trading captains" were like European generals, exerting permanent authority over all those who accompanied them to the fort. In reality, Matonabbee and other leaders held sway only over their own extended families; the cleverest of these leaders would forge temporary alliances to induce respect and extract higher prices.

To travel faster across inhospitable territory, Matonabbee now left the old and the young in the care of a few men who could provide for them and who would guide them to Catha-wha-chaga to wait. The travellers resumed their journey at a brisker pace. As the weather warmed and thawed the lakes and rivers, they dispensed with snowshoes and built canoes. Animals were scarce. Some men, weakened by hunger and unable to carry as much weight as usual, stashed furs in caves and crevices and kept going. Others turned back. Still, the overall numbers increased as various families joined the larger group.

One band declined to join. The last time they had visited Prince of Wales Fort, they had taken goods in advance, on trust. Instead of returning now and discharging that debt, they proposed to carry their furs to Knapp's Bay, far north of Churchill. There, by trading with the HBC men who visited annually in the sloop, they would receive full price. Hearne noted that the most adroit Dene had been practising such frauds as long as the Company had been sending its sloop north.

As May wore on, even the ablest hunters could find only geese and small birds, and so expended a great deal of powder and shot. Some ran out of ammunition. Hearne and his immediate allies could afford to help some people but not others, and a few women died: "It is a melancholy truth, and a disgrace to the little humanity of which those people are possessed, to think, that in times of want the poor women always come off short; and when real distress approaches, many of them are permitted to starve, when the males are amply provided for."

Hearne and his fellow travellers scrambled across the Catha-wha-chaga River just before the ice broke up. That night, May 30, 1772, rain came down in torrents. The river overflowed its banks and flooded the camp. Around three in the morning, the men had to dismantle their tents and retreat to a nearby hill. There, the wind blew so strongly that no tent would stand. The travellers, Hearne among them, could only huddle with their backs to the wind and tent cloth wrapped around their shoulders—a situation that endured for three days and nights.

When finally the weather changed, the travellers felt so numb in their feet and legs that they could hardly walk. But at last they encountered deer—not enough, initially, to feed so many, but soon in greater numbers, along with geese, partridges, and gulls. For the first time in weeks, they had enough to eat. Now the worst problem was the driving rain, which came in heavy showers.

By this time, Hearne well understood that the Chipewyan were jealous of their role as middlemen between the HBC traders and those Dene who lived farther west. He knew that often when Yellowknife and Dogrib travelled to the Bay, Chipewyan bands would plunder them, sometimes both coming and going.

Yet he didn't register the ruthlessness involved until early June. Portaging across an island in the middle of a river, the travellers came upon human remains picked clean by animals. Matonabbee told Hearne that these were the bones of some Yellowknife who, a few years before, had ventured east to trade at Churchill. Keelshies had taken charge of these dozen strangers, who were carrying valuable furs. After coercing the strangers into exchanging their largesse for provisions, the wily Chipewyan insisted that they carry the furs to Churchill. At the fort, Keelshies took credit for bringing in the Yellowknife and promised to bring more. Governor Norton gave the newcomers many gifts as an inducement to return.

Keelshies and the rest of his execrable gang, not content with sharing all the furs those poor people had carried to the Fort, determined to get also all the European goods that had been given to them by the governor. As neither Keelshies nor any of his gang had the courage to kill the Copper Indians [the Yellowknife], they concerted a deep-laid scheme for their destruction; which was to leave them on an island. With this view, when they got to the proposed spot, the Northern Indians took care to have all the baggage belonging to the Copper Indians ferried across to the main, and having stripped them of such parts of their clothing as they thought worthy of notice, went off with all the canoes, leaving them all behind on the island, where they perished for want.

Just a few days from Prince of Wales Fort, Hearne witnessed a manifestation of similar attitudes. One Yellowknife man had joined the travellers with a view to trading at the fort. For ten hours, gale-force winds delayed the crossing of a river. Finally, after all the Chipewyan had been ferried across as well as the man's bundle of furs, this native man was left alone on the river's north bank. Nobody but Matonabbee would go back to fetch him. Hearne writes, "The wind at that time blew so hard, that Matonabbee stripped himself quite naked, to be ready for swimming in case the canoe should overset; but he soon brought the Copper Indian safe over, to the no small mortification of the wretch who had the charge of him, and who would gladly have possessed the bundle of furs at the expense of the poor man's life."

A few days before, at the Egg River, on Matonabbee's suggestion, Hearne had sent a final letter post-haste to Prince of Wales Fort advising the governor of their imminent return. At the Pocotheekisco River, roughly two days out of Churchill, the explorer received a reply, together with a little tobacco and some other articles he had requested. The party walked until ten o'clock that night then camped on one of the Company's goose-hunting islands.

The next morning, June 30, 1772, Samuel Hearne set out on his final march to Prince of Wales Fort. With Matonabbee, he had been travelling for eighteen months and twenty-three days. From his initial departure in 1769, he had been rambling in the Barrens for two years, seven months, and twenty-four days. During this time, he had journeyed at least 3,500 miles, and probably closer to 5,000 miles.

As finally he approached Prince of Wales Fort, an exhausted and hungry Hearne realized that the ramparts were lined with people. Someone fired a cannon, a great hurrah went up, and old friends and acquaintances, people he had not seen in two years, began streaming out of the fort. Despite his protestations, several young men wrestled him up onto their shoulders and carried him into the fort.

Samuel Hearne had completed his quest.

9

CUMBERLAND HOUSE

HALF A CENTURY would elapse before another European would visit the mouth of the Coppermine. In 1821, having descended that rough river, John Franklin would lead a Royal Navy expedition east along the coast of the continent in a bungled operation that would cost the lives of ten men and necessitate a last-minute rescue by the Yellowknife. And as late as 1911, almost 140 years after Samuel Hearne returned to Churchill, J.B. Tyrrell set out to trace a section of his route while proposing to visit "parts into which no white man had ventured during the intervening time."

Hearne's maps would come under attack as inaccurate, but considering the conditions under which he created them and the instruments he had to use, they proved remarkable accomplishments. By determining that the Coppermine River was unexploitable—worthless at least to the Hudson's Bay Company—Hearne put an end to a fantasy that had drained HBC coffers of tens of thousands of pounds and would have siphoned off more.

Even more importantly, by travelling with First Nations peoples, adopting their methods, and writing about the experience, Hearne showed Europeans how to explore the north. He wasn't the first to apprentice himself, but his three-year trek was easily the most ambitious any outsider had undertaken. Within the context of northern exploration, Hearne was a prophet who pointed the way forward. He was the first articulate adventure traveller, the first "winterer" fully to communicate—in *A Journey to the Northern Ocean*—that Europeans could survive in the Barrens only by learning from native peoples. Seven decades would elapse before the indomitable John Rae would fulfill the promises inherent in Hearne's approach, adopting native methods while serving as leader and chief hunter of his own expeditions.

Finally, Samuel Hearne had answered the most pressing question then pertaining to northern exploration. Did a Northwest Passage run westward out of Hudson Bay? Andrew Graham, the master at York Fort, recognized his achievement:

Mr. Samuel Hearne, a young gentleman of a good education, being employed by the Hudson's Bay Company to examine the country to the NW of Churchill River, in order to find whether or not there were any passage by water from the Bay to the South Seas; after being absent three years returned, having travelled to Copper-mine River ... without crossing any river worth notice.... This great undertaking has fully proven that no passage is to be expected by the way of Hudson Bay.

To this, we must add a corollary. The Northwest Passage was a European conception. By becoming the first explorer to reach the Arctic coast of North America, Samuel Hearne established a first point along a coastal waterway that extended to the Pacific Ocean. At the mouth of the Coppermine River, he discovered the only Northwest Passage that could accommodate ships of his own century or the next. And early in the twentieth century, when Roald Amundsen became the first explorer to navigate the Northwest Passage, he would sail directly past the mouth of the Coppermine, where, in July 1771, Samuel Hearne had stood gazing out.

IN 1772, the Hudson's Bay Company turned to more immediate concerns. During the three years that Samuel Hearne had been voyaging overland, the Company had awakened to a major challenge—indeed, a threat to its continued existence: increasing competition from Montreal-based fur-traders. In 1759, during the latest round of English-French hostilities, when Hearne had been sailing under Captain Samuel Hood, Great Britain had gained control of the French colony of Quebec. During the past dozen years, Scottish and English merchants newly based in Montreal—men with names like Frobisher, McGill, and Mackenzie—had begun financing a fur-trade initiative. They were building trading posts to the west and south of Hudson Bay and intercepting fur-bearing native people before they reached Company posts around the Bay. These aggressive Canadians, whom the HBC men referred to as "pedlars," were reducing profits. What to do?

On August 26, 1772, the insightful Andrew Graham wrote to London recommending that the Company respond by immediately building an inland trading post. This would require unusual energy and intelligence, and he suggested "that no persons other than Hearne of Churchill" or Thomas Hutchins, designated "surgeon" at York Fort, be charged with this undertaking. Two days later, possibly after receiving some communication from Graham, Hearne wrote HBC headquarters stating that he did not wish to be employed in the black whale fishery—the folly of which he had long since recognized—and that he would be of more service inland.

Earlier that month, Hearne had written asking the company to "pay to Mrs. Diana Paine the balance of my last three years wages; and as your Honours mentioned that a gratuity would be granted me at the return from the inland journey, that also please pay to Mrs. Paine, all of which she is to put out for my benefit." The following year, having awarded Hearne £200 "as a gratuity for his great labour and pains" in journeying to the Coppermine River—fully eight times his original salary, and twice the current base salary of the governor of a post— the Company responded:

Being desirous that you should hereafter enjoy the benefit of your labours in the early stage of life, we did not comply with your order in paying your balance of wages and the gratuity to be allowed you but as the whole sum due to you is £272.16.6, we have £258 part thereof in the purchase of £300 Bank Consolidated three per cent annuities, which will produce you £9 a year until such times as you shall choose to alter the mode of the present investment.

Samuel Hearne had clearly stated that his mother would invest the money on his behalf. The HBC itself having done so, he made no attempt to change the arrangement, although he did request that the interest be paid to his mother.

In 1769, before Hearne went north, the Committee had indicated that if they hadn't needed him to undertake the overland expedition, they would have made him master of the brigantine *Charlotte*, pride of the local fleet. On arriving back at Prince of Wales Fort in 1772, Hearne received a more recent letter stating, "We have appointed Mr. Magnus Johnston to be master of the *Charlotte*, and yourself to be mate of that vessel, for the present."

Johnston was a long-time friend of Moses Norton. But with his gratuity yet to be decided, Hearne chose not to question the decision, indicating only that he would prefer to work inland. Such a move would serve the additional purpose of putting distance between himself and Governor Norton. In 1770, when Hearne had stood up to him, refusing to take Norton's relatives along with Matonabbee, he had revealed his mettle.

The governor had realized that he was dealing not only with someone who was intelligent—perhaps even smarter than himself—but with an officer he could no longer intimidate. Such an individual could prove dangerous. Such an individual, being situated at close quarters, might chance upon any number of peccadilloes and blow them out of proportion. Such an individual would not shrink from making accusations against a superior officer, casting him in a negative light with the London committee. Norton found this prospect unwelcome. Better to keep Mr. Hearne at a distance from Prince of Wales Fort—the farther away, the better.

Having arrived at Churchill on June 30, 1772, Hearne spent most of July organizing his field notes and drafting his report, a version of which would survive as the Stowe manuscript. In mid-August, Norton sent him to Sloop's Cove, three miles upriver, to camp and to supervise repairs to the sloop *Churchill*, which had been leaking badly. Early in September, the governor sent Hearne with Magnus Johnston and a dozen men back to the cove to lay the *Charlotte* up for the winter. In October, with that work completed, Norton sent Hearne to supervise ten men in salvaging firewood; and the month after that, he sent him with a dozen men to establish a hunting camp at a lake some distance away. On November 24, Norton received ninety partridges from "Mr. Hearne's tent," and on February 11, 1773, sixty more.

Hearne remained at the lake through March. Early in April, Norton sent him with Johnston to supervise twenty-one men cutting ice from around the *Charlotte*. In May and June, he was back at Sloop's Cove, overseeing five men fitting out the brigantine for its annual six-week voyage. In mid-July, preparations complete, Hearne sailed north as mate on the *Charlotte*, travelling as far as Knapp's Bay and Whale Cove, and trading with native people from the surrounding regions.

On August 22, 1773, when the *Charlotte* arrived back at Prince of Wales Fort, Samuel Hearne, now twenty-eight, received the news he had been anxiously awaiting: the Company had appointed him to lead an expedition inland from Hudson Bay, leaving from York Fort. He was to depart as soon as possible, select a suitable location, and build the Company's first inland post. One week after he arrived back in Churchill, accompanied by a capable young man named Robert Longmoor, Hearne sailed for York Fort, three days to the south.

SAMUEL HEARNE had been told that he might find two giant birch-bark canoes waiting. In these, he could immediately make a dash inland with great quantities of trading goods. But he knew it was too late in the season, and also that it was one thing for Andrew Graham to ask groups of Western Cree, who had their own priorities, to build these craft and bring them to the factory; it was quite another actually to have the canoes on hand.

On September 2, 1773, when Hearne arrived at York Fort, he found no large canoes waiting. Nor could anybody build canoes at that location, if only because the stunted woods nearby contained neither white birch nor cedar, both of which were necessary. Lack of expertise was also a problem—one the HBC men would eventually resolve by learning from Cree masters.

In the absence of large canoes, and backed by the Governing Council, Hearne decided to remain at York Fort through the winter and to proceed inland the following spring. He would travel to a place known variously as Basquiau, Pasquia, and, eventually, La Pas or The Pas, about 450 miles southwest. From there he would scout around, find the best location, and build the post.

Soon a competent man named Isaac Batt, who had canoed out

Samuel Hearne drew this sketch of York Fort while waiting to proceed inland to Cumberland House, either late in 1773 or early in 1774. Over the years, the drawing has been repeatedly misidentified as Prince of Wales Fort, probably because somebody made that mistake early on, and later viewers have trembled to tamper with received documentation.

ahead, returned to York Fort. He had been unable to continue inland because freeze-up was making the rivers impassable. During the ensuing winter, Hearne consulted with Ferdinand Jacobs, now the master at York, as well as with Matthew Cocking, the fort's second-in-command, and Thomas Hutchins, surgeon.

Hearne had become friends with Hutchins three years before, when they had gone hunting together with the mathematician William Wales. With Hutchins, an amateur naturalist, Hearne shared a keen interest in plants and animals. This did not preclude hunting, however, and when the two hunted golden plover, they "killed in one afternoon as many as two men could conveniently carry."

In the spring of the new year, Hearne donned snowshoes and trekked to the bottom of Hudson Bay, visiting Severn House and Albany and Moose forts—a return journey of over 1,400 miles. He knew that because of the ice in the rivers he would not be able to leave

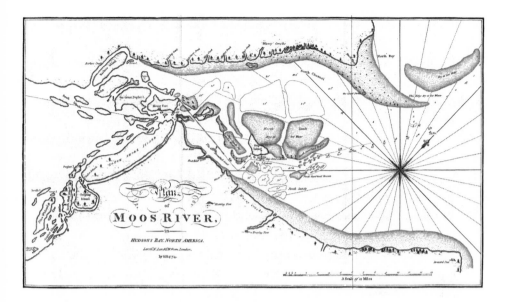

Early in 1774, the ever-restless Hearne donned snowshoes and trekked seven hundred miles south to Moose Fort, where the ice always melted earlier. He used his time to chart both the Moose and Albany rivers, including many details of interest specifically to mariners—channels, shoals, landmarks, soundings. As an experienced navigator, he indicated more than half a dozen quasi-islands that lay two fathoms deep, and also two extensive sandy areas that "dry at low water."

York Fort until summer. The ice melted earlier in the southern reaches of the Bay and, insatiably curious, the sometime mariner took the opportunity to chart the Moose and Albany rivers. For both, he drew not simple land maps but detailed seaman's charts, indicating channels, shoals, soundings, and landmarks.

He also discussed his undertaking with Andrew Graham, now at Severn, and with Edward Umfreville at Albany, a man who would later fall out with the HBC and write scathingly about it. Neither had travelled inland extensively, and they drew up a fanciful "loading table" enumerating the goods Hearne could carry inland in the large canoes Graham had requested from various "Upland Indians," or Western Cree.

These imaginary canoes would resemble those the "Canadian pedlars" brought from Montreal, the largest of which could carry an astonishing two tons—more than four thousand pounds' worth of goods. Graham conceived of more modest but still large craft, each of which could transport one thousand pounds in fifty-pound packs. However, because of the rough rivers and countless portages involved in reaching York Fort from the interior, the Western Cree used much smaller canoes, which normally held two men, their camping gear, and perhaps one hundred beaver skins—a total of 250 to 300 pounds.

Back at York Fort, knowing that Graham was thinking wishfully, and aided by Matthew Cocking, who would travel inland as his second-in-command, Hearne made more realistic calculations. At thirty-one, Cocking was two years older than Hearne. He had arrived at York Fort in 1765 as a clerk and writer, and by 1770 had become the fort's second-in-command. He had wintered recently in the targeted area and knew the river system and some of the people. Cocking predicted that come spring, the Western Cree would bring no large canoes, only their usual small ones. These craft could carry nothing but easy-to-handle packs of twenty pounds each, and Hearne planned accordingly.

In May, one month before departure, some of the Company men, most of them hardy souls from the islands of Orkney, protested that they had not signed on for inland service. They rightly suspected that an undertaking of this nature would prove far more onerous than maintaining a well-established post on Hudson Bay. Some flatly refused to go.

Eventually, by promising what he later described as "a trifling gratuity," Hearne mustered the requisite dozen volunteers—but not before he determined that one man, who adamantly refused to winter inland, should be sent home "as an example to others not to deny their duty." He also recommended that in future contracts, the HBC stipulate that inland service might be required.

Shortly before he left, Hearne received encouraging words from the London committee, as well as a decoration "by which particular mark of distinction we hope the Indians will more readily assist you towards promoting our interest in every respect." His reaction to this is not recorded.

In June, when the rivers had thawed, small groups of traders began arriving with furs—some Assiniboine, a few Ojibwa, many Western Cree. These last, most of whom arrived from the parklands, plains, and boreal forests to the west and north of Lake Winnipeg, included people from six major groups: Susuhana, Sturgeon, Pegogamaw, Keskach-ewan or Beaver, Athabasca, and Missinipi. Each of these groups comprised small, autonomous bands who inhabited different regions.

Eighteenth-century British fur-traders, accustomed to a central-ized and hierarchical world, failed to grasp this or to understand its implications. They lumped all Western Cree together as "Upland Indians" and assumed the existence of some overarching governing body wielding ultimate authority. The Cree, like the Dene, recog-nized that this misapprehension might prove useful and did what they could to preserve it.

A couple of Western Cree band leaders had promised Andrew Graham that they would build large birchbark canoes, and accepted a downpayment. But many families would make the onerous journey to York Fort only every second year, and those in question did not show up. After trading, the Cree began leaving as usual in small groups, four or five canoes at a time. Since he had no other means of reaching the interior, Hearne decided to hire various visitors to transport him, splitting his own men into groups and distributing trading goods among them.

Meanwhile, several Swampy Cree had arrived from Churchill with astonishing news: Governor Moses Norton had fallen sick and died. Andrew Graham travelled north from Severn House to take tempo-rary command of Prince of Wales Fort, but he was anxious to retire to England. On June 21, 1774, shortly before journeying inland, and recalling that the Committee had recently expressed great satisfac-tion with his three-year trek, his journal, and his maps, Hearne wrote a letter to HBC headquarters offering himself as a candidate to com-mand Prince of Wales Fort when Graham was retired, "which he intends to be very soon." He also asked that £20 be paid to his mother's account.

TWO DAYS LATER, accompanied by Robert Longmoor and a carpen-ter named Andrew Garrett, Hearne climbed into a canoe and started a 450-mile journey. In his notebook, he observed with some frustration that the five small canoes, although heavily laden, could carry only

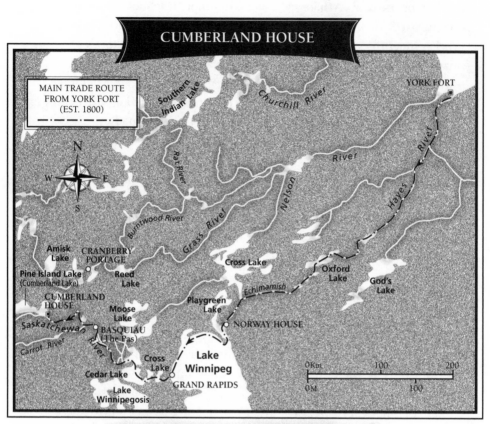

CUMBERLAND HOUSE

MAIN TRADE ROUTE
FROM YORK FORT
(EST. 1800)

YORK FORT

Southern Indian Lake

Churchill River

Rat River

Nelson River

Hayes River

Burntwood River

Grass River

Amisk Lake

CRANBERRY PORTAGE

Reed Lake

Cross Lake

Oxford Lake

God's Lake

Pine Island Lake (Cumberland Lake)

CUMBERLAND HOUSE

Moose Lake

Playgreen Lake

Echimamish

Saskatchewan River

BASQUIAU (The Pas)

NORWAY HOUSE

Carrot River

Cross Lake

Lake Winnipeg

Cedar Lake

GRAND RAPIDS

Lake Winnipegosis

0 Km   100   200

0 M   100

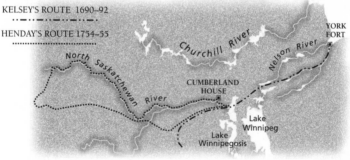

KELSEY'S ROUTE 1690–92

HENDAY'S ROUTE 1754–55

YORK FORT

Churchill River

Nelson River

North Saskatchewan River

CUMBERLAND HOUSE

Lake Winnipeg

Lake Winnipegosis

180 pounds of Brazil tobacco, 130 pounds of powder, 200 pounds of shot, 6 gallons of brandy, and a few trifling articles for trade. For provisions, the men carried only 2 pecks of oatmeal and 12 pounds of biscuit. And, on the second day out, when he discovered that the rivers were too shallow to accommodate even this much weight, Hearne wisely but regretfully abandoned the oatmeal.

Travelling up the Hayes River, Hearne encountered another challenge: the shortage of game in the region. The "Canadian pedlars" regularly canoed and portaged thousands of miles—from Montreal to Ottawa, Mattawa, the Great Lakes, and westward—but they augmented their diet of dried peas and pemmican with game. Hearne and his men travelled twelve days before they found any, and then it wasn't moose or caribou but a few swans. This was typical.

During the trip to York Fort, Cree traders carried food. Excellent hunters, they could usually bag at least some game. By the time they returned inland, however, game would have grown scarce along the river, and often they endured near starvation before reaching their families near the parkland borders. There, they would abandon their canoes and travel on foot so as to hunt more effectively.

Hearne and his party travelled up the Hayes and Fox rivers, paddling, tracking, and portaging, and then proceeded west via the Nelson River and Moose Lake, following a variation of what later became known as the Middle Track. (The main trade route, the Lower Track, developed along the Hayes River.) Rain poured down continually, and even Cree hunters could locate no game. Later, Hearne wrote, "During the whole time we had nothing to eat except berries, which, when eaten in so large a quantity as to stop hunger, are of such astringent quality (especially to strangers) that me and my two men were much disordered by them. At the same time, hunger obliged us to have recourse to a still greater quantity, let the consequence prove as it may."

On August 19, 1774, after eight weeks on the rivers, Hearne reached Basquiau, or The Pas, so named because it is a narrow place between steep banks. From here, he could look out over a broad lowland plain—perfect camping grounds in a wilderness of lakes and rivers, with trails winding away north and south to higher country.

Henry Kelsey had visited The Pas in the early 1690s. Sixty years later, Pierre Gaultier de Varennes et de La Vérendrye had built the first trading post in the area. And in 1754, the HBC's Anthony Henday had passed this way en route to visit the Blackfoot of the western plains. He had urged them to come to York Fort to trade, but they had answered that game was too scarce along the way, and "the natives who went down to the Bay were often-times starved while on their journey." Having travelled the route, Henday observed, "Such remarks I thought exceeding true."

Now, in 1774, Hearne found the remains of a chimney on the south side of the river, and on the north side, near where he camped, "an old Canadian House laying in ruins"—probably the place built by La Vérendrye. Hearne considered building the new Company post on this spot, but much of the nearby woods had been cleared as a result of continual visitation. Also, local Cree told him that an intersection used by three different bands, the heart of the entire system of waterways, lay sixty miles up the Saskatchewan River at "Pine Island Lake," now called Cumberland Lake.

Proceeding there, Hearne stood at the edge of a fine, broad bay that offered a commanding view of the lake. To the west lay the plains and the Rockies; Athabasca country lay to the north, Prince of Wales Fort to the northeast, Lake Winnipeg to the southeast—and from here, all these fur-rich lands were accessible by water. Pine Island Lake itself was ringed with pines, poplars, and birches—all the requisite raw materials. Samuel Hearne said yes. On September 3, 1774, he and his two men began clearing a site and building a temporary log house.

What to call this place? Having chosen the site for its strategic importance in controlling the routes of the fur trade, Hearne remembered visiting an impressive star-shaped fortification on the outskirts of Old Portsmouth—a place called Fort Cumberland. And he named the new outpost Cumberland House.

THIS FIRST permanent inland trading post marked the beginning of the Hudson's Bay Company's westward expansion. It was a turning point in the history of the Company and, by extension, that of North America. At this time, the HBC operated a dozen trading posts in Rupert's Land, none more than one hundred miles from Hudson Bay.

By 1821, when it absorbed its competition, the Company would control the North American fur trade with a chain of posts extending from Montreal to Victoria.

The building of Cumberland House in 1774 launched the transformation. In September of that year, Samuel Hearne expected to be joined by reinforcements at any time. He watched with particular eagerness for his three most experienced men. Matthew Cocking, his second-in-command, knew the surrounding area; Isaac Batt had undertaken to supervise the collecting of birchbark and the building of large canoes; and Charles Thomas Price Isham, the "half-breed" son of James Isham, had proved himself an excellent hunter.

On October 9, a group of Canadians landed two large canoes one hundred yards from the house. With them, they brought Robert Flatt, an HBC man who had left York Fort shortly after Hearne. The Canadians had found him alone at the head of Lake Winnipeg. In his journal, Hearne wrote, "The Indians who brought him from the fort, after taking all the goods from him, treated him very cruelly and then went their ways, and had not the Canadians happened to have come that way, probably he never would have been heard of."

This was a classic case of cultural misunderstanding. Early HBC traders did not appreciate that the First Nations really did function in small, autonomous groups and that, having journeyed inland from York Fort, various bands would disperse to rejoin families at different hunting grounds. Flatt had travelled inland with a party that turned south at Lake Winnipeg. When he insisted that they bring him farther west, naturally they responded with derision. Who was this pale stranger? What made him think he could order them about in their own lands? This response was common to the First Nations. The present-day Dene Stephen Kakfwi has explained, "When non-Dene came to our land, we saw them as curious strangers who had come to visit; we shared with them and helped them to survive. We could not conceive that they would not see the world as we do. . . . The Dene had no experience or understanding of a people who would try to control us, or who would say that somehow they owned the land we had always lived on."

Samuel Hearne surmised that the other men sent to build Cumberland House had run into difficulties like Flatt's. Now, he could only welcome the Canadians who had rescued the HBC man—and use the occasion closely to examine their *canots du nord*. These craft were half the size of the *canots de maître* that served around Montreal, but were still twenty-four feet long, four feet eight inches broad, and one foot eight inches deep. Each required four paddlers but carried sixty-five or seventy pieces weighing more than two tons in all, including one hundred gallons of rum and wine and at least ten weeks' worth of provisions. Each year, from beyond Grand Portage, the Canadians would send out sixty such canoes—and a sea of rum and wine.

After two days, when the visitors departed, the Cree faced a difficult choice. They could remain at Cumberland House and continue to work as hunters for a few impoverished Englishmen, or they could follow the Canadians and join in the revelry that was bound to ensue before long. They made the choice that young men everywhere have always made, leaving Hearne not a little disgruntled: "The Indian captain who brought me from the fort and has been tenting by me ever since, was so affected with the smell of the Canadians' New England rum that he and his crew embarked and followed after them, before they were out of sight."

Given his small, inexperienced crew—none of his three men had previously ranged farther from a trading post than a wooding or hunting tent—Hearne could not even dream of procuring birchbark and building the large canoes he needed to transport great quantities of goods. A couple of band captains promised to build these craft, but having exhausted his meager supply of brandy, Hearne could not induce them to deliver. As the northern winter took hold, bitterly cold and dark, he drew on his three-year training in hardship to steady his men. In mid-December, faced with a shortage of food, he introduced short rations, putting himself on exactly the same two-meals-a-day diet as the others. He also told the men to cease grumbling and behave like Dene, because obviously he had no power to change matters.

When Robert Longmoor suffered badly frostbitten toes, Hearne performed an impromptu operation and laid them open to the bone—though he felt the absence of the medicine chest, which was with some of his absent crew. After six weeks, the tough lowland Scot went back to work. As soon as he got a chance, acting on Hearne's advice, Longmoor began working with an expert Cree canoe builder.

He learned to start by building a frame, cutting, steaming, and bending cedar or white spruce into ribs, gunwales, and planks. He would peel the bark from mature birch trees, stitch these peelings together, and, using a handmade awl, lash the large sheets to the gunwales with cords or *wattape* made of spruce roots—roots that Cree women had collected, soaked, and stripped of their outer layers. Finally, he would slather the lacing with pitch made of boiled spruce sap mixed with charred caribou hair and animal fat. Within two years of arriving at Cumberland House, Longmoor had become an efficient builder of large canoes—the Company's first.

By mid-January 1775, Hearne and his crew were surviving on a daily ration of one handful of the dried, beaten meat he called *thewhagon* and four ounces of other meat. Three weeks later, the Englishman observed that this scanty subsistence, so different from the normal allowance at a company fort, "is so alarming to my men in general, that it is with the greatest difficulty I can persuade them from thinking that entire famine must ensue."

Partridges, rabbits, and fish had all but vanished. Yet Hearne, having survived long stretches on nothing but water and tobacco, remained sanguine: "I'm not without hopes of some relief before long as I daily expect some Indians in." Two days later, a Cree hunter arrived to report that a dozen of his companions had killed five moose and were hauling in the meat.

The rest of the winter passed without incident. Toward the end of May, when the ice began to melt, Hearne set the men to work building a permanent log house and embarked with a large group of native people bringing furs to York Fort. He needed to acquire trading goods for the following year, and also to investigate the absence of his most experienced men. After four weeks on the river, paddling steadily, he arrived at York Fort on June 23, 1775, a year to the day since he had departed. Nobody had heard anything of the missing men—a discovery that alarmed everyone.

Just four days later, Matthew Cocking and Charles Isham arrived to tell their story. The previous year, Isham and Isaac Batt had travelled a more southerly route than Hearne and had found themselves at the mouth of the Saskatchewan River. This was near where their guides wished the new post to be built—southwest of Cumberland

House and, not surprisingly, much closer to their own hunting grounds. Again, the frustrated Cree had left the Englishmen to their own devices.

Cocking had come up behind the other two, but his canoes were so heavily laden that he could not provide transport. Neither could he leave the men to starve, and so all three camped through the winter on the Assiniboine River. Early in June, with the ice melting, and just before they embarked for York Fort, the Company men encountered some short-handed Canadian pedlars. These men offered Isaac Batt better wages than the HBC was paying, so he said goodbye and joined the competition.

Samuel Hearne stayed one week at York Fort, enjoying the company of friends. The London committee might by now have responded to the vacancy situation at Prince of Wales Fort, where Andrew Graham was waiting to retire, but communications were so slow that no response had yet arrived. Hearne could hardly wait around doing nothing. On July 8, with a flotilla of canoes and a few Company men, he embarked once again for Cumberland House.

The first two weeks on the river went well enough. Then came an evening when, complaining of the heaviness of the goods and the difficulty of the work, the Cree requested some brandy. Unlike the Chipewyan, who were relatively indifferent to alcohol and with whom he had done so much travelling, many of the Western Cree had acquired a taste for strong drink. To encourage the men in their duty, Hearne distributed three gallons—"which though quite sufficient for a much greater number of reasonable beings, were so far from satisfying them that t'were with great difficulty we could prevent them from taking more by force."

The next day proved clear and sunny, but the native men refused to embark, some "being a little quamish and some sulky." The day after that, Hearne got them going, but not without difficulty. One man was still hungover from the drunken bout. A friend insisted on changing canoes to help him, but that left two weaker men to paddle alone. Only one of these could steer a little, and they complained of being only two while the other large canoes had three. To settle the matter, Hearne gave them one man out of his own canoe, the largest in the company.

Early in August, kept in camp by a heavy rain, the native men had a falling out amongst themselves. When finally departing, Hearne's canoe mate decided to switch canoes without explanation, insisting on travelling in convoy with his friends, "so that I were then left with the largest canoe heavy laden, to paddle by myself . . . and as several got disabled in their squabbles, I could get no one to assist me except a young female who was not of any material service."

On August 11, the men again pressed Hearne for more brandy. They were making good time and, despite misgivings—and, indeed, despite suspicions that had been troubling him for some time—he gave them a little. When they had finished that, they broke out their own small containers and drained those—only hadn't he seen them do that already? Hearne's worst fears were confirmed: while pretending to hunt, the native men had broached the large kegs of brandy, filled their containers, and made up the difference with river water.

Examining all the kegs, Hearne discovered that, of those carried by the native people, only one remained intact. He had left with a flotilla of thirty-odd canoes, but while travelling and camping in small open areas along the river, this large number necessarily resolved itself into parties of two, three, or four canoes. Bad weather would sometimes force a riverside sojourn of two or three nights. Then, he determined through questioning, those carrying the brandy would make use of it: "Some of the remaining kegs were little better than water."

Nine times out of ten, this inland journey proved arduous and joyless and involved going hungry for weeks. Faced with such different circumstances and with so much temptation, few groups of young men would have resisted the temptation to siphon off a taste of euphoria. As the man responsible, of course, Hearne could not see it that way.

On departing this latest camp, he and his fellow HBC men removed all the brandy kegs into their own canoes. Some of the Cree were affronted. If they couldn't carry brandy, they wouldn't carry any goods at all. But here, within a three- or four-day paddle of his destination, Hearne refused to back down. If necessary, he would post a guard, paddle to Cumberland House, and return with more men "rather than put it again in their power to make a dupe of me after being apprised of their villainy."

Of the many evils the fur trade brought from Europe, alcohol abuse was one of the worst. Having discovered this vice, some of the Cree

This 1952 painting by Franklin Arbuckle, Hearne Builds Cumberland House, 1774–75, *makes the construction of the Hudson's Bay Company's first inland post look as neat and orderly as the creation of a contemporary suburban tract house. The realities included a dearth of food, equipment, and men, but again Hearne persevered and overcame all obstacles.*

had been drinking. They tossed around trading goods and talked of staving the brandy kegs. Hearne and his men surrounded the kegs and a scuffle ensued, "and though we were much inferior in number, yet had greatly the advantage, being all sober and they much intoxicated. We were careful not to take any offensive weapons, and only gave them a little old English Play, which had so good an effect that we soon drubbed them into a seeming good humour again, though some of them were a little sulky."

When he arrived at Cumberland House, Hearne found that, led by the carpenter, Andrew Garrett, the three men left behind had made great progress. They had roughed in the various apartments and begun framing the roof. Hearne doled out extra rations.

He expressed considerably less pleasure when, two days later, he finished taking stock of the company stores. Two large bundles of trading goods had gone missing, one containing forty-three pounds of Brazil tobacco, the other fifty-six pounds of ball and shot. He sampled the kegs of brandy and confirmed his worst fears. Some kegs were almost pure water, while the brandy in others was no stronger than grog, notoriously low in alcohol content. Of the two hundred gallons of brandy with which he had departed York Fort—brandy being now necessary to trading in this vicinity because of the competition from Montreal-based traders—he had arrived with less than half.

Samuel Hearne was slow to anger, but this made him furious. As he saw it, this was precisely the kind of misadventure that had turned the Hudson's Bay Company into "the make game and laughingstock of every trader from Canada." He would not allow that judgment to stand. By building Cumberland House, he had made a beginning. He had yet to solve the problem of transporting large quantities of trading goods inland, but to that he would turn his attention.

LATE IN THE AFTERNOON of October 4, 1775, from the roof of Cumberland House, where with the carpenter he was admiring the new chimney, Samuel Hearne caught movement out of the corner of one eye. He rose to his feet, shielded his eyes, and pointed across Pine Island Lake: "Two canoes." After a while, as the craft became more visible, with some puzzlement he added, "Matthew Cocking?"

His mind racing—could this mean what he scarcely dared hope?— Hearne climbed down the rough wooden ladder and walked to the landing area, anxious to greet Cocking like the friend he had become.

"Governor Hearne!" Cocking cried as he jumped out of the canoe.

Hearne scratched his head, then said, "Prince of Wales Fort?"

"The command is yours!" He looked up at Cumberland House. "And thank you for this! Most impressive!"

"You are to succeed me?"

Cocking nodded and shouldered his valise: "Dispatches from London."

The two Englishmen started up the hill toward the log house.

A few hours later, a jubilant Samuel Hearne stood gazing out over Pine Island Lake. The London committee had given him command of one of the HBC's most important establishments—and he was just thirty years old. At York Fort, the much older Humphrey Marten would succeed Ferdinand Jacobs, who like Graham wished to retire. According to Cocking, Marten had initially expressed some dismay— not at Hearne's promotion, but rather that Hearne's energy and resourcefulness would no longer be available at Cumberland House.

For the sake of Andrew Graham, who wished to depart that autumn, Hearne was to travel to Prince of Wales Fort as soon as possible. He tried to induce some of the Cree camped nearby to travel directly to Churchill, but they would have none of it. Hearne did not blame them. If they left this late in the season, they would have to winter at that northerly post, hundreds of miles from their wives and children. His only recourse was to return to York Fort with the Homeguard who had come with Cocking and then to trek north on snowshoes when freeze-up made that possible.

Hearne turned and looked proudly at Cumberland House, rising quite grandly against the woods. Part of him felt sorry to leave. Yet he had finished his work here. And Prince of Wales Fort was his to command. Governor Samuel Hearne. Yes, that had a ring to it. He strode up the hill to pack.

10

THE GOVERNOR'S
MAGIC

⁕

BATTLING FREEZE-UP, which always brought the most challenging travelling conditions of the year, Samuel Hearne descended the river system from Cumberland House to York Fort. There, impatiently, he waited for the waters of Hudson Bay to freeze solid enough that he could trek north along the coast. Finally, in January 1776, he snowshoed to Prince of Wales Fort and took charge.

Three months later, he and his men were still dealing with snow-drifts that reached "nearly as high as the windows of the second storey." As spring came on, Hearne described the increasing bustle of activity, which included renovating his own quarters:

Armourer employed stocking hunting guns. Smith doing some necessary jobs in his own branch, shipwrights making of boats. . . . House carpenter making a window frame for the porch leading to the chief's apartment, mason cutting fire stones for the chief's fire-place, some men with the horses hauling snow out of the yard, the others grinding oatmeal and doing other necessary jobs. . . . Cooper and one man making and repairing small sleds, sawyer and one man sawing boards, and the tailor with one man at work for trade; the others clearing away the snow from the outer gates, and digging the boats from under the snow ready for the carpenter to repair them.

Before long, and although swamped with a backlog of work, Hearne gave dramatic evidence of the change of regime by taking as his "country wife" the widely admired Mary Norton, daughter of the late Moses Norton.

Of all First Nations women, British fur-traders found Cree girls the most attractive. According to HBC officer James Isham, they were well shaped, "very frisky when young," and often had beautiful eyes: "large and grey yet lively and sparkling, very bewitchen." As a mixed-blood Cree, Mary Norton was probably lighter skinned than most, another characteristic admired by Company men, whose racial prejudices were never far below the surface.

No portraits survive, although Samuel Hearne, confident of his abilities as an amateur artist, must certainly have tried his hand. Mary Norton probably resembled the sixteen-year-old mixed-blood girl who would later entrance fur-trader John McNab: "She was neither bold nor bashful; her behavior was free, unconstrained and remarkably modest. She was, with regard to her person, a handsome brunette, fine black expressive eyes, arched eye brows, high forehead, shaded with natural ringlet of black flowing hair, an aquiline nose, pretty mouth, teeth exquisitely beautiful, and the contour of her face of an oval form. She was tall and slender, well proportioned but very delicate."

Mary Norton, too, was sixteen. At thirty-one, Hearne might appear, to contemporary Westerners, to be something of a cradle-robber. But in eighteenth-century Rupert's Land, as Isham observed, "Maidens are very rare to be found at thirteen or fourteen and I believe [I may say there are] none at fifteen." At sixteen, having been kept from other men by her father, Mary was now being courted by every HBC officer in the fort and not a few Cree.

Hearne could remember Mary Norton as a dark-eyed girl of eight or nine, laughing and joyful, running around the governor's quarters. A few years later, when he returned from his trek to the mouth of the Coppermine River, he noticed changes—not just that she had begun to fill out, but that she had grown quiet and serious. He had talked with her frequently and knew her well enough that, when she was fourteen, he could observe, as if light-heartedly, that soon she would probably take a husband.

She had looked at the ground. "My father will not allow it."

Not long afterward, while talking business with Moses Norton, Hearne noticed the governor's daughter on the ramparts. "You'll soon be thinking of finding a husband for Mary," he said to Norton.

The older man reddened and declared his daughter far too young.

The precise, efficient Samuel Hearne had a romantic streak. Still, he would have regarded The Trapper's Bride, *a depiction of marriage "in the fashion of the country" by Victorian Alfred Jacob Miller, as ludicrously saccharine: white horse, war bonnet, tipi, adoring lovers—surely the rationalists of the Enlightenment would never fall to this?*

Because at heart he remained a sailor, Samuel Hearne would spend more time than most standing on the ramparts, gazing out to sea and deeply inhaling the salty air. One afternoon, not long after he had been chosen to establish Cumberland House, Hearne stood at a spot from which he could observe the entrance to the kitchen. When Mary Norton emerged, he waved and invited her to join him.

After a few moments of pleasantry, Hearne said, as if in passing, "I may have irritated your father, Mary, by observing that soon you will be old enough to marry."

"What did my father say?"

"That you are far too young."

"All my friends are already married!"

"It's certainly best that you wait, Mary." Hearne had been staring out to sea, but now, as he spoke, he glanced at the young woman beside him. "Perhaps you will wait?"

"Wait for what, Samuel?" Suddenly understanding, Mary blushed and looked away. "I'm late! I must go!" In confusion, she started away down the stairs, but then turned and raced back up. She embraced Hearne and kissed him. "You know I will."

With that, Mary Norton, age fourteen, fled down the stairs.

Now, in 1776, Mary was sixteen—practically an old maid. With her father dead, and despite the vying of other suitors, Samuel Hearne carried the day.

THE LONDON COMMITTEE expressly prohibited Hudson's Bay Company men from having intimate relations with First Nations women. On several occasions, the Committee argued, such involvement had led to trouble. Earlier in the century, for example, eight Canadians based at a post on the Severn River had carried off several Cree women against their will and were subsequently murdered.

Yet such fatalities were the exception rather than the rule. They invariably resulted from breaching customs, not from following them. The Committee may have repudiated "immoral behaviour," but what it really disliked was expense. In 1750, an HBC officer named Robert Pilgrim had become the first to bring home to England not only a child but a Cree wife. A few months after settling on the outskirts of London, Pilgrim died. His will stipulated that his son remain in England with relatives but that Thu-a-Higon, if she so desired, be returned to Churchill to live among her own relatives. The HBC grudgingly acquiesced. Not long afterward, it issued strict orders to ships' captains prohibiting them from carrying native passengers to England without London's written permission.

As long as "country marriages" cost the HBC nothing, the Committee was prepared to turn a blind eye. And as Sylvia Van Kirk demonstrates in *No Tender Ties*, the Company would never have survived, much less flourished, without these marriages *à la façon du pays*, "in the custom of the country." The First Nations approved and encouraged long-term relationships between traders and native women because they could see that such affiliations benefited both groups. The native peoples gained privileged access to European goods; the British gleaned knowledge of how to survive in this harsh environment.

Some of the HBC men treated their country wives shabbily, abandoning them when they returned to England. Decades after Hearne, Governor George Simpson would prove especially despicable. But most Company officers behaved honourably. Matthew Cocking, for example, had had three wives, and he provided in his will for the two who survived him.

Another of Hearne's contemporaries, the surveyor Philip Turnor, would later flatly inform the London committee that the master of any given post would face endless difficulties if he did not take a wife,

as above half the Indians that came to the house would offer the master their wife, the refusal of which would give great offence to both the man and his wife, though he was to make the Indian a present for his offer, the woman would think herself slighted, and if the master was to accept the offer, he would be expected to clothe her and by keeping a woman it makes one short ready answer (that he has a woman of his own and she would be offended) and very few Indians make that offer when they know the master keeps a woman.

In practice, common sense prevailed—even though, as products of hierarchical Europe, the traders introduced class restrictions. The governors or masters of the various posts, later called chief factors, would frequently support two or three country wives, clothing, housing, and feeding all of them. Junior officers would usually be permitted to entertain women in their apartments but not to keep them overnight; and "servants," or working men, would be compelled to disappear over the walls.

Having contended with these double standards as a junior officer, Hearne proved a liberal governor, allowing the younger men far greater latitude than he had enjoyed. Yet even Hearne, who shrank from nothing when describing the First Nations—eating habits, religious beliefs, sexual behaviour—offered no description of country marriages, probably because doing so would have meant betraying HBC men who remained in the field.

Fortunately for us, the Montreal-based traders felt less constrained. As in Scotland, where a couple could establish a legal marriage simply by declaring their consent before a witness, customs and ceremonies were not elaborate. Yet these modest rituals could be ignored only at peril. Usually, the HBC man would visit the bride's parents and request their consent. Probably, he would pay a "bride price"—one horse, for example, or three muskets—and seal the new alliance by smoking the peace pipe with the family. All this Hearne well understood. Given his sense of propriety, and indeed of chivalry, he naturally embraced tradition.

And this was a spectacular match—the tall, handsome, and energetic new governor, the most powerful man in the region, and the gentlest, best-educated, and, to the European eye, most beautiful of all the young women. Mary's father was dead. But at an appointed time, probably around March 1776, Hearne went to visit her relatives, most notably her mother, Meo-See-Tak-Ka-Pow. Mary Norton would have preceded him to the encampment, located within walking distance. Hearne undoubtedly brought along his second-in-command, and also a company servant to haul a sledge bearing gifts.

The rest is not hard to imagine. In the largest tipi in the camp, the three Englishmen sat and smoked the calumet with Mary's mother, aunts, and uncles. Hearne recognized the new alliance by inviting all those present to visit the fort as they wished, having previously stipulated, through Mary, that they arrive no more than four at a time. Hearne distributed the many gifts he had brought, as befitted the status of Mary Norton—weapons, clothes, and utensils, as well as tobacco and brandy.

In addition to gift-giving, the Cree practised the custom of "bride service," according to which the newly married couple would live with the wife's relatives until a child was born, the husband proving himself by supplying his in-laws with game. It's tempting to imagine one of Mary's uncles teasing the good-natured Hearne, smoking the calumet and asking, straight-faced, when the Englishman would begin hunting caribou for his mother-in-law. In truth, nobody expected "bride service" from the Europeans, though the white men were expected to understand that an alliance had been created that involved responsibilities on both sides.

The calumet smoked and the gifts distributed, thirty or forty Homeguard Cree accompanied Samuel Hearne and Mary Norton back to the fort, drumming and singing as they went. Usually, the bride would now go through a cleansing ritual performed by women at the fort, who would wash off paint and bear grease and exchange her native garments for a shirt, a short gown, a petticoat, and leggings. But as Mary Norton already dressed in a European style and employed no

Hearne would have felt comfortable with the rustic realism of Paul Kane, who depicted a chief factor celebrating his country marriage by setting out on snowshoes with a team of dogs to enjoy an extended wedding trip.

ointments, her friends contented themselves with dressing her in a fabulous new dress ornamented with quillwork and beads.

That evening, Samuel Hearne and Mary Norton, dining together publicly for the first time, inspired toast after toast at an elaborate dinner. The new governor provided a dram of whisky for every man at the fort, and probably a tad more, and the revelry had hardly begun—the fiddlers sawing away and the men jigging with female visitors—when Hearne and his wife retired to their quarters.

Next morning, perhaps, if the weather remained fine, Hearne would hitch up half a dozen dogs. He would bundle Mary Norton into a sled, cover her with furs, and, just for the fun of it, whisk her away to one of the hunting tents. When he suggested this, Mary Norton said, "Tomorrow, Samuel, we go. Tonight, come!"

She took his hand and led him to bed.

* * *

THE GOVERNOR of Prince of Wales Fort was not unlike the captain of a ship. Within the stone walls of the fort, he controlled the lives of only a few dozen men, but he also supervised two sloops and a brigantine and the functioning of a network of river travellers that extended thousands of miles into the western plains and the Arctic barrens.

Having finally abandoned the black whale fishery launched by Moses Norton, on which it had wasted £20,000, the HBC was urging Samuel Hearne to expand the inland fur trade and also the white whale fishery, which had always been reasonably profitable, "Particular attention to be paid to the procuring of oil, a very valuable article of trade." For the sake of business, Hearne was also to encourage the various Dene groups, the Athabasca Cree, and the Inuit to cease warring amongst themselves.

All this Samuel Hearne would do. He would also get into a wrangle with Humphrey Marten, who had joined the Hudson's Bay Company in 1750. Sixteen years older than Hearne, Marten had recently succeeded Ferdinand Jacobs as master at York Fort. In 1777, the scrupulously honest Hearne called attention to a discrepancy of £400 in Marten's accounts. The following year, Marten accused Hearne of using brandy to entice native people, notably those who owed debts at York, to trade instead at Prince of Wales Fort. One of the ship captains, Magnus Johnston, had done precisely that on at least one occasion. Hearne told him not to do it again and otherwise ignored the complaint.

In 1779, when the older man was departing to spend a year in England, he repeated his allegations—and then was prevented by ice from escaping the Bay. This time, Hearne told the London committee airily that Marten's accusations were of "so peevish a nature as not to claim the notice of my pen." For the next couple of years, the written communications between the two, so necessary to conducting Company business, betray an unsurprising frostiness.

Eventually, a shared calamity would unite the two masters. And in the end, when Marten was suffering from gout and a "bilious disorder," he would write to Hearne as to his last honest friend, complaining that although ill health was destroying the few pleasures remaining to him, "yet consciousness of being honest to my masters doth as it must to you, soothe the pains of the body and blunt the points of the rancorous darts hurled at us by those bad men, who think we injure them by being honest to our masters. But whilst this feeble hand can hold a pen, until these eyes are closed for ever, or at least whilst you and I remain in the service, I will join with you heart and hand in preventing as much as in me lies all illicit practices."

AS GOVERNOR of Prince of Wales Fort, Samuel Hearne, that reflective man of action, found he could make time to pursue his broader interests. In one of the letters that flowed regularly between HBC outposts, Hearne mentioned to Humphrey Marten—this before their imbroglio—that he had undertaken to help young George Hudson "by way of learning him to draw a little."

In June 1776, when he sent London the rough field notes he had written at Cumberland House, the newly appointed governor also thoughtfully addressed the greatest impediment to inland expansion, the challenge of transporting sufficient goods. Without resorting to supplying an ocean of brandy, a strategy Hearne could not recommend, the HBC would never induce the native people to build large canoes in sufficient numbers, making it "necessary to have recourse to some other methods, and the only one that remains is to try what can be done in light shells made of wood after the canoe form; and I am apt to believe that expert wherrey builders could make vessels ⌈capable of carrying⌉ upwards one ton burthen, so portable that two men may carry them one fourth of a mile at least without resting."

Hearne specified what woods to use, and recommended that these craft be built, tested for portability, and sent out immediately. Again, he drew on his experience as a sailor:

As a number of such slight vessels would be very unhandy stowage on board of a ship and liable to many accidents on the passage, it would be more convenient to send out two expert workmen with proper wood etc. for their use, and as they could prepare all the timbers and planks in the winter, ready for setting up in the summer, they would in a year or two have a considerable number made fit for use and will with care last several years, whereas the best birch rind canoe that can be built will not last longer than one year.

The London committee built a few skiffs according to Hearne's specifications and sent them to York Fort in the summer of 1778. The native people and inland men refused to use them, however, fearing that they would break up in the rough rapids where no shipwright would be available to make repairs. Instead, Company men like Robert Longmoor began learning canoe-building from the native peoples.

Even so, as historian J.B. Tyrrell later observed, in Hearne's remarks we have the first recommendation by an HBC officer that the Company build small wooden vessels "to transport goods inland, instead of depending on the birch bark canoes of the Indians." As a result, Hearne is often credited with having "invented" the York boat, which, modelled on craft developed in Orkney, "that island universe in the northern reaches of Scotland," later became synonymous with the HBC. To be precise, he was first to envisage and call for the development of such craft.

Meanwhile, Hearne began expanding and reworking the narrative of his journey to the mouth of the Coppermine River. Not long after completing that trek, he had sent London a bare-bones account— little more than expanded field notes. But already, sensing the possibilities and significance of the project, he felt dissatisfied: "I would have inserted the sketch of my two former journeys in the draft, but on leaving the fort in a hurry in December 1770, I left the principal of my remarks relative thereto in an old journal book, which I gave the surgeon of the fort for waste paper, and on my arrival found that I had no remarks left concerning my last draft, otherwise would have laid the lakes and river down in their respective places with their communication with the sea."

Besides adding clarifications, observations, and cries from the heart, most of which would never be properly integrated into the narrative of the *Journey*, Hearne began preparing a vocabulary of the Dene language—essentially, an English-Athapaskan dictionary. To those members of the London committee who showed an interest, he sent artifacts, among them a bayonet and a knife he had found in the tents of the Inuit at Bloody Falls, "the former in shape like the ace of spades, with the handle of deer's horn a foot long, and the latter exactly resembling those described by [David] Crantz," who had written extensively about the Inuit of Greenland.

Influenced by Enlightenment thinkers, especially Voltaire, Hearne adopted a scientific attitude toward living in the north. This coloured even his friendship with Matonabbee, who brought more furs to Churchill "than any other Indian ever did, or ever will do." In his book, while explaining that native leaders felt under pressure from friends and relatives, he describes how, in October 1776, Matonabbee arrived to trade at the head of a large contingent.

After the usual ceremonies, according to which the HBC governor gave the leaders gifts of brandy, tobacco, and various edibles, Hearne honoured his old friend with a new captain's uniform of military design, so signalling his status and authority. It consisted of a lined blue coat with regimental cuffs and collar, a waistcoat and breeches of green baize, a white shirt, yarn stockings gartered below the knee, a pair of English shoes, and a hat bedecked with colourful feathers and tied round with a bright worsted sash that hung down to the shoulders. He also outfitted Matonabbee's six wives from head to toe.

Over the next ten days, and in response to requests, Hearne gave Matonabbee still more gifts: seven lieutenants' coats, fifteen other coats, eighteen hats, eighteen shirts, eight guns, 140 pounds of gunpowder along with shot, ball, and flints, as well as much tobacco, cloth, and paint, and many hatchets, ice-chisels, files, bayonets, knives, awls, blankets, combs, looking glasses, stockings, handkerchiefs, and needles. In all, using the standard fur-trade measure of a single adult beaver pelt, he gave Matonabbee goods worth more than seven hundred made beaver.

But the most extraordinary of his demands was twelve pounds of powder, twenty-eight pounds of shot and ball, four pounds of tobacco, some articles of clothing, and several pieces of ironwork, etc., to give to two men who had hauled his tent and other lumber the preceding winter. This demand was so very unreasonable that I made some scruple, or at least hesitated to comply with it, hinting that he was the person who ought to satisfy those men for their services; but I was soon answered, that he did not expect to have been *denied such a trifle as that was*; and for the future he would carry his goods where he could get his own price for them. On my asking him where that was, he replied, in a very insolent tone, "To the Canadian traders." I was glad to comply with his demands; and I here insert the anecdote as a specimen of an Indian's conscience.

Hearne naturally took this line in writing to his HBC superiors, the men in Fenchurch Street who paid his salary—and who were profiting hugely from the fur trade. In truth, he admired Matonabbee for driving a hard bargain, and clearly enjoyed his brashness. To the London committee, however, he needed to justify his expenditures, and here we see him hard at work, portraying himself, despite appearances to the contrary, as a faithful and thrifty steward of Company resources. Where Matonabbee was concerned, Hearne preferred to err on the side of generosity and to concoct justifications later.

IN HIS SPARE TIME, Hearne proved less a Company man than an amateur anthropologist—and this in an age before anthropology was born. In *A Journey to the Northern Ocean,* he frequently turns to describing and analyzing what, following Voltaire, he calls the "superstitions" of the First Nations he encounters—material that would later intrigue Coleridge.

At one point, Hearne suggests that although the Chipewyan Dene showed great confidence in the supernatural power of their conjurors, religion had yet to dawn among them. None of them expressed any belief in life after death, he explained, nor any hope of reward or fear of punishment—two essentials, for this eighteenth-century Englishman, of any religion. He marvelled that Matonabbee "could tell a better story of our saviour's birth and life than one half of those who call themselves Christians; yet he always declared to me, that neither he, nor any of his countrymen, had an idea of a future state."

Hearne returned repeatedly to the belief system of the Dene. Lacking the conceptual framework of a French *philosophe* or an Oxbridge intellectual, he never quite understood that the Dene, like other First Nations, were spiritual rather than religious, that for them, all things were connected, and the world was both natural and supernatural. He could only report that nearly all of the Dene, including Matonabbee, shared a firm belief in the power of their magicians:

When these jugglers take a dislike to, and threaten a secret revenge on any person, it often proves fatal to that person; as, from a firm belief that the conjurer has power over his life, he permits the very thoughts of it to prey on his spirits, till by degrees it brings on a disorder which puts an end to his existence: and sometimes a threat of this kind causes the death of a whole family; and that without any blood being shed, or the least apparent molestation being offered to any of the parties.

Hearne offers an arresting example, and this third supernatural anecdote is the one from which Coleridge would take most in writing "The Three Graves"—not in specific details but, as he himself would indicate, in spirit and storyline. In the winter of 1778, Matonabbee arrived at Prince of Wales Fort sounding uncharacteristically worried. Another Dene warrior—possibly the giant with whom he had tangled previously—was speaking of him in a manner that made him fear for his life. He implored Hearne to kill this individual, who was then several hundred miles away:

To please this great man to whom I owed so much, and not expecting that any harm could possibly arise from it, I drew a rough sketch of two human figures on a piece of paper, in the attitude of wrestling. In the hand of one of them, I drew the figure of a bayonet pointing to the breast of the other. This is me, said I to Matonabbee, pointing to the figure which was holding the bayonet; and the other is your enemy. Opposite to these figures I drew a pine tree, over which I placed a large human eye, and out of the tree projected a human hand. This paper I gave to Matonabbee, with instructions to make it as publicly known as possible. Sure enough, the following year, when he came in to trade, he informed me that the man was dead, though at that time he was not less than three hundred miles from Prince of Wales Fort. He assured me that the man was in perfect health when he heard of my design against him; but almost immediately afterwards became quite sick and gloomy, and refusing all kind of sustenance, in a very few days died.

Hearne adds that after this, visitors frequently sought his supernatural intervention, but he never complied, "by which means I not only preserved the credit I gained on the first attempt, but always kept them in awe, and in some degree of respect and obedience to me." He adds that the story could be verified by William Jefferson, now his second-in-command at Prince of Wales Fort, as well as the other officers and many of the men then serving.

LATE ONE SPRING AFTERNOON, carrying eight or ten geese, and with Mary Norton conveying half a dozen more, Samuel Hearne strode happily through the front gates of Prince of Wales Fort. To those who greeted him, he answered, yes, the hunting had gone exceedingly well. He and Mary had spent the past three days camping near the wintering tents. Hearne enjoyed these sojourns not only because he loved being out on the land—the expanse, the solitude, the sense of frontier—but because he savoured the nighttime privacy, which was greater than that afforded by his own quarters.

Now, bent on investigating a mystery that intrigued him, Hearne went directly to the Company kitchen, where he dropped off all but two geese. Carrying these two fowl—one notably larger than the other—Hearne led the way to his apartment, which he had partitioned into four areas: sitting room, bedroom, kitchen/dining room, and study.

While Mary plucked and cleaned the geese, Hearne prepared the table he used as a desk, covering it with a worn deerskin. He returned his microscope to its case and dug out an old straight razor and two small bowls. When Mary produced the geese, Hearne laid out the first, a common grey goose weighing perhaps ten pounds. He made a precise incision, extracted the bird's testicles, and deposited them in one of the bowls.

The larger goose, which had not been grey but rusty brown at its head and breast, weighed fifteen or sixteen pounds. While Mary watched at his shoulder, Hearne carefully took out this bird's testicles. "Aha! Just as I thought!"

"Samuel, what?"

"Look at the testicles, Mary. See how much smaller these ones are? That's why Barren Geese don't breed!"

Having washed his hands and cleaned the table, Hearne sat down at this desk, picked up his quill pen, and wrote in the notebook he reserved for flora, fauna, and wildlife. Later, preparing his book for publication, he would draw on these notes when writing about "Barren Geese"—an entry that, like a score of others, demonstrated not only his scientific curiosity but his attention to detail:

[Barren Geese] never make their appearance in the spring till the greatest part of the other species of geese are flown northward to breed, and many of them remain near Churchill River the whole summer. This large species are generally found to be males, and from the exceeding smallness of their testicles, they are, I suppose, incapable of propagating their species. I believe I can with truth say that I was the first European who made that remark, though they had always been distinguished by the name of the Barren Geese; for no other reason than that of their not being known to breed. Their flesh is by no means unpleasant, though always hard and tough; and their plumage is so thick before they begin to moult, that one bird usually produces a pound of fine feathers and down, of a surprising elasticity.

In noting the bird's small testicles, Hearne drew attention to a scientific curiosity that would not be fully explained until 1965, when naturalist H.C. Hanson published *The Giant Canada Goose.* Hanson determined that some immature geese would fly one thousand miles north from Minnesota to moult in the area around Churchill, so arriving much later than other geese, as Hearne had observed. Too young to breed, they grew large as a result of exercise but remained immature.

During his tenure as governor of Prince of Wales Fort, Hearne conducted countless scientific experiments like the one described above. One winter, he used his "excellent microscope" to examine the lice and other parasites that plagued the northern lemming, finding the work difficult because of the cold: the moisture from his breath made the lens foggy. Hearne persevered. He examined the windpipes of the whistling and the trumpeter swan, described their convoluted shapes, and concluded that the two species were anatomically identical—which is not quite correct.

Hearne was not infallible. But he did determine that the pouch at the base of the pelican's beak could hold three quarts of liquid, and that Canada geese would often nest in abandoned muskrat houses. He provided one of the earliest accounts of the passenger pigeon, and was the first to recognize that there are two different species of curlew, the Hudsonian and the Eskimo. Also, he understood bird migration at a time when leading English scientists were wondering whether swallows spent the winter underwater.

At Prince of Wales Fort, Samuel Hearne thus established himself as a pioneering naturalist. Here, too, he was able to indulge his love of animals. In his *Journey*, he would describe how one Swampy Cree man learned to tame moose, rendering them as friendly as domesticated horses, so that these large, antlered animals would follow the man anywhere and return at his call.

This remarkable trainer sometimes led moose to Churchill. In summer 1777, he paddled down a river with several companions while two especially tame moose followed along on the bank. At night, when he camped, these creatures would turn up and he would fondle them like dogs. One afternoon, to cross a deep bay, the Cree party paddled from point to point. The trainer remained with his companions, assuming that the moose would follow around as usual. That night, the young animals did not arrive, and as the trainer heard wolves howling, he dejectedly drew the obvious conclusion.

Hearne not only regarded this anecdote as worth communicating, but while ensconced in the governor's quarters, himself maintained a revolving menagerie of extraordinary pets, among them lemmings, mink, fishers, muskrats, red squirrels, ground squirrels, Arctic foxes, eagles, snow buntings, Lapland buntings, and horned larks, as well as canaries, which he imported.

The friendliness of the mink "made them troublesome as they were always in the way and their so frequently emitting a disagreeable smell [when frightened] made them quite disgusting." Fishers, by comparison, "are easily . . . domesticated, are very fond of tea leaves, have a pleasant musky smell and are very playful." Red squirrels disappointed, "though several of them became so familiar as to take anything out of my hand and sit on the table where I was writing and play with the pens etc., yet they never would bear to be handled and were very mischievous, gnawing at the chair bottoms, window curtains, sashes, etc." Ground squirrels, on the other hand, soon became very friendly: "by degrees they will bear handling as well as a cat: are

As an amateur naturalist, Hearne not only studied beavers but kept them as pets. He delighted in wryly correcting the errors of supposed experts who advanced grandiose claims about the creatures' social organization, observing that little remained to be added but "a vocabulary of their language, a code of their laws, and a sketch of their religion."

exceedingly cleanly, very playful and by no means so restless and impatient of confinement as the Common Squirrel."

Eventually, Hearne would devote more than fifty pages to describing the mammals, fish, and fowl of the western subarctic. Now, with Mary Norton, he lived and learned what he later communicated. And he pronounced the beaver the best pet of all:

In respect to the beaver dunging in their houses, as some persons assert, it is quite wrong, as they always plunge into the water to do it. I am the better enabled to make this assertion, from having kept several of them till they became so domesticated as to answer to their name, and follow those to whom they were accustomed, in the same manner as a dog would do; and they were as much pleased at being fondled as any animal I ever saw. I had a house built for them, and a small piece of water before the door, into which they always plunged when they wanted to ease nature; and their dung being of light substance, immediately rises and floats on the surface, then separates and subsides to the bottom.

When the winter sets in so as to freeze the water solid, they still continue their custom of coming out of their house, and dunging and making water on the ice; and when the weather was so cold that I was obliged to take them into my house, they always went into a large tub of water which I set for that purpose; so that they made not the least dirt, though they were kept in my own sitting room, where they were the constant companions of the Indian women and children, and were so fond of their company, that when the Indians were absent for any considerable time, the beaver discovered great signs of uneasiness, and on their return showed equal marks of pleasure, by fondling on them, crawling into their laps, laying on their backs, sitting erect like a squirrel, and behaving to them like children who see their parents but seldom.

In winter, Hearne adds, the beaver showed themselves "remarkably fond of rice and plum pudding; they would eat partridges and fresh venison very freely, but I never tried them with fish, though I have heard they will at times prey on them." Drawing on his own thorough studies, he repudiated the assertion that beaver build two doors to their houses, pointing out that this would open them to attack by wolverines. He corrected the mistakes of those who had written of non-existent beaver apartments and "slave-beavers," and then showed his sense of humour in addressing the ludicrous notion that beaver can "drive stakes as thick as a man's leg into the ground three or four feet deep."

I cannot refrain from smiling, when I read the accounts of different authors who have written on the economy of those animals, as there seems to be a contest between them, who shall most exceed in fiction. But the compiler of the *Wonders of Nature and Art* seems, in my opinion, to have succeeded best in this respect; as he has not only collected all the fictions into which other writers on the subject have run, but has so greatly improved on them, that little remains to be added to his account of the beaver, beside a vocabulary of their language, a code of their laws, and a sketch of their religion, to make it the most complete natural history of that animal which can possibly be offered to the public.

HEARNE'S STEPFATHER, Samuel Paine, had died in 1768. He left virtually his entire estate to his "loving wife, Diana Paine." Eight years later, according to records at England's national archives, she herself passed away, bequeathing almost everything to Hearne's sister, who had married one Joseph Le Petit. The following year, while serving as governor of Prince of Wales Fort, Hearne began sending small sums of money to his sister, Mrs. Sarah Le Petit. During the next several years, from 1777 through 1786, he would sporadically direct the Company to send her ten, twenty, or thirty pounds, to a total of £160.

Additionally, once each year in 1781 and 1782, Hearne would direct odd payments of £4.4 to "Richard Hearne," about whom absolutely nothing is known. Perhaps he was a relative who twice shipped the explorer a desired specific. Perhaps not. Certainly, it must be remembered that, official regulations notwithstanding, HBC officers who fathered children with native women—Humphrey Marten, for example—would often contrive to send those youngsters to Britain for schooling. It is conceivable that Hearne was sending his sister money to pay for the education of a son named Richard—so called, perhaps, after his grandfather, Richard Norton. Well aware of HBC policy, Hearne would have kept any "half-breed" son out of business correspondence. Given the high mortality rate among children in eighteenth-century England, Richard Hearne might well have contracted some illness and died young, which would explain his subsequent disappearance from the public record.

This much is certain: during his tenure as governor at Prince of Wales Fort, Samuel Hearne came to love his "country wife," Mary Norton, more than life itself. In his published *Journey*, he would reveal this with a heartfelt eulogy. Before that, drawing on secrets that Mary shared with him in the late 1770s, Hearne would write the only passage in his work that, for sheer, unadulterated emotionalism, would even begin to rival his subsequent paean. That passage, a word-portrait of Moses Norton, is fiercely angry—as savage and denunciatory as his eulogy is loving and broken-hearted.

Scholars have puzzled over this. Why such furious passion? Why such hatred?

Born around 1720, Moses Norton had spent nine years of his young manhood in England, acquiring some education. Probably he resided in east-end London, home of the Cockney accent, because later, as Richard Glover noted, he had trouble spelling words beginning with the letter *h*. In 1744, Moses was apprenticed to an HBC sea captain who sailed between England and Hudson Bay. Eight years later, as mate of the sloop *Churchill*, he sailed up and down the coast, trading with the Inuit.

Late in 1762, after sailing around Chesterfield Inlet and ruling it out as a Northwest Passage, he became governor of Prince of Wales Fort—and so he remained until he died in December 1773. Years later, when writing his eulogy of Mary, Hearne would mention that Moses Norton had been indulgent and overprotective: "Her father was, undoubtedly, very blamable for bringing her up in the tender manner which he did, rendering her by that means not only incapable of bearing the fatigues and hardships which the rest of her country-women think little of, but of providing for herself."

Yet in his denunciation, written earlier, Hearne describes Norton as living "in open defiance of every law, human and divine." He charges that while forbidding other HBC officers any contact with native women, he "kept for his own use five or six of the finest Indian girls." He describes the governor's lectures in praise of sexual abstinence "as the hypocritical cant of a selfish debauchee, who wished to engross every woman in the country to himself." And he asserts that, as a lecherous older man, the governor "actually poisoned two of his women because he thought them partial to other objects more suitable to their ages."

With palpable satisfaction—and perhaps some fictional embellishment, as he was not present—Hearne writes that, on December 29, 1773, Moses Norton died of an inflammation of the bowels,

and though he died in the most excruciating pain, he retained his jealousy to the last. For a few minutes before he expired, happening to see an officer laying hold of the hand of one of his women who was standing by the fire, he bellowed out, in as loud a voice as his situation would admit, "God d—n you for a b—h, if I live I'll knock out your brains." A few minutes after making this elegant apostrophe, he expired in the greatest agonies that can possibly be conceived. This I declare to be the real character and manner of life of the late Mr. Moses Norton.

As a rule, Samuel Hearne was empathetic and fair minded—which is why scholars have found this word-portrait intriguing. Hearne doesn't even mention that in his final month, Moses Norton added a codicil to his will stipulating that Mary receive an annuity of £30. That Norton's executrix—his English wife, Sarah—permitted only £10 annually to be shared between Mary and her nominal "aunt," really her mother, was not the dead governor's fault.

In his 1911 edition of *Journey*, editor J.B. Tyrrell suggested that "in the warmth of dispute, when endeavouring to overcome criticisms or objections of others, [Hearne] was liable to be carried beyond the points of strict accuracy and, in order to strengthen his argument, fill in the blanks in his record from his imagination."

Fur-trade historian E.E. Rich expresses even greater skepticism about the portrayal, arguing that, in caricaturing Norton as a lecherous old man, Hearne laboured under strong personal dislike. Rich acknowledges that Norton's annual letters to the Company contained a "sycophantic emphasis on the encouragement of virtue and the suppression of vice which the other Bay governors found unnecessary.... But whether he was such a gross and dangerous hypocrite as Hearne painted must be open to question, for Moses Norton was a man of uncommon energy and perception." Rich concludes that although Committee members "obviously felt that all was not above suspicion at Churchill they can have no reason to envisage anything like the ludicrous and bitter bacchanalia which Hearne described."

Writing in the mid-twentieth century, Richard Glover would allow the energy of Moses Norton, but not his vaunted perceptiveness. Besides encouraging the myth of the fabulous copper mine, Norton dispatched two moose to live in London and persuaded the HBC to launch the disastrous black whale fishery. Yet even Glover, struck by the ferocity of Hearne's portrayal, pronounced the portrait "so lurid that one would welcome corroboration."

In those sections of his book he wrote in the early 1770s, when describing an altercation with Norton, Samuel Hearne even-handedly observes that the governor, "to his honour, and whatever our private animosities might have been ... did not suffer them to interfere with public business." At another point, he expresses baffled dismay that Norton had apparently taken a dislike to him, attributing it to his own refusal to bring the governor's relatives on his trek with Matonabbee.

Hearne's outrage erupts only later, in an extended footnote he wrote in the late 1770s. Clearly, he had revised his opinion of the late governor radically downward. Why had he done so? That's what baffled Tyrrell, Rich, and Glover.

But none of these scholarly figures had developed an imagination dark enough to engage Hearne's portrait of Norton at face value, and to look where, in the only language available to him—that of the eighteenth century—he was so clearly pointing. Hearne was far from prudish about sexual matters and mores. At one point in *A Journey to the Northern Ocean,* while coolly analyzing differences between the First Nations, Hearne observes that in some groups, men occasionally cohabit "with their own mothers, and frequently espouse their sisters and daughters. . . . Few of those who live under the protection of the English ever take either their sisters or daughters for wives, which is probably owing to the fear of incurring their displeasure; but it is well known that acts of incest too often take place among them."

When treating matters closer to home, he would naturally respond less analytically. Samuel Hearne loved Mary Norton. And when, after the death of her father, she became his country wife, inevitably she told him her secrets. The record shows that Mary had grown up within the walls of Prince of Wales Fort. The record also shows that, with numerous other young women, she had spent her nights locked inside her father's quarters.

At one point in *A Journey to the Northern Ocean,* Hearne defends polygamy as a survival strategy well suited to the Barren Lands. But the explorer never attempts to make a case for incest. In his view, fathers who used their daughters as wives were living, as he wrote of Moses Norton, "in open defiance of every law, human and divine."

Finally, Hearne's outrage makes sense.

EUROPEANS brought many useful technologies to North America. They also introduced horrible diseases, among them cholera, measles, influenza, syphilis, and scarlet fever. But in devastating effect, none of these could compare with smallpox. In 1781 and 1782, Samuel Hearne listened with increasing dismay to reports that an epidemic was sweeping north through the First Nations—the worst epidemic in history.

Most Europeans had inherited some resistance, but the native peoples, never exposed, had none whatsoever. The only HBC man to catch smallpox was the half-breed Charles Isham, and he recovered. Among native peoples, the merest exposure usually brought death.

The epidemic had begun late in 1780, when Sioux living in the Missouri River valley came into contact with infected white travellers. From there the disease swept west and north, like wildfire in a gusting wind. By October 1781, it was killing Blackfoot and Assiniboine around the South Saskatchewan River. Then it coiled back eastward and attacked the Western Cree, wiping out six identifiable subgroups.

The plague drove north into Dene lands, causing panic and hysteria. Stricken with high fever, many First Nations sought relief by throwing themselves into lakes and rivers, so hastening their own demise. As soon as people showed symptoms, friends and family abandoned them as lost. Scores of Western Cree lay unburied in their tents.

From Prince of Wales Fort, Samuel Hearne estimated that the disease killed 90 per cent of all Chipewyan. Perhaps he exaggerated. His detailed reports would soon be lost, for while Hearne was coming to terms with this catastrophe, another was about to strike still closer to home.

ON AUGUST 8, 1782, at three o'clock on a cold, grey, blustery afternoon, and in response to the excited shouts of young Company men, Samuel Hearne hurried to the ramparts of Prince of Wales Fort. Putting a looking glass to one eye, he peered across the choppy waters of Hudson Bay. Directly off "Eskimo Point," on which the fort stood, he saw three warships approaching, all flying the Union Jack—one ship of the line with seventy-four guns and two frigates with thirty-six guns each, the *Sceptre*, the *Astrée*, the *Engageante*.

Not for nothing had Samuel Hearne spent six years in the Royal Navy. Even before he lowered his looking glass, he knew the truth.

The seventy-four gun Sceptre *that led two well-armed frigates to Prince of Wales Fort looked a lot like this French-built battleship. All three vessels, in an attempt at subterfuge, flew British flags. Because of his experience in the Royal Navy, Hearne recognized immediately that the ships were French, and that their intentions were hostile.*

Despite the British flags and pennons, these were not His Majesty's Ships that had somehow chanced into Hudson Bay and were now coming to pay a social call. These were French men-of-war—and they were coming, incredibly but certainly, to sack Prince of Wales Fort.

In 1778, France had joined the American colonies in their revolutionary war against England. But to deploy three valuable warships to these remote regions? And for the sake of a season's furs? To Hearne, it made no sense. Nevertheless, here was reality.

"You may cease rejoicing," he told his excited men, "and prepare the cannons. These are French warships come to wreak havoc."

Even as he spoke, Hearne realized that he faced impossible odds. To mount a defence, he had forty-two cannons, including two spares—ten 24-pounders, twenty-four 12-pounders, and eight 6-pounders. Theoretically, the largest of these could hit a target at a distance of one thousand yards—though in truth, accuracy became problematic

Each of these cannons, still extant on the ramparts at Prince of Wales Fort, required a crew of at least ten or twelve men. When the French arrived, Hearne had thirty-nine men at the fort—none of them trained as fighters, many of them out duck-hunting.

beyond six hundred. The cannons were decades old, but teams of well-trained artillerymen would be able to fire such weapons once every three or four minutes.

The biggest problem—the insurmountable problem—was the shortage of men. How many times, while serving with Hood, had Hearne sailed into battle? He had lost count. Nonetheless, he had long ago mastered the art of war. He knew that to fire even sporadically, each cannon required a crew of ten or twelve men—at the very least half a dozen. But the "crowning weakness," as one commentator would call it, was the lack of water. A decade earlier Andrew Graham had observed, "No springs near; drink snow water nine months of the year." How long could defenders endure without water?

Prince of Wales Fort had no protective glacis, or sloping bank, and no surrounding moat. Given 250 men, it might be able to hold out for a few hours against forces like these, perhaps one whole day. As it stood, in addition to a handful of visiting Dene and two or three Home-guard Cree, Hearne had thirty-nine men—many of whom were out hunting ducks. Those he sent for immediately. But that gave him six gun crews of untrained civilians—blacksmiths and masons and labourers. Hearne well knew that firing a cannon was precise, danger-ous work that involved swabbing out the barrel, measuring charges accurately, and mixing gunpowder properly. Perhaps, though no governor in history had ever done so, he should have conducted train-ing drills? Too late now.

Hearne understood the firepower of the warships that lay just out of range of the fort's cannons. Such vessels would carry between four and five hundred trained fighting men. A competent commander would mount a two-pronged attack. He would land a fighting force on the Bay side of the fort, then sail his ships into the mouth of the Churchill River. As the ships commenced firing, blazing away with more than one hundred powerful guns, the ground troops would advance from Bay side and overrun the fort. What could be simpler?

As well, Hearne knew what would result if he offered resistance. The invading Frenchmen, having seen their comrades die in agony, would commence a murderous rampage, committing atrocities and outrages. He had seen it before. Despite himself, he remembered Bloody Falls. Here and now, such a debacle might well ensue. What would Voltaire counsel? The philosopher regarded patriotism as a sentimental fallacy. He mocked the vanity of war and its justifications. The only rational course was quick surrender.

Hearne posted sentries, called his officers to his quarters, and explained the situation. None could find fault with his reasoning. Around eight o'clock, the three French vessels dropped anchor about five miles from the fort and began sounding the Churchill River, gauging its depth by firing cannons.

As darkness fell, Hearne dispatched scouts, among them both HBC and native men. At three o'clock in the morning, these men returned to report that a French force had landed—perhaps three or four hun-dred men. And on the Bay side, as Hearne had predicted.

At dawn, Hearne knew, the end-game would begin.

Releasing his officers to organize their affairs, Hearne went to Mary

Norton. He explained that the best course would be to offer no resistance. Probably, the French would destroy the fort and take him prisoner. "Mary—perhaps you should come with me."

"Come with you?"

"The French will take me prisoner." Hearne began pacing the floor. "But after a time, they will offer an exchange and return me to England. If you come with me, Mary, if I tell them you are my wife, they will take you, too. Perhaps this is our chance. We will live together in England."

"Are you mad, Samuel? What about my sisters? No, I cannot leave—not like this."

Hearne resumed pacing, running his fingers through his hair. "Perhaps you are right, Mary. We don't know what the French will do. But one thing you must remember." Hearne seized her shoulders and looked into her eyes. "Whatever happens, I will return. It might take me a year, it might take me two. You must never despair, Mary. You must trust me: I will return."

"Samuel, I do."

Hearne did a final tour of inspection. A few Dene remained within the fort, having come to trade, but their leader was Keelshies—a man he distrusted. How he wished Matonabbee were present! But he wasn't. To Keelshies, Hearne said, "Take care of Mary Norton. Probably I will leave for a time. But when I return, and I shall, I will richly reward those who have cared for my wife. Do you understand?"

Keelshies nodded. "Why must you go?"

Hearne could see that the Dene leader had no idea of the catastrophe that was about to unfold. No matter: he would see soon enough. "Take care of Mary Norton. When I return, I will reward you."

Shortly after seven o'clock in the morning, with the day dawning bleak and cold, Hearne watched from the ramparts as two Frenchmen approached the fort—a young officer accompanied by a drummer, waving a white flag and carrying a letter. One of the young HBC men asked whether, when they got within range, he should open fire. Hearne said, "Put that weapon down! You'll get us all massacred to no purpose."

Through his looking glass, he watched as the Frenchmen halted one hundred yards away. They had come to demand his surrender in the face of a manifestly superior force. Hearne took grim comfort in the knowledge that these men came from the land of Voltaire. Faced with fellow Europeans, they would adhere to European conventions. Unless they met resistance, they would murder no innocents, commit no atrocities.

Hearne told one of his officers to tie a white shirt to a stick.

Turning again to his beloved wife, Hearne said, "Do not fear, Mary. If they take me prisoner, do not fear. And do not despair. My darling, believe me, I will return."

"My husband, I will wait."

Samuel Hearne glanced around Prince of Wales Fort. Within these walls he had spent the happiest years of his life. Now, with shocking abruptness, the idyll had ended. He ordered the front gates thrown open. Then, alone and unarmed, holding aloft his makeshift flag, Samuel Hearne marched through the gates of Prince of Wales Fort to meet the invaders.

Part Three

ANCIENT
MARINER

11

VOYAGING
WITH NOBILITY

No ACCOUNT by Samuel Hearne of the sacking of Prince of Wales Fort has survived. But on August 9, 1782, one eyewitness—probably William Jefferson, his second-in-command—wrote that "after agreeing on such capitulations as Mr. Hearne thought necessary, or could obtain both for Europeans and natives, [the French] were permitted to come within the fort, for we were in no ways capable of defending the settlement from three ships on one side of the fort and six hundred regulars on the other."

After hoisting their colours, French troops ransacked the warehouses and destroyed the embrasures of the cannons: "Nothing but a scene of destruction all over the factory this whole day, and in the evening five different places were set fire to."

The next morning, as prisoners, Hearne and the thirty-nine other "English Europeans" were brought aboard the *Sceptre*, the largest of the French ships. At seven o'clock that evening, the Englishmen "saw & heard part of the factory blow up; at the same time, many of our people felt the ship shake under them with the explosion. Cannon rendered unserviceable by spiking, breaking and burning the carriages. The private men pilfering from us all they could lay hold of."

Two days later, when French troops had finished bringing aboard furs, ammunition, and provisions, the three warships began sailing south along the coast of Hudson Bay, bound for York Fort. As the senior authority on the English side, Samuel Hearne sat down to talk with the captain of the *Sceptre*, who was also commander of the French expedition: Jean François de Galaup, the comte de La Pérouse.

Hearne discovered that he shared much with the French nobleman,

the quintessential gentleman sailor. La Pérouse was a skilful combat-
ant, a superb navigator, and a charismatic leader. Above all, he was a
rationalist who took a scientific approach to the pursuit of knowledge.
He, too, had learned much from Voltaire.

Four years older than Hearne, La Pérouse had joined one navy
shortly before Hearne joined another. Between 1757 and 1763, the
two Young Gentlemen may well have participated in the same naval
battle on opposite sides. A few months before, in April 1782, La
Pérouse had fought under Admiral François de Grasse against
George Rodney and Hearne's old mentor, Samuel Hood—part of a
French force that had suffered a crushing defeat. It was one of those
disasters, according to an English eyewitness, in which "the sharks of
the Caribbean leaped from the water and struggled with each other to
feast on the dead and dying Frenchmen among flaming hulks and
fallen rigging."

A few years from now, when this latest warring ended, La Pérouse
would lead a notable voyage of discovery to the Pacific Ocean. He
would survey the west coast of North America from Alaska to California, then cross the Pacific Ocean and become the first European to
navigate the waters between China and Japan. He would visit
Australia and then, in Polynesia, get caught by a cyclone, his two
ships going down with all hands. Before that happened, however, he
would have the foresight to send home the journal of his expedition.
Published in 1797, *Voyage de La Pérouse autour du monde* would be recognized as a classic of discovery. As Captain James Cook was to
England, so the comte de La Pérouse was to France: the greatest
mariner of his age.

With this man of stature, Hearne established an immediate rapport.
After discussing broader matters, notably the treatment of the Hudson's Bay Company employees and where they could expect to be
taken (France), Hearne made one request on his own behalf: that the
comte de La Pérouse return his journal, a work-in-progress about his
trek to the Northern Ocean. The comte agreed to consider the
request.

Meanwhile, as the three French vessels sailed south along the
rocky coast, La Pérouse wondered if Monsieur Hearne could lend him
some navigational help. Hearne respectfully declined. Surely the

comte would understand that a gentleman could not betray his country. The Frenchman acquiesced, though it cost him to do so. In fact, he did understand. Also, he listened when Hearne said he was desperately worried about the innocents left behind at Churchill. He spoke not of Mary Norton but of "Homeguard Indians," explaining that during the past couple of years, a smallpox epidemic had killed half of the Western Cree and a far greater percentage—he feared as much as 90 per cent—of the Chipewyan Dene. Without food or ammunition, he said, many people would not survive the winter.

Having considered the matter further, Hearne wished to urge all the Cree and Dene around the fort to travel inland, where game was more abundant and where they might encounter the great leader Matonabbee. He had written a letter to one among them who could read, he said, strongly advising them to do this. He hoped that La Pérouse would allow him to send this missive from York Fort.

At five o'clock the following morning, French sailors spotted an HBC sloop travelling north, bound apparently for Churchill. La Pérouse ordered one of his frigates, the thirty-six-gun *Engageante*, to pursue and seize the vessel. But also, moved by the urgency of the Englishman's solicitations, he gave the frigate captain Hearne's letter. This captain sailed north into the fog and lost sight of the HBC sloop (the *Prince Rupert* would escape to Great Britain). The *Engageante* then sailed all the way back to Churchill, where the captain found about sixty native people sheltering in the ruins of the fort. He gave one of them Hearne's letter and, as La Pérouse had instructed, left some provisions and ammunition.

Back on the *Sceptre*, the well-educated La Pérouse had begun reading Hearne's journal. This rough manuscript, he realized, contained irrefutable proof that no Northwest Passage flowed westward out of Hudson Bay, and also evocatively portrayed a hitherto unknown people and way of life.

La Pérouse invited Hearne onto the quarterdeck, met him on the starboard side where nobody would interrupt, and told him he had perused the journal. One could argue, he said, that the manuscript belonged to the Hudson's Bay Company, which had sponsored his adventure, and so retain it as the legitimate spoils of war. Hearne responded that he had long ago sent a report about the trek to the

HBC. Since then, he had been revising and expanding, so that the journal had become a new work entirely—certainly his own property and not that of the HBC.

"I accept that argument, Monsieur." La Pérouse produced the work and handed it over. "I return your journal on one condition."

"Monsieur?"

"That you publish it as soon as possible."

Hearne was astonished. "You think it has merit, then?

"More than that, Monsieur. It is important. You must publish it immediately."

A few years later, the editor of *Voyage de La Pérouse autour du monde* would mention Samuel Hearne's epic trek in his introduction:

An account of this journey was found in manuscript among the papers of the governor [Hearne], who was very pressing that it should be returned to him as his private property. As the journey was undertaken, however, by order of the Hudson's Bay Company, with a view of obtaining knowledge of the northern part of America, the journal of it might have been considered with propriety as belonging to the Company, and now of right devolved to the conquerer; yet the goodness of La Pérouse's heart induced him to yield to the urgent solicitations of Governor Hearne, and he returned the manuscript to him; on the express condition, however, that he should print and publish it immediately on his arrival in England. This agreement does not appear to have been fulfilled to the present day.

Now, at York Fort, La Pérouse proceeded as at Churchill. He landed several hundred troops—though with considerably greater difficulty, because here the surrounding land was not rocky but swampy. One HBC man, later referred to as "Old John Irvine," had identified the best way to approach the fort, but the suspicious French did not trust him and forged their own, more arduous route. Meanwhile, one HBC ship, the *King George*, slipped away under cover of darkness, carrying most of the season's furs to England.

Early on the afternoon of August 24, La Pérouse sent an emissary to York Fort carrying a letter similar to the one he had sent at Churchill. Humphrey Marten, recently returned to resume command, described the missive as "offering us our lives and private property but threatening the utmost fury should we resist." Less familiar than Hearne with the conventions of making war, Marten agreed to surrender but, standing outside the fort while a cold rain beat down, sought to negotiate a formal agreement, neatly signed and sealed.

A French officer, one of the few who spoke English, served as translator. He wrote later that some of his senior colleagues lost patience. The officer in charge, Monsieur de Rostaing, saw the sloop *Severn* moving and feared that it might try to escape on the ebb tide. As the vessel hove to in response to shouted orders, this excitable officer ordered his troops to open fire. They wounded one HBC man.

The translator understood de Rostaing's sense of urgency: "the weather was vile, it rained, and the cold was intense. Everybody was soaked to the skin, which checked perspiration, and all were terribly fatigued by the hard march we had just made."

He understood also that Humphrey Marten wanted La Pérouse to formally sign the preliminary articles of surrender. When he relayed this to de Rostaing, that officer grew enraged. He "seized one of the posts of the barrier with violence, and seemed as if he were about to break it down in his rage." The translator, "disgusted with [de Rostaing's] unrestrained impatience," tried to reassure Marten. He knew the volatility of the French troops, how anxious some of them were to break down the gates with their hatchets, and feared precisely the kind of conflagration that had worried Hearne at Churchill. Any assault "might arouse the butcher's instinct for which I saw plenty of material all around us, and finally bring us to all sorts of horrors and atrocities."

This man told Marten,

Ten paces from you, you will notice men armed with axes. Take care that the order to use them not be given. Nothing could then save you and your men from the fury of the soldiers, inflamed as they are by privation and suffering. Just look at us, see our tattered clothes almost dropping off us, and you can easily guess how we have suffered during the three days that we have been exposed to the cold, the rain, the dense fog and the dampness of the ground. At this moment we are more anxious for rest than for booty. You can judge for yourself whether this place is suitable for tired men, and you will not be astonished that we show so much impatience to get under cover in your fort, and even a little bad tempered when we see you resisting our efforts.

My little speech made the old man laugh, perhaps because of some uncouth English that I made use of, but what was still better, it made him change his mind. He ordered the keys to be brought and the gates thrown open.

The French proceeded into York Fort. They opened the stores, which were better stocked than at Churchill, and distributed shirts, socks, and shoes among themselves. Because La Pérouse had been sent north from the Caribbean with sealed orders, opened only off the coast of Newfoundland, the troops had arrived in Hudson Bay wearing only their tropical kit, totally unprepared for the cold, wet weather.

During the voyage to Churchill, La Pérouse had faced an additional problem. Unfamiliar with the waters of Hudson Strait, he had encountered icebergs and pack ice. His ships had sustained considerable damage. Now, with August ending, he rightly feared that his vessels might get trapped in the Bay by ice. He realized that the help of an HBC navigator familiar with these waters might make all the difference. So far, none had agreed to help him. To Samuel Hearne, he expressed his misgivings.

After some reflection, Hearne responded with a proposal: he and Humphrey Marten would convince an HBC sloop captain to guide the French through Hudson Strait if, in exchange, the comte de La Pérouse would set free all the HBC men to sail home to England in the *Severn*. None of the English prisoners were military men, after all. In addition, both Hearne and Marten would give their word of honour as gentlemen that an equal number of French prisoners would be returned to France.

Normally, the sloop *Severn* plied between York, Moose, and Severn forts. The vessel had not been designed to cross the Atlantic Ocean, especially not in late autumn. La Pérouse warned of the risks Hearne would face—the dangers *"qu'il encourrait dans cette longue navigation, vu la saison ou nous étions; il persista obstinément dans sa resolution"* (the dangers "which they would face on this long journey, given the season we were in; he persisted in his resolution").

Hearne had spoken with John Turner, captain of the *Severn*. "Can you get us safely through Hudson Strait?"

"Yes, Sir. I've sailed it often enough."

"And beyond that? Could you sail the *Severn* to Stromness?"

Hearne and thirty-two other men crossed the Atlantic Ocean in a single-masted sloop built along these lines.

"I could sail her across the Atlantic, Sir—though I'm not certain I could hit Stromness."

"What if I were to handle the navigating? We could do it then?"

"Indeed, I believe so."

Faced with Hearne's "obstinate resolve," the comte de La Pérouse accepted his proposition. However, he could not justify relinquishing the *Severn* to the HBC as it was part of the spoils of war. Hearne suggested that he give it to the sloop captain, John Turner, if he got them through Hudson Strait. La Pérouse agreed.

On September 2, the three warships sailed out of York Fort with the English prisoners distributed among them, the *Sceptre* towing the *Severn*. The Englishmen found conditions miserable. The vessels were swarming with vermin. Food was scarce, with each man receiving barely enough to survive—a daily ration of two ounces of beef or pork, or else a few beans boiled together, Jefferson wrote, "with some maggoty biscuit almost capable to walk itself." Inevitably, scurvy was rampant. Every day, sailors threw two or three dead bodies over the side.

After four days, with Turner showing the way, the ships entered the icebergs of Hudson Strait. And, when four days later still they emerged into the Atlantic Ocean, Hearne acquired a letter of safe passage from La Pérouse. On October 10, off Cape Resolution, he and Humphrey Marten and thirty-one other men—as many as the sloop could carry—boarded the *Severn* and sailed for Stromness in the Orkney Islands, in the northern reaches of Scotland.

In a letter to his superiors, La Pérouse outlined what he had done, noting that he had permitted Hearne, Marten, and the others "to return to England in a little boat I had taken in Hudson's Bay." He enclosed written promises from the two HBC governors that they would send from England the same number of French prisoners. These promises would eventually be honoured.

Meanwhile, on October 15, 1782, after an uneventful passage that afforded Hearne an opportunity to employ his navigational skills, the *Severn* arrived in Stromness. Nine days later, carrying "a proper pass" from the comte de La Pérouse for use in the event that he encountered a continuing French blockade, Hearne sailed that vessel southward. Late in October, after an absence from England of sixteen years, and with decidedly mixed feelings, Hearne took the wheel of the *Severn* and guided her into Portsmouth harbour. The mariner had arrived safely home.

LATE IN 1782, around the time Hearne reached London, Great Britain was negotiating a peace treaty with its American colonies, as well as with France and Spain. For six years, the colonies had been fighting for independence. In October 1781, seven thousand British troops had surrendered to George Washington at Yorktown, Virginia, effectively ending the war. In February 1783, while Hearne was in London, Britain would officially proclaim an end to hostilities. That September, the Treaty of Paris would recognize the independence of the United States of America, and also cede certain possessions to France and Spain. Great Britain would retain control of Quebec, Upper Canada, and Rupert's Land.

As negotiators hammered out these agreements, the Hudson's Bay Company faced crucial decisions of its own. The destruction of Prince of Wales and York forts, which the Committee regarded as gratuitous and outrageous, had served nobody more than the Montreal-based fur-traders. In the interior, where Cumberland House had begun spawning satellite posts, the HBC men had received no supplies or trading goods. Farther north, the Dene would soon begin bringing their furs to the Canadians at Fort Chipewyan, so establishing a pattern that would prove difficult to break.

In London, at meeting after meeting with the HBC's Governing Committee, Samuel Hearne—eager to return to the woman he loved—developed a plan to rebuild the forts, or "factories," as some forts were now being called, at both York and Churchill. The site at York had been well chosen. But at Churchill, Prince of Wales Fort had been erected on Eskimo Point, a rocky peninsula that was cold, inaccessible to Company sloops, and, worst of all, devoid of drinking water, which had to be transported from upriver.

Hearne recommended building a new post five miles up the Churchill River, at the site originally chosen by Jens Munck early in the previous century. Supported by Humphrey Marten, his fellow officer and former nemesis, he urged that dwellings be prefabricated in England, according to his own design and drawings. These frame houses could be dismantled, shipped in pieces to Hudson Bay, and there reassembled. The Governing Committee not only agreed, it quickly assigned carpenters to do as Hearne advised.

In recent years, before Hearne arrived back in London, Samuel Wegg, the governor of the HBC, had been lending copies of his journal and maps to select individuals. The Admiralty had taken these seriously enough that in 1778, when Lord Sandwich drafted instructions for the third voyage of Captain James Cook, he advised him "not to lose time in exploring rivers or inlets" along the western coast of North America until he reached a latitude of 65 degrees—a mark just south of the Arctic Circle.

Now, suddenly, Hearne had appeared in person. The author of that unpublished but influential journal, having spent three years walking to the Arctic Ocean, the only European among native peoples, had not only been taken prisoner by the comte de La Pérouse, but had engineered a miraculous return to England aboard a tiny sloop. Here was a tall, handsome man, plain-spoken but articulate, even compelling, who—dressed in three-quarter-length coat with matching vest and breeches, as well as silk stockings, square-buckled shoes, and white periwig—could grace any drawing room.

Several times, Hearne met Dr. John Douglas, canon of St. Paul's

Cathedral and later bishop of Salisbury, who had been engaged by John Montagu, earl of Sandwich, to prepare for publication the journal of the third voyage of Captain James Cook. In his long introduction to that work, Douglas would not only summarize Hearne's three-year trek, but quote two long passages from it. Douglas would write that Wegg "was particularly obliging to the Editor by giving him repeated opportunities of conversing with Governor Hearne." The canon showed an especially keen interest in the mariner's descriptions of the customs and beliefs of the Dene, and encouraged Hearne to write more about them—advice that would give rise to the penultimate chapter of Hearne's own book. Like the comte de La Pérouse, Canon Douglas deemed Hearne's journal worthy of wider circulation, though he revealed his own supercilious racism in saying so: "The publication of this would not be an unacceptable present to the world, as it draws a plain artless picture of the savage modes of life, the scanty means of subsistence, and indeed of the singular wretchedness, in every respect, of the various tribes, who, without fixed habitations, pass their miserable lives, roving throughout the dreary deserts, and over the frozen lakes of the immense track of continent through which Mr. Hearne passed."

The explorer also met Thomas Pennant, a zoologist of some standing. Pennant's *Tour in Scotland*, based on a 1769 visit, had encouraged the redoubtable Samuel Johnson to travel north into the Hebrides with James Boswell to explore "the wild and savage life of the region." Pennant was still collecting material for his *Arctic Zoology*, and with Hearne he found much to discuss. Pennant contributed systematic knowledge of current systems of animal classification, though obviously he enjoyed nothing like the mariner's first-hand knowledge of northern wildlife. The zoologist supplied English names for animals that Hearne had registered only in Athapaskan, and convinced him to devote a separate chapter to animals. Eventually, Pennant, too, would go on record: "To Mr. Samuel Hearne, the great explorer by land of the *Icy Sea*, I cannot but send my most particular thanks, for his liberal communication of my zoological remarks, made by him on the bold and fatiguing adventure he undertook from Hudson's Bay to the *ne plus ultra* of the north on that side."

During these winter months in London, while worrying incessantly about Mary Norton and preparing to return to Churchill,

In June 1780, during the Gordon Riots, a fire at the northern end of London Bridge engulfed the waterworks and a toll house. By late 1782, when Hearne got a chance to investigate, most of the damage had been repaired.

Samuel Hearne also renewed his friendships with two men he had met in Hudson Bay—and with whom, over a dozen years before, in the winter of 1769, he had gone on at least one extended hunting trip. The first was Thomas Hutchins, for seven years the surgeon at York Fort. Hutchins had joined the HBC in 1766, the same year as Hearne. In the mid-1770s, as chief factor at Albany Fort, he had organized the establishing of Gloucester House. A few months before, he had returned from Hudson Bay to become secretary to the Company in London. A keen naturalist and botanist, Hutchins would write one of a dozen volumes of "Observations on Hudson's Bay," and would, for his scientific work, receive a gold medal from the Royal Society.

The second "old friend" was none other than William Wales, the eminent mathematician and astronomer Hearne had got to know in 1768 and 1769, just before he departed on his great trek north. Wales had come to Prince of Wales Fort to observe the Transit of Venus and later published a paper about his sojourn. In 1772, the Royal Society had appointed Wales to sail as astronomer and co-navigator on the second voyage of Captain James Cook. On his return to London in

1775, Wales had become master of the mathematical school at Christ's Hospital, a London Blue Coat School for boys—a position he maintained while publishing articles on mathematics and navigation.

Wales was assisting Canon Douglas in preparing Cook's journal for publication. He was a scientific humanist who heartily endorsed Hearne's conduct in having immediately surrendered Prince of Wales Fort. In 1774, while on Easter Island, Wales had watched while a young draughtsman sketched a view of the island. Rising to depart, Wales had picked up his musket—and just then a native man raced past his companion "and snatched off his hat from his head and ran away with it. I cocked and pointed the musket without thought of anything but firing at him; but when I saw a fellow creature within twenty yards of its muzzle, I began to think his life worth more than a hat, and as to the insult, rot it."

Later, Wales would become Hearne's best friend. Now, along with Wegg, Douglas, Pennant, and Hutchins, the mathematician was one of several notable figures with whom the explorer shared lively, wide-ranging discussions.

As well, Hearne undoubtedly visited his sister in Peckham, just south of London. There, with her husband and their son, Samuel Hearne Le Petit, Sarah lived in one of the houses she had inherited from Diana Paine. Hearne would have asked to see his mother's last will and testament. Almost certainly, his older sister found an excuse to avoid showing it to him.

On November 26, 1776, Diana Paine had written that she did "give and bequeath unto my son Samuel Hearne now resident at Hudson Bay one hundred pounds of lawful money of Great Britain, to be paid unto him if he demands it within twelve calendar months after my [death], hoping nevertheless that as he is well provided for he will not distress by the receipt thereof his sister, Sarah Le Petit." Hearne's mother appointed this same "dearly beloved daughter" the sole executrix of the will, bequeathing her "all the rest and residue of my estate and effects both real and personal, particularly my two houses with the stables and land thereunto"—those establishments being in Peckham and elsewhere in the parish of Camberwell—together with all her household goods, apparel, money, and other effects.

One hundred pounds was no insulting bequest. Many London families lived for a year on less. But that sum, hedged about with the expressed desire that Hearne not demand it, certainly did not compare with Sarah's inheritance. Had Hearne alienated his mother? Could he have done so by sailing away to Hudson Bay in 1766, soon after she married and moved to Peckham, perhaps hoping to reside nearer to him? Such a breach is unlikely; through the years, Hearne had continued to send money to his mother.

The tone and tenor of Diana Paine's will suggest another scenario, as does the stunning alacrity with which it was executed. The will was "proved" in London on December 2, 1776—just six days after the dying woman signed it. Obviously, Hearne's mother had been writing on her deathbed. Possibly, she was doing so in response to the dictates of her daughter, who grudgingly allowed her to at least leave £100 to her long-departed son.

Hearne probably suspected all this and let it pass. What would he have done, at this stage, with a house in or near Peckham? From the time he arrived in London in November 1782 through the ensuing winter and spring, Hearne remained focused on returning to Churchill, there to rebuild not just the HBC trading post, but his life among the native peoples and the animals—and, above all, his life with Mary Norton.

Late in June 1783, after eight months in England, having selected a crew of competent men and supervised the stowing of a prefabricated house aboard the *King George*, an anxious Samuel Hearne set sail for Hudson Bay.

ON SEPTEMBER 14, 1783, following a rough Atlantic crossing, and in the midst of a driving rain, the *King George* reached the mouth of the Churchill River and dropped anchor near the ruins of Prince of Wales Fort. Despite the storm and the risk of capsizing, Hearne insisted on going ashore in a boat. He felt driven to explore the fort for some sign of Mary Norton. He accomplished that, but found no communication tucked away in the ruins of his former quarters— indeed, no sign of any living soul.

Hearne returned to the supply ship. He had advised the Committee—

This woodcut depicts Jens Munck's Winter-Haven *in 1623. One hundred and sixty years later, Hearne rebuilt Fort Churchill on the same spot.*

and secured instructions—to erect the new trading post five miles upriver from the ruins of the fort, on the spot selected in the seventeenth century by that competent but ill-fated Danish explorer Jens Munck. This put the factory just beyond the reach of the saltwater tides of Hudson Bay and gave it ready access to wood, fresh water, and rich hunting grounds. Having brought a house "in frame" from England, Hearne set his men to erecting it.

Anxious for news of Mary Norton, Hearne forayed ever farther into the woods and also kept one eye on the river. On September 27, he spotted four people paddling past in two canoes. Recognizing Home-guard Indians, he hailed them ashore. After exchanging friendly greetings in Cree, Hearne asked, "And Mary Norton? Where is my wife?"

The four Cree exchanged solemn glances. The eldest of them said, "Come, Hearne."

The man turned and walked along the riverbank, picking his way sure-footedly among the rocks. Filled with anxiety, Hearne scrambled after him. "Where are you taking me?" He almost had to shout against the wind. "Are you taking me to Mary Norton?"

After a couple of minutes, having arrived at a difficult outcropping of rocks, the old man stopped, turned, and faced the governor. "I must tell you sad news, Hearne. Mary Norton died last winter."

"That is not possible! I told her I would return."

"Starvation took many, Hearne. Your wife was among them."

"Not Mary."

"She refused to take another husband."

He felt his knees buckle. "I—promised to return."

With an effort of will, Hearne regained control. He heard seagulls crying and looked up, saw the white birds wheeling on the wind high above. Mary Norton had loved seagulls. He looked back along the river where the other three Cree stood talking with Company men. Several of these were looking in his direction.

Without speaking—because he could not speak—Hearne nodded, then turned and left the old man. He crossed the rocky outcrop and continued along the river, concentrating on stepping carefully from one large rock to another. After a few minutes, when he looked back, he could no longer see the fort or even the old man who had spoken with him. Except for the seagulls, he heard nothing. While travelling with Matonabbee, Hearne had seen old women fall sick and then die of starvation—a terrible death. Not a death for his beloved wife.

Alone beneath the blue sky, Samuel Hearne fell to his knees on a flat rock. Invisible here, and with the Churchill River sweeping past, he buried his face in his hands, and he wept.

YEARS LATER, revising his journal in London, Samuel Hearne would write a celebration of Mary Norton—a long passage that, in a work striving constantly for scientific detachment, stands almost alone in its emotionality. He was well aware that half the Homeguard Cree had perished during that terrible winter, and elsewhere in his book he declared as much. But when it came to the loss of his beloved wife, he could not pretend to detachment and even-handedness.

Mary, the daughter of Moses Norton, many years chief at Prince of Wales Fort, in Hudson Bay, though born and brought up in a country of all others the least favourable to virtue and virtuous principles, possessed them, and every other good and amiable quality, in a most eminent degree.

Without the assistance of religion, and with no education but what she received among the dissolute natives of her country, she would have shone with superior lustre in any other country; for, if an engaging person, gentle manners, an easy freedom, arising from a consciousness of innocence, an amiable modesty, and an unrivalled delicacy of sentiment, are graces and virtues which render a woman lovely, none ever had greater pretensions to general esteem and regard: while her benevolence, humanity, and scrupulous adherence to truth and honesty would have done honour to the most enlightened and devout Christian.

Dutiful, obedient, and affectionate to her parents; steady and faithful to her friends; grateful and humble to her benefactors; easily forgiving and forgetting injuries; careful not to offend any, and courteous and kind to all; she was, nevertheless, suffered to perish by the rigours of cold and hunger, amidst her own relations, at a time when the gripping hand of famine was by no means severely felt by any other member of their company; and it may truly be said that she fell a martyr to the principles of virtue. This happened in the winter of the year 1782, after the French had destroyed Prince of Wales Fort; at which time she was in the twenty-second year of her age.

Recalling Voltaire and his crusade against superstitious optimism, Hearne despaired of "accounting for the decrees of Providence on such occasions as this," and went on to quote from a poem by Edmund Waller:

> Stranger alike to envy and to pride,
> Good sense her light, and Nature all her guide;
> But now removed from all the ills of life,
> Here rests the pleasing friend and faithful wife.

In this heartfelt footnote, Hearne also accused Moses Norton of having overprotected Mary and of failing to teach her to provide for herself—though he assumed no responsibility for having failed to rectify the situation. Also in this entry, whose authorship is beyond dispute, Hearne demonstrates, yet again, that he was no illiterate scribbler. By quoting Waller, a middling seventeenth-century poet, Hearne conveys to posterity what, in the context of late-eighteenth-century England, he could not speak aloud: that Mary Norton, native North American, had been his beloved wife. To communicate this by quoting poetry is to take a literary approach; indeed, such a strategy is the very hallmark of literacy.

SAMUEL HEARNE encountered no "Northern Indians" until the following spring. Then, on May 2, 1784, having learned of the return of the English traders, about forty Chipewyan Dene arrived with a small cache of furs. From them, Hearne heard more devastating news. Matonabbee, his old friend, mentor, and business partner, had taken his own life. When he discovered that the French had razed Prince of Wales Fort and had taken Hearne prisoner, he hanged himself, "saying he [did not wish to] live any longer as he was sure I was dead. Poor man. He was a stranger to the lenity of European warriors, but naturally thought the French had taken us all out to sea into deep water and murdered us, or threw us into the sea."

To his journal, Samuel Hearne would add a second moving obituary. This one, too, surfaces as a long footnote, which, in a professionally edited manuscript, would have been integrated into the text. The Englishman would describe his friend as "the most sociable, kind, and sensible Indian" he had ever met. He would review his heritage and describe his singular boyhood, during which he lived not only among the Dene, but also among the English and the Cree. Having a gift for languages, Matonabbee spoke Cree and some English, as well as his native Athapaskan. During his youth,

he gained a knowledge of the Christian faith; and he always declared that it was too deep and intricate for his comprehension. Though he was a perfect bigot with respect to the arts and tricks of Indian jugglers, yet he could by no means be impressed with a belief of any part of our religion, nor of the religion of the Southern Indians [Cree], who have as firm a belief in a future state as any people under the Sun. He had so much natural good sense and liberality of sentiment, however, as not to think that he had a right to ridicule any particular sect on account of their religious opinions. On the contrary, he declared, that he held them all equally in esteem, but was determined, as he came into the world, so he would go out of it, without professing any religion at all. Notwithstanding his aversion from religion, I have met with few Christians who possessed more good moral qualities, or fewer bad ones.

Glossing over Matonabbee's temper and celebrating his positive qualities, Hearne described his friend as reliable, punctual, and honest, "while his benevolence and universal humanity to all the human race, according to his abilities and manner of life, could not be exceeded by the most illustrious personage now on record." Matonabbee had avoided gossiping about and slandering his neighbours. After noting that his friend was unusually handsome—six feet tall, his face unmarked and expressive—Hearne did think to observe, "As no man is exempt from frailties, it is natural to suppose that as a man he had his share; but the greatest with which I can charge him is jealousy, and that sometimes carried him beyond the bounds of humanity."

Hearne would describe how, in his youth, Matonabbee created a lasting peace between the Chipewyan and the Athabasca Cree. And in 1772, after Matonabbee had guided Hearne to the mouth of the Coppermine River—a service "he performed with greater punctuality, and more to my satisfaction, than perhaps any other Indian in all that country would have done"—the HBC recognized him as leader of all the Dene. He continued to serve the Company by bringing more furs to Churchill "than any other Indian ever did, or ever will do."

Matonabbee had visited Prince of Wales Fort in the spring of 1782, several months before the arrival of La Pérouse, and he returned the following winter;

but when he heard that the French had destroyed the Fort, and carried off all the Company's servants, he never afterwards reared his head, but took an opportunity, when no one suspected his intention, to hang himself. This is the more to be wondered at, as he is the only Northern Indian who, that I ever heard, put an end to his own existence. The death of this man was a great loss to the Hudson's Bay Company, and was attended with a most melancholy scene; no less than the death of six of his wives, and four children, all of whom were starved to death the same winter, in one thousand seven hundred and eighty-three.

JANUARY 1785. On the windswept bank of the Churchill River, clearly visible among a few sparse trees, and with grey smoke wafting skyward from its chimney, a small frame building sat half covered by drifting snow. Eighteen months before, almost laid low by grief at the news of Mary Norton's death, Samuel Hearne had persevered in his duty and had lost himself in constructing this trading post.

Now, inside the house, some two dozen bearded, rough-looking men sat before a blazing fire on wooden chairs and benches, listening to a sermon delivered, without style or grace, by a man in a "toggey," or long fur coat. The speaker, William Jefferson, second-in-command of this lonely outpost, might have talked of the miracle of the loaves and fishes or the turning of water into wine. Perhaps he revisited the parable of the prodigal son or the story of how Jesus called a dead man out of a cave, crying, "Lazarus! Come forth!" Or maybe he drew on the Old Testament, recalling Abraham and Isaac, or how Moses had led his people to within sight of the promised land.

Among the listeners, at one side of the room near the back, sat a weather-beaten, clean-shaven man, six feet tall, lean but powerfully built, set apart from the others not just by the determined neatness of his appearance, but by his air of distracted tolerance. Samuel Hearne, the thirty-nine-year-old governor of this rebuilt post, bowed his head respectfully but remained silent as, together, the other men mumbled the Lord's Prayer.

The service over, the majority of men, the tradesmen and labourers, shuffled reluctantly out of the relatively comfortable room that served as the governor's quarters. Two men remained behind: Jefferson, who had served Hearne as second-in-command for the past eight years, and a fourteen-year-old boy named David Thompson, recently arrived from London, where as an orphan at a charity school he had excelled in Bible study.

The governor poured three glasses of brandy.

"Oh, no, Sir!" Young Thompson said. "Not for me."

"Good lad." Hearne nodded and said, "Jefferson, to the King!"

The two men drank, and then Jefferson spoke. "Really, Samuel, I do wish that you would resume delivering the Sunday sermon. You're so much better at it than I."

"You do very well, William."

Young Thompson said, "Did you used to lead the service, Mr. Hearne?"

"He did that," Jefferson said. "And wonderfully well, too."

"Why did you stop, Sir?"

"Because I could no longer do it in good conscience."

"Sir, I don't understand?"

Hearne stood with his hands clasped behind his back, gazing into the wintry morning through a small clear patch in the icy window. "You have seen what remains of Prince of Wales Fort, Mr. Thompson?"

"Of course, Sir."

"Then you have seen the least of the tragedy." Hearne continued to gaze at the frozen river, the swirling snow. "Quite incomprehensible, the decrees of Providence."

"Mr. Hearne, one thing puzzles me about the destruction of the fort."

"Come, Thompson. Let us leave the governor."

"I understand that you had too few men, Sir."

"Too few men to work the cannons, yes." Hearne turned and addressed the young man. "Also, no water within the walls, three warships on one side, several hundred troops on the other."

"What I don't understand, sir . . . is why you didn't put your faith in God."

"Put my faith in God?"

"Think of the Holy Bible, Sir. Of David and Goliath. Or the miracles of our Saviour. Turning water into wine, raising Lazarus from the dead."

Hearne resumed looking out the window. Faced with the death of Mary Norton, and despite the skepticism of Voltaire, he had yet retained a slim hope of a future state of some kind—one that did not abrogate the laws of nature. But then he had learned of the death of Matonabbee, and of the deaths of his wives and children, and the vestiges of his faith had crumbled. "You would have me believe in miracles, Mr. Thompson? In divine intervention?" Hearne reached over, plucked a dog-eared volume from the top of his desk, and showed it to the orphanage-educated youth: "Here is my Bible, Mr. Thompson."

"The Philosophical Dictionary." Having read the title aloud, the young man cried, "But that's . . . surely you jest!"

"I am sorry to shock you." Hearne laid the book back on his desk. "But no, I do not jest."

"But Voltaire is—an unbeliever!"

"You wish me to believe in miracles?" Hearne placed one hand upon the *Dictionary.* "Here is my belief, Mr. Thompson. Here is my belief, and I have no other."

SEVERAL MONTHS BEFORE, in August 1784, as David Thompson had debarked, Samuel Hearne had suffered yet another disappointment. A much-anticipated shipment of timber had failed to arrive from England. He had written to the London committee requesting the wood to add an extension to the small frame building he had brought to Hudson Bay in the Company supply ship. That house was far too small to accommodate furs, supplies, and men. The sparse woods in the vicinity could produce nothing resembling the necessary beams and posts, so Hearne had drawn up a detailed plan for a twenty-three-foot addition that would serve the contingent as a main residence.

But instead of sending the timber, the Committee had reprimanded him: why couldn't he expand Fort Churchill in the same way as others were developing York Factory, using local materials? With the final return ship, Hearne sent a tart reply:

That I knew the size of the house before I left England is most certain, and the number of men it could contain, but at the time it was looked upon in no other light than a temporary residence till a more convenient place could be built, and the sole reason for its being so contracted was done with a view that the ship and sloop might the more easily bring it out. I confess it was no small disappointment in not receiving the timber, and I apprehend the price at this time would have been trifling in proportion to what it would have been when the houses [inside the stone fort] were built.

Fort Churchill in the late 1800s. The original dwelling house, which Hearne found less than satisfactory, was the building nearest the top left corner. Housed in such cramped and miserable quarters, he felt little inducement to remain.

At that time, as he correctly observed, the Company men had been unable to find enough timber to build a house. Since then, five decades had passed. The sparse woods had been further depleted, so that "we can at present scarce find fuel to cook our victuals and keep us from freezing during the winter."

The London committee, unconvinced, sent no timber the following year. In August 1785, backed by his officers, Hearne wrote a still stronger letter, suggesting that the Committee must be "entirely unacquainted" with the situation at Churchill to compare it with York Factory. The men at that more southerly post had erected a dwelling within the old stockades, using old bricks and timber and working with the same ovens as before: "Our situation was quite different, being at least five miles from the stone fort, so that every article was obliged to be brought in boats, which could only be done in fine weather on account of the high seas that always infest the shores of this river in the fall of the year."

In denying his request, the London committee had also suggested that, while attempting to win back business, Hearne had proved too liberal with the Company stores. Specifically, he had distributed too much imported brandy to the men when the factory could have been brewing its own beer. This rebuke sparked a rebuttal signed by all the officers:

Mr. Hearne feeling himself extremely hurt by the many and repeated, though unmerited, accusations of abuse of his charge and authority ... thinks it a duty incumbent on himself in vindication of his conduct to assert in this public manner that after nineteen years hard servitude in a variety of stations and places of trust, he can with the strictest truth and boldest confidence assert that *your interest* in preference to his own ease, happiness and emolument has ever been the direction of his conduct. With equal confidence he defies his most implacable enemies to charge him with the smallest breach of fidelity on any occasion whatever.

In 1786, as these tensions continued to swirl, a disappointed Hearne apologized for sending an incomplete report, claiming that bad health had caused his "writings to be so backward when the ship arrived that it is not in our power this year to send you so minute an account of the expense of trading goods as usual." He added, "My health being greatly on the decline makes me desirous to return to England by the next ship; and hope your honours will appoint a person to succeed me."

The following spring, the London committee gave him permission to return, adding, "we have great reason to be offended at the answers we received to the seventh and thirteenth paragraphs of the general letter last year, and we certainly should have manifested our displeasure in a manner no ways agreeable, could we have imagined that any officer (besides Mr. Hearne) was capable of being the author or abettor of sentiments and expressions so disrespectful to us and disgraceful to themselves."

A decade before, in March 1777, while enjoying his life of goose-hunting and scientific experiments, his days and nights with Mary Norton, Hearne had written to a fellow officer proclaiming himself in excellent health—"but that is no wonder since the pureness of the air and the wholesomeness of the diet makes it the healthiest part in the known world; and what is very extraordinary at this place, some of us think we never grow any older."

The following year, writing to London, Hearne had complained of ill health—perhaps legitimately, perhaps as a way of laying the groundwork for a leave of absence that would enable him to bring Mary Norton to England. Either way, late in 1785 or early in 1786, Hearne might well have fallen ill. At some point, certainly, he contracted a viral infection, in either his kidneys or his liver, and this could have been when it happened.

Having taken to his bed, Hearne might have stayed there, unable to do the Company accounts, tormenting himself over the death of Mary Norton. Should he have insisted that Mary come with him when he was taken prisoner? Should he have counselled her to take another husband? Hearne might well have slid into what today we would call a clinical depression. What reason did he have to get out of bed? What reason to live?

In this scenario, Hearne could have realized that unless he acted, unless he departed these memory-laden shores, so rich to him once, so meaningless now, he would not survive. And he had to survive, he had finally realized, for at least one reason: he had to see his journal through to publication. He had to tell his story.

On August 16, 1787, Samuel Hearne ceded command of Fort Churchill to William Jefferson, his second-in-command. On the twenty-fifth, having boarded a Company supply ship called the *Sea Horse*, and having waited out a storm, he departed for England. Hearne stood on deck as the vessel passed the ruins of Prince of Wales Fort. Twenty-one years before, he had arrived here for the first time. Now he sailed away for the last, knowing he would never see these shores again.

12

A LONDON FAREWELL

Eighteenth-century London is not remembered as a mecca of health and sophisticated medicine. Still, the metropolis was superior to Churchill. Not long after arriving back in London late in 1787, and despite his sorrow over the death of Mary Norton, Samuel Hearne soon found himself serving as an adviser to the Governing Committee of the HBC, activity for which he received a modest stipend. He also resumed working intensively on his journal, the only thing in the end that had kept him alive.

Three weeks after he arrived, the Company paid him a small fortune (more than £520) in back salary and gratuities, and for at least two years the HBC continued to pay him small sums accruing from the northern trade. As a result, for the first time in his life, Samuel Hearne could relax in one favourite coffee house or another and contemplate the changing world.

The newly invented steam engine meant that for the first time, people had a reliable source of energy that involved neither muscle nor wind. They could mine deeper coal seams and haul heavier loads out of the ground. They could drive blast furnaces hot enough to burn not just coal but coke, so facilitating year-round production. While a large windmill might generate thirty horsepower, a typical steam engine would give them ten times that energy. Steam engines revolutionized paper mills, breweries, and flour mills. They drove spinning and weaving machines. Hearne realized that the cottage-industry England in which he had grown up was passing away.

In January 1788, Hearne witnessed the birth of *The Times*, a notable event even though the *London Gazette* had been appearing since 1666.

That August, he regretted the death of landscape artist Thomas Gainsborough, who had rivalled Joshua Reynolds in portraits. And he probably read the fifth and final volume of *The History of the Decline and Fall of the Roman Empire*, the masterwork by Edward Gibbon, whose first volume he had perused years before.

In November, following a ride in the rain, King George III suffered convulsions and begun talking gibberish and behaving erratically. Doctors tried lectures, threats, and straitjackets; they applied poultices of Spanish fly and mustard, hoping that the ensuing blisters would draw out the evil humours. In February 1789, despite these treatments, the king regained his sanity. On March 10, Londoners celebrated the king's return to health. James Boswell reported that the city burned with "a general blaze of light . . . coloured lamps, transparent figures. . . . Every street was crowded with people rejoicing. The effect was to make me forget all anxious uneasiness for the time."

Boswell, having inherited a rich estate in Scotland, was among those who denounced the British republicanism that now arose in response to the French Revolution. Where Samuel Johnson was a fierce Tory, a believer in hierarchy to the point of expressing approval for India's caste system, Boswell in his middle age went further still. A proud aristocrat and monarchist, he joined at least two right-wing societies and wrote screeds and songs attacking English support for the "horrible anarchy" that had arisen across the Channel. Indeed, he became so enraged that his friends feared his denunciations "at times seemed almost unbalanced."

Hearne paid closer attention to Edmund Burke, a Whig parliamentarian who, in October 1790, published a more rational critique in his *Reflections on the Revolution in France*. Burke condemned the revolution's philosophical basis as false and flatly rejected Rousseau's notions of a social contract and of natural rights in a state of nature. He predicted bloodshed, civil war, and tyranny, and suggested that eventually a military dictatorship would emerge to restore order.

When Thomas Paine responded with *The Rights of Man*, defending the philosophical principles of the French Revolution and arguing that men are born free and equal in rights to liberty, property, security, and resistance to oppression, Hearne knew he had found his spokesman. In the coffee houses of London, enjoying far better health than in Churchill, he found himself vigorously debating these issues, siding, inevitably, with those who took most from Voltaire.

The Age of Revolution had begun. Down with oppression and exploitation! Emboldened by the American Revolution, Frenchmen were calling for limits to royal power and for the establishment of property rights and individual freedoms. Early in 1789, French troops killed three hundred Parisians after riots erupted in response to the announcement of a wage cut at a wallpaper factory. In Marseilles, rioters seized control of the city's three forts and killed one of the commanders. Then came July 14, 1789, when a Parisian mob stormed and seized the Bastille, the grim prison that symbolized tyranny.

Noble ideals were giving rise to harsh realities. A new invention, the guillotine, captured the public imagination as an efficient way of putting people to death. A French mob smashed its way into the royal palace and humiliated the monarch, forcing him to don a red woollen cap, the symbol of the revolution, and proclaim a toast to his unexpected guests. The escalating madness culminated in the killing of Marie-Thérèse-Louise de Savoie-Carignan, princesse de Lamballe, a friend of the queen. The mob cut off her head, stuck it on a pike, and paraded it before the temple in which the king and queen were held.

Hearne followed these developments with appalled amazement. Never in the wilds of North America had he seen such savagery. Perhaps the European monarchy was not, after all, such a terrible institution.

To naval developments the ex-mariner naturally devoted special attention. He was intrigued that a Staffordshire ironmaster had built a "wonder boat" of iron—not the first iron-hulled boat, but at seventy feet in length, by far the largest. And he sorrowed to learn, early in 1791, of the death of the comte de La Pérouse. While attempting to circumnavigate the globe, La Pérouse had disappeared with his two ships, *L'Astrolabe* and *La Boussole*, believed to have sunk during a cyclone in the Pacific.

The following year, Hearne again heard the siren call of distant lands, when Captain George Vancouver, who had previously sailed with his friend, William Wales, began surveying the west coast of North America. In July one of Vancouver's seamen wrote, "We have now reached a latitude level with Newfoundland, exploring the inlets between a large island and the mainland which is dominated by a huge range of snowcapped mountains covered with pine forests. Today we were visited by natives in canoes who traded otter skins and salmon for our buttons and beads. . . . This beautiful country reminds us of Scotland and looks ideal for British settlement."

That splendiferous coast, Hearne knew, lay some distance to the west of the Barren Lands he himself had explored. He could not help wondering, how far?

Later in 1792, he read that ten mutineers from HMS *Bounty* would soon face court martial. Three years before, driven mad by abuse, these sailors had helped force Captain William Bligh and eighteen supporters into a twenty-three-foot longboat in the South Pacific. Given food but no map, Bligh had survived forty-seven days at sea, sailing 3,600 miles to the island of Timor. Hearne had to admire this navigational feat, though he detested everything else he heard about the captain. Bligh, who had sailed with both Vancouver and Wales, had arrived back in England late the previous year. Now, when Hearne read in *The Times* that the captured mutineers would face a naval panel headed by Samuel Hood, he told Wales, "Those poor devils will swing from a yardarm."

Around this time, Hearne was reading Boswell's recently published *Life of Johnson*. While not especially interested in the life of Johnson, the mariner was avid to read what Boswell wrote of the man's death. In 1784, the celebrated literary man had died of "dropsy"—precisely the incurable illness with which, since his return to England, he himself had been diagnosed.

Today, dropsy, or edema—an excess accumulation of bodily fluids—is recognized as a symptom of liver or kidney infection. Late in the eighteenth century, it remained mysterious. Hearne knew only that his own decline and death would resemble those of Johnson—not, he realized, an especially pleasant prospect.

DURING THESE YEARS, Samuel Hearne lived frugally in lodgings at N° 8 Leigh Street in Red Lion Square. A man of modest tastes, he ate most meals in a handful of coffee houses scattered around the city near his favourite destinations. Once a week, he would dine at the well-appointed table of William Wales and his wife, where he would often entertain guests with tales of his adventures. Every two or three months, he would travel by coach to Peckham and spend a few days with his sister and her family.

Hearne was no atheist, but neither was he a practising Christian. He had been unable to reconcile the notion of a caring god with the horrific deaths of innocents, like those he had witnessed at Bloody Falls. Since the death of Mary Norton, he felt this contradiction even more strongly. He found the deism of Voltaire more congenial than Christianity, embraced natural law as paramount, and could not be induced to attend church services.

From Red Lion Square, Hearne could walk to the British Museum, where he enjoyed exploring the antiquarian and natural history collections, open six hours a day to "studious and courteous persons." He spent far more time, however, at Hudson's Bay House, then situated in the heart of the city on the north side of Fenchurch Street. Hearne had discovered, as he wrote later, "that several learned and curious

London, here viewed from the Southwark side of the Thames, remained a city of church spires and sailing ships. It was still small enough that, having established himself in Red Lion Square, Hearne could walk to most of his regular destinations.

gentlemen are in possession of manuscript copies of, or extracts from, my Journals, as well as copies of my Charts."

To revise his book, Hearne had applied to the HBC Committee for permission to peruse these documents. Previous tensions had been resolved, or at least set aside, for "this was granted with the greatest affability and politeness." Eventually, the explorer would dedicate his book to George Samuel Wegg, who served both as governor of the HBC and as vice-president and treasurer of the Royal Society; to Sir James Winter Lake, deputy governor of the HBC; and also to "the rest of the committee of the honourable Hudson's Bay Company."

Once into the Company archives, Hearne did not confine himself to his own field notes and journals. He also examined—and would obliquely answer—the works of HBC critics like Joseph Robson, an ex-officer who charged that the Company showed no interest in exploration but "slept at the edge of a frozen sea." Hearne also paid careful attention, as he demonstrated in his finished work, to journals, logbooks, and letters pertaining to the mysterious fate of Captain James Knight.

When visiting the HBC archives, Hearne would often eat at the nearby Elephant & Castle, a public house in which, during the late 1720s, a young William Hogarth had lived and struggled, earning his living as a painter of tavern signs. In exchange for board and lodging, Hogarth had embellished the walls with a variety of large, colourful paintings, among them one called *The Hudson's Bay Company's Porters Going to Dinner*, later described as "full of spirit and original character." In the background, this painting depicted another of Hearne's favourite haunts, a public house called the Magpie & Punchbowl.

There is virtually no chance that during this period Hearne wasted a moment cavorting with the "the famous and noble Order of Bucks," as David Thompson, that disgruntled cartographer, would flippantly suggest. Created around 1739 as an offshoot of the Freemasons, this "noble order" was an extravagant men's club with a reputation for gambling, drunkenness, and debauchery. Its membership comprised a dozen chapters of wealthy young men forbidden by custom from wearing the same waistcoat to a club meeting more than once.

The abstemious Hearne, who had declined to imbibe alcohol even when travelling in the Barren Lands and who had perhaps indulged only when sorrowing over Mary Norton, was unlikely to begin seriously drinking now, when he was battling a debilitating dropsy. If Thompson's allegation contains any kernel of truth, it would consist in the possibility that back in 1783, while sojourning in London as a minor celebrity, the mariner had addressed a chapter of Bucks as a guest speaker.

WHEN HE WROTE the introduction to *A Journey to the Northern Ocean*, Samuel Hearne positioned the work as a vindication of the Hudson's Bay Company. He responded directly to criticisms, for example, that the Company had sponsored no exploration. Meanwhile, as an officer with extensive experience in the field, he blossomed into a valuable adviser. Since the early 1780s, despite Hearne's rebuilding at Churchill, the HBC had seen a dramatic decline in trade with the Dene. Business had suffered as a result of both the razing of Prince of Wales Fort and the devastating smallpox epidemic of 1781–82, which Hearne deplored as part of a European legacy that included alcohol abuse, venereal disease, whooping cough, and scarlet fever. The ex-governor's observations and remarks on the smallpox epidemic had been lost when the French sacked the fort, but elsewhere Hearne estimated that the disease had killed 90 per cent of the Chipewyan.

Hearne told the Committee that fur-traders based in Montreal, so long active in southern and western regions, and now organized as the North West Company, had recently begun intercepting northern native people who traditionally travelled to Churchill. These "pedlars" had established trading posts on Lake Athabasca in the very heart of Dene country. Why would these native traders paddle hundreds of miles to the Bay when they could do business so close to home? Hearne insisted that the solution lay in building an HBC post on Lake Athabasca, and possibly another on Great Slave Lake, which he had visited with Matonabbee while returning from the Arctic sea.

Two problems presented themselves. First, the route Hearne had travelled between Great Slave Lake and Churchill was far too difficult to serve for the transport of supplies and trading goods. Second, the precise locations of those two distant lakes had become a matter of dispute. Alexander Dalrymple, the influential hydrographer and mapmaker employed by the East India Company, had challenged the accuracy of Hearne's original map. Accustomed to the geographic scale of Great Britain and continental Europe, he could not believe the gargantuan size of North America, or that Great Slave Lake lay so far to the west.

If a man can be situated socially not only by his friends but also by his enemies, certainly Alexander Dalrymple, who now became Hearne's principal nemesis, moved in the highest circles. He was the younger brother of David Dalrymple, Lord Hailes, an early mentor to the affluent James Boswell. Employed by the East India Company since 1752, Alexander Dalrymple had been recommended as "particularly suitable" to lead the 1769 naval expedition to Tahiti to observe the Transit of Venus. He was bitterly disappointed when Captain James Cook was chosen instead. Nor did Dalrymple care much for Hearne's closest friend. William Wales had not only observed the famous Transit in Rupert's Land, but had served as co-navigator on Cook's second voyage and then helped prepare the journal of that expedition for publication.

Working from his armchair in London, Dalrymple decided that a navigable Northwest Passage must extend westward out of Hudson Bay—the very notion that Hearne had demonstrated to be false by travelling to the Arctic Ocean. If such a southerly Northwest Passage had existed, he would have encountered it. Dalrymple refused to accept this. Perhaps the ex-mariner was prevaricating. Or perhaps his maps were inaccurate. Maybe he had not travelled so far north as he claimed. If so, the elusive Passage might exist after all. Dalrymple offered this suggestion in *Memoir of a Map of the Lands about the North Pole*, a pamphlet that infuriated Hearne.

Eventually, in a brief preface, the explorer would respond to the hostile hydrographer: "Mr. Dalrymple, in one of his Pamphlets relating to Hudson's Bay, has been so very particular in his observations on my Journey, as to remark, that I have not explained the construction of the Quadrant which I had the misfortune to break in my second Journey to the North. It was a Hadley's Quadrant, with a bubble attached to it for an horizon."

After explaining that he had not expected his as-yet-unpublished

journal to come under the close scrutiny "of so ingenious and indefati-
gable a geographer as Mr. Dalrymple," Hearne admits to feeling
"rather hurt at Mr. Dalrymple's rejecting my [most northerly] latitude in so peremptory a manner, and in so great a proportion, as he
has done." After answering certain specific criticisms Hearne writes,

I do not by any means wish to enter into a dispute with, or incur the displeasure of Mr. Dalrymple; but thinking, as I do, that I have not been treated in so
liberal a manner as I ought to have been, he will excuse me for endeavouring to
convince the Public that his objections are in a great measure without foundation. And having done so, I shall quit the disagreeable subject with declaring,
that if any part of the following sheets should afford amusement to Mr. Dalrymple, or any other of my readers, it will be the highest gratification I can
receive, and the only recompense I desire to obtain for the hardships and
fatigue which I underwent in procuring the information contained in them.

Also in his preface, Hearne regretfully reports the loss of "a considerable vocabulary of the Northern Indian Language, containing sixteen folio pages." In 1790, he had lent this dictionary to his friend
Thomas Hutchins to copy for the use of a looming HBC expedition;
"But Mr. Hutchins dying soon after, the Vocabulary was taken away
with the rest of his effects, and cannot now be recovered."

WHILE THE HBC had sound commercial reasons to inquire into the
precise locations of Lake Athabasca and Great Slave Lake, Samuel
Hearne had excellent personal ones, thanks to Alexander Dalrymple.
And he brought his long experience of the north to Company strategy
sessions. Governor Wegg convened and chaired most of these. Early
on, attendees included Hutchins, the Company's corresponding secretary and an old friend of Hearne who had served at York and Albany
forts before returning permanently to London in 1782. The Committee also included Wales, who frequently served the Company as an
outside consultant. In 1770, he had been the prime mover behind a
Royal Society request that the HBC collect natural history specimens.
These four men—Wegg, Hutchins, Wales, and Hearne—decided

that the Company should send a surveyor to pinpoint the locations of Lake Athabasca and Great Slave Lake and to identify transportation routes to and from those areas. For Hearne, such an expedition would serve the additional purpose of vindicating the rough accuracy of his own most important map. The man to send, the four agreed, was Philip Turnor, a well-experienced surveyor and yet another protégé of Wales. In 1778, the Company had sought the mathematician's assistance in hiring young men "well skilled in the Mathematics and in making Astronomical Observations." Wales had referred them to Turnor, who became the first man employed solely as a surveyor by the HBC.

Based initially at York Factory, Turnor had surveyed and mapped the territory around York, Moose, and Albany forts, concentrating on areas south and west of Hudson Bay. Samuel Hearne was at that time stationed farther north, governing Prince of Wales Fort, and so the two men may not have met, though the record is inconclusive because some journals have been lost.

Even so, the connections were many. In 1779, for example, Turnor had stayed at Cumberland House, founded by Hearne five years before. An entry in his journal suggests that he first heard the mariner's name pronounced by a Scot, and also hints at what Hearne had been up against: "Having found a Compass at Cumberland House which was left by Mr. Herron it appears by that Compass, that the Variation of the Compass is about 12 degrees Easterly."

In mid-October 1787, around the time Samuel Hearne returned to England from Fort Churchill in the *Sea Horse,* Turnor arrived from York Factory in a sloop called the *Beaver.* If Hearne had not previously met Turnor, he did so now, in London, and discovered he had much in common with the slightly younger man. Of Turnor, who had travelled extensively in Rupert's Land, one HBC officer had written, "He did not grumble at the hardships he had to encounter, and his attitude in adapting himself to primitive conditions of life was one of great courage." The same could have been written of Hearne. As well, the two men shared many friends and acquaintances—not just Wales and Hutchins, but also Humphrey Marten, Matthew Cocking, Robert Longmoor, and the embittered Edward Umfreville, whom neither liked.

The idiosyncratic spellings of the times obscure a still more special bond. Philip Turnor, born in the early 1750s, was the older brother of John Turner, who in 1782, while captain of the *Severn*, had been taken prisoner at York Fort by the comte de La Pérouse. Philip Turnor knew from his brother that Hearne had not only secured the release of the *Severn*, but had then acted as navigator and guided that vessel to Stromness.

Throughout 1788 and into 1789, Hearne, Wales, Hutchins, and Turnor spent countless hours together at HBC headquarters, analyzing journals and maps. They spent even more time at the Elephant & Castle down the street, where, far more comfortably ensconced, and surrounded by the early works of Hogarth, they debated geographical probabilities. They contemplated the rough map of Montreal fur-trader Peter Pond, who in 1785 had wintered south of Athabasca Lake and who speculated about whether that lake drained northward into Arctic waters or westward into the Pacific.

Turnor had returned to London after complaining for years of bad health. But on May 16, 1789, persuaded by Hearne and the others, and apparently quite recovered, he renewed his contract as inland surveyor for three years at £80 per year. Two weeks later, carrying a copy of the map Samuel Hearne had created in the early 1770s—still the only representation of most of the area northwest of Churchill—Turnor sailed from the Thames on the *King George*, bound for Hudson Bay.

The surveyor understood the commercial nature of his mission. He also understood that his friend Hearne, while certain of his discoveries, was counting on him for geographical vindication—if only because the lack of such vindication was delaying the publication of *A Journey to the Northern Ocean*.

TWO DECADES previously, before even he left Prince of Wales Fort, Samuel Hearne had believed that a northward trek across vast lands unknown to Europeans—a quest to find a fabled copper mine and a Northwest Passage—would almost certainly constitute a memorable achievement. When he had accomplished the feat, the enthusiastic reaction to his first reports confirmed this opinion. Through the

1770s, Hearne had worked on developing his field notes into a journal suitable for publication, becoming aware not only of the magnitude of the task but also of his limitations as a writer. His encounter with the aristocratic comte de La Pérouse, who had returned the journal to him on condition that he publish it, had reinforced his commitment to the project.

By now Samuel Hearne understood that to conceive a book was one thing; to complete, revise, and publish it was quite another. Writing a book, Hearne realized, was not unlike embarking on a journey to the northern ocean. He knew that somewhere in the distance there lay a fabulous sea—publication, recognition, his name remembered. But how to get there from here? Two decades before, lost in the Barrens, lacking snowshoes, freezing and starving to death, Hearne had inspired the supremely competent Matonabbee to take him where he needed to go. As in the frozen north, where arrogance and assertiveness would have availed nothing, so now in the swirl of cosmopolitan London Hearne needed the humility and wisdom to recognize that he would never achieve his objective alone.

During his London sojourn of half a decade before, several notable figures had supported his literary undertaking, among them the zoologist Thomas Pennant, the cleric John Douglas, and such HBC leaders as Samuel Wegg and Thomas Hutchins. As well, he had received enthusiastic support from William Wales, whom he had met at Prince of Wales Fort so long ago. Wales, now in his early fifties, a married man roughly a decade older than Hearne, was well respected as a mathematician, astronomer, meteorologist, and demographer. Born in Yorkshire in humble circumstances, Wales, too, was a self-made man.

In 1769, the first scientist to winter at Hudson Bay, Wales had kept observations on the winds and the weather, and also published, in the Royal Society's *Philosophical Transactions*, a brief but perceptive journal about life in the north. Three years later, as co-navigator and meteorologist, he had sailed with Captain Cook on his second great voyage, circumnavigating the world in the *Resolution*. As secretary to the Board of Longitude, Wales also had the crucial duty of maintaining chronometers being tested for accuracy, one of which had been developed by the clockmaker John Harrison.

William Wales was Hearne's best friend in London. This portrait was painted in 1794 by John Russell, in return for Wales's help in preparing a map of the moon.

On returning from this 70,000-mile voyage, the sedentary Wales put sailing behind to become the mathematics master at Christ's Hospital. This so-called Blue Coat School, where student uniforms consisted of yellow stockings and blue coats, prepared some boys for university, others for a naval career. Wales taught both mathematics and navigation.

In a history of Christ's Hospital, Wales's grandson, William Trollope, described him:

A practical sailor himself, and the co-navigator of Captain Cook, he knew the requisite qualifications of a seaman; and his whole aim was to fit his boys for the profession in which they were destined to embark. . . . Strict and punctual in his discipline, he was frank and open in his temperament; and he was more loved for the goodness of his heart than feared for the heaviness of his hand. There was a fund of genuine humour about him, and a joyous expression of countenance, which took hold upon the affection; and his ready wit, expressed in a pleasing provincial dialect, frequently elicited the hearty mirth of his juvenile auditors.

The essayist Charles Lamb (1775–1834), in *Recollections of Christ's Hospital,* paints a similar portrait: "All his systems were adapted to fit them [his students] for the rough element they were destined to encounter. . . . To make his boys hardy, and to give them early sailor habits, seemed to be his only aim. . . . There was in William Wales a perpetual fund of humour, a constant glee about him, which, heightened by an inveterate provincialism of North country-dialect, absolutely took away the sting from his severities."

Wales also taught Samuel Taylor Coleridge, who wrote in a letter of the older man, "Two or three times a year the mathematics master beats up recruits for the King's Boys, as they are called, and all who like the navy are drafted into the mathematical and drawing schools, where they continue till sixteen or seventeen and go out as midshipmen and schoolmasters in the navy." Coleridge also described Wales as "a man of uncommonly clear head," recalling that in his 1781 paper on demographics, *An Enquiry into the Present State of the Population in England and Wales*, he repudiated a confused essay which argued, erroneously, that England was experiencing a rapid depopulation.

Now, in London in the late 1780s and early 1790s, Wales and Samuel Hearne spent many long hours talking about the distant northern world in which the mathematics master had passed one memorable year but in which the ex-mariner had spent most of his adult life. They talked often about Hearne's work-in-progress, *A Journey to the Northern Ocean*, and Wales was foremost among those who, having realized how much Hearne knew about the flora and fauna of the north, as well as about the native peoples, urged the intrepid traveller to add chapters on these matters.

In William Wales, Samuel Hearne had found a man who knew his way around the London book-publishing world better than he himself ever would. He suspected that the HBC, jealous of its proprietary interests and geographical secrets, loath to disseminate knowledge of the north to its competitors, would delay publication as long as it could. But when the time came, when he finished revising and the Company agreed to publish, Wales would be the man to make the book a reality. In William Wales, Hearne had found an autonomous lieutenant who understood his quest and could help him achieve it. He had found the European equivalent of Matonabbee.

*　*　*

Christ's Hospital in Newgate Street. In 1791, at this Blue Coat School, the eloquent Samuel Hearne met an impressionable eighteen-year-old student named Samuel Taylor Coleridge, and dazzled the youth with his harrowing tales of adventure and the supernatural.

ONE GREY AFTERNOON in the spring of 1791, a tall, slim, and weathered man in a slightly old-fashioned beaver hat climbed out of a public coach in Newgate Street. He was respectably though not stylishly dressed in a blue three-quarter-length coat with matching waistcoat and white breeches, all slightly worn, and he strode through the gate of Christ's Hospital careless of any impression he might make, and happy to find that he was breathing without difficulty.

Not yet forty-six, Samuel Hearne knew that his recovered health was now deteriorating. Until recently, he might enjoy five or six good days out of seven—days when he could visit the museum or the HBC archives, or perhaps walk to his favourite coffee house, there to read the newspapers and to trade stories and opinions; lately, he could expect only three or four such days in a week. Today was one of the good days, however, and as he walked through the cloisters crowded with blue-coated boys, most of them heading in the same direction as he was, he realized that, thanks to William Wales, he had come to know the school well.

In the late eighteenth century, as in contemporary times, schoolmasters and teachers made a practice of bringing notables into their classrooms whenever possible, and William Wales had more than once invited Samuel Hearne to address the older students. Hearne was an accomplished raconteur, after all—and what a story he had to tell. He had grown up in the Royal Navy and sailed with one of England's most illustrious fighting captains. He had worked in the merchant marine and the whale fishery. And, he had travelled thousands of miles with fantastical "Indians," the sole European among them. Now he was preparing an account of his adventures for publication.

At first, Samuel Hearne had resisted his friend's overtures. In the early 1780s, during his reluctant sojourn in London, he had been feted as an ex-prisoner-of-war who, having been captured by the French, had contrived to negotiate both his own release and that of many others. Around London, he realized in retrospect, he had cut a dashing figure. Now, as a result of his illness, his dropsy, Hearne had lost weight. Beneath his periwig, his blond hair had grown thin and grey. He felt old and exhausted.

William Wales had persevered in inviting Hearne, as much for the sake of the odd-spoken and reclusive ex-mariner himself as for the boys. Since 1788, Hearne had visited Christ's Hospital any number of times and had spoken to countless Blue Coat boys. He had been invited today—some school occasion marking he knew not what— simply to enjoy himself as a dinner guest. As he made his way into the well-lit dining hall, enjoying the vitality, the jostling and noise of the boys, he heard someone call, "Samuel! Over here!"

Hearne spotted Wales, rotund and jovial, standing in a circle of adults, most of them obviously visitors like himself. He made his way to this group, some of whom he knew slightly. The guests had been discussing the paintings hung in the dining hall, the most impressive of which had been done by Antonio Verrio—a huge representation of James II, surrounded by courtiers and presiding at a convocation of graduating students. As a gifted amateur artist, Hearne stood admiring the intricacies of this work and the way Verrio used colour. He was still lost in it when Wales said, "Ah, Coleridge!" And then, "Samuel? I don't believe you have met Samuel Taylor Coleridge—a young man with a keen interest in adventure."

Hearne was struck by the intensity of the awkward youth who appeared before him, pudgy and black haired yet alert. Wales spent too long summarizing Hearne's history, mentioning his Royal Navy service and also that he had survived some amazing adventures during a journey of exploration, about which he was now preparing a narrative for publication. Coleridge, he told Hearne, was this year's Grecian, the leading classical scholar in the Upper Grammar School. He had earned two scholarships that would pay most of his expenses to Cambridge.

Samuel Hearne congratulated the young man—Coleridge would turn nineteen in October—and wondered that they had not previously met. Coleridge explained that he had spent far too much time in the sick-ward, suffering from jaundice and rheumatic fever. As well, he had recently endured the sudden deaths of two people close to him. The inquisitive Hearne now learned, to his surprise, that he had much in common with young Coleridge, whose closest brother, Frank, had joined the Navy at eleven. While still a child, and like Hearne himself, Coleridge had lost his father to sudden illness—an event that had changed his life. Both men had also spent countless boyhood hours perusing *Robinson Crusoe*, imagining themselves lost and alone on some deserted island.

Coleridge, also insatiably curious, wanted to hear more about the ex-mariner's voyages and amazing adventures—and what about the book he was working on, the tale of his overland voyaging in the north? Hearne at first offered brief responses, but when Coleridge asked if he could recall a moment of inspiration, when he felt absolutely driven to tell a particular story, Hearne recognized something in the younger man.

And so, almost despite himself, he launched into his tale, telling young Coleridge how, while working for the Hudson's Bay Company, he had embarked on a quest to discover a fabled copper mine and a Northwest Passage. Soon enough, and as had happened before, Hearne found himself caught up in his story. Wales and several other guests had stopped talking and stood listening, rapt, as Samuel Hearne, swept away by the power of his own tale, recounted his three-year odyssey in the northern barrens, evoking the hardship but also the magic, and gravitating ineluctably to the massacre he had witnessed at Bloody Falls.

Two warriors had killed a young woman at his feet, he told the wide-eyed Coleridge and half a dozen others. Since that moment, he had felt haunted, and that feeling of guilt never left him but had only intensified. Could he not have prevented the massacre? Should he not have tried harder? "The massacre of those innocent people," he said, dabbing at his eyes. "The senseless killing of that young girl. That moment changed me forever."

IN THE EARLY 1790s, Samuel Hearne ran into financial difficulties. Shortly after arriving in England from Hudson Bay, the explorer had collected over £520 in outstanding wages. During the next couple of years, he had received another £70—nearly the equivalent of the annual salary paid to surveyor Philip Turnor. As chief at Prince of Wales Fort, while earning £130 a year and augmenting that with bonuses reflecting the amount of trade he conducted, Hearne had amassed considerable savings, if only because he had no place to spend money.

Two decades before, for example, the Company had purchased a £300 annuity on Hearne's behalf, investing the "gratuity" he had earned with his epic trek. Even if he had not troubled to collect the £100 allotted by his mother's will, the funds he had saved should have enabled him to live out his days in reasonable comfort. According to the obituary published in *The European Magazine and London Review*, it was the explorer's generosity that created the problem:

He had saved a few thousands, the fruits of many years' industry, and might, had he been blessed with prudence, have enjoyed many years of ease and plenty; but he had lived so long where money was of no use that he seemed insensible of its value here, and lent it with little or no security to those he was scarcely acquainted with by name. Sincere and undesigning himself, he was by no means a match for the duplicity of others. His disposition, as may be judged by his writing, was naturally humane; what he wanted in learning and polite accomplishments he made up in native simplicity and innate goodness; and he was so strictly scrupulous with regard to the property of others that he was heard to say a few days before his death, "He could lay his hand on his heart and say he had never wronged any man of sixpence."

By late 1792, Hearne was less concerned with money than with failing health. Eighteenth-century medicine did not recognize dropsy as symptomatic of liver or kidney failure, but regarded it as a malady in its own right. Doctors observed that, starting with the feet and legs, the body accumulated fluids—and so they drew off blood. They prescribed fasting, diuretics, purgatives, and, eventually, opiates, which were readily available.

In 1784, Samuel Johnson had died of dropsy, and Hearne's sufferings undoubtedly followed a similar pattern. The swelling in his legs slowly worsened, and he found breathing increasingly difficult. By October 1792, the once athletic explorer would have struggled while walking short distances, pausing to rest and catch his breath. If he caught the least cold, he felt such constriction in his chest that he could not lie down in his bed but would be compelled to sit up all night so he could breathe. In the end, only laudanum or opium syrup would induce sleep.

Samuel Johnson, considerably older, had suffered a paralytic stroke that was not, strictly speaking, symptomatic. Hearne would doubtless have identified with Johnson's other complaints: "I am sleepless; my legs grow weary with a very few steps." Once in a while, the "painful fatigue" would ease, and Johnson would move about almost as normal. And yet, "My sleep is little, my breath is very much encumbered, and my legs are very weak. The water has increased a little, but has again run off. The most distressing symptom is want of sleep." Toward the end, Johnson felt such excruciating pain in his swollen legs that, in an attempt to release fluids, he stabbed them with a surgical knife and scissors. Hearne, too, would have suffered—though without these histrionics. From the Dene people, while travelling in the Barren Lands, he had learned courage in the face of suffering, and now he took pride in demonstrating that stoicism.

Probably because he was younger than Johnson, Hearne remained mobile until very near the end. And shortly before he died, he savoured one last sweet victory. From Hudson Bay, in July 1792, Philip Turnor had submitted a report of his travels. Having arrived at York Factory late in August 1789, he had spent the ensuing winter at Cumberland House, where he taught David Thompson astronomy and inspired the young man's first survey. In September 1790, after finally receiving supplies, and accompanied by an assistant named Peter Fidler, Turnor started north. He wintered on the Churchill River, then started west toward Athabasca and Great Slave lakes. Fidler wrote in his journal that the "sole motive for going to the Athapescow [Athabasca] is for Mr. Turnor to survey these parts in order to settle some dubious points. . . . [Both Samuel Hearne and Peter Pond of the North West Company] fixes these places on their maps far more West than there is good reason to think them."

In so surmising, however, Fidler proved wrong. He was following Alexander Dalrymple, who fondly imagined that if Hearne had misplaced Athabasca Lake or Great Slave Lake, he might have done the same with the mouth of the Coppermine River. Essentially, Turnor's observations vindicated the pioneering navigator—or so it appeared from his preliminary report.

Subsequent readings, still more precise, would determine that Hearne did place the mouth of the Coppermine too far north, but only by 275 miles. Given the geography of Hudson Bay, the error was not significant. In travelling to the Arctic Ocean, Hearne would have encountered any passage emerging out of that Bay no matter how faulty his instruments. He had determined the truth: south of the Arctic waters of Coronation Gulf, there exists no navigable Northwest Passage.

Given this vindication, the HBC at last allowed William Wales to negotiate the sale of Hearne's manuscript to Strahan and Cadell, the well-respected publishing company that had brought out Cook's *Third Voyage*. On Wednesday, October 3, 1792, Hearne wrote publisher Andrew Strahan:

I am sorry my health will not permit me to wait on you. I saw Mr. Wales previous to my calling at your house; who informed me of your proposals which I accept; and anything in reason should be allowed to the person that prepares the Work for the Press. With respect to the agreement you mentioned I wish for nothing more than it shall specify that the Book shall be sent into the World in a style that will do credit to you, and myself; and that Mr. Wales be presented with one Copy, and myself Two.

This handwritten missive, sealed with red wax and sent by hand, is now at the British Library in London. On October 8, the Monday after he dispatched his note, the bedridden explorer signed the contract and watched as Wales witnessed it. For £200—the same amount he had received as a gratuity for his three-year trek—Hearne awarded the publisher the copyright to *A Journey to the Northern Ocean.*

Scholars have observed that, eleven years later, Jane Austen would receive only £10 for *Northanger Abbey,* and that, for the *Vicar of Wakefield,* published in 1762, Oliver Goldsmith, facing debtor's prison, had accepted a mere £60. On the other hand, James Boswell—now clearing £900 a year in rents from his estate—had refused "a cool thousand" for the copyright to *Life of Johnson* and instead negotiated an advance against royalties of £400.

In any event, Hearne's contract, also held at the British Library, reveals that mariner himself never received a penny, if only because no funds were payable until after publication: "The said Andrew Strahan ... doth hereby covenant with the said Samuel Hearne his executors administrators and assigns to pay to the said Samuel Hearne the said sum of two hundred pounds at the expiration of three months from the Day of Publication of the said Work."

An obscure contemporary named William Goldson would later mention in an overview of North American exploration that Hearne's manuscript had been "purchased by Mr. Wales, who intends committing it to the press." If Hearne was having financial difficulty, Wales may well have loaned him money against publication. The publishing contract, however, is clearly between the explorer and the publisher. And to Hearne, who was dying, the money did not much matter. He cared only about the book. He was hoping that *A Journey to the Northern Ocean* would etch his name into the history of northern exploration. In this, despite contention and controversy, the book would succeed beyond his wildest dreams.

In November 1792, breathing with increasing difficulty and with the pain becoming intolerable, Hearne realized that he could not hold out much longer. From his bed, he communicated as much to William Wales. This faithful visitor told him to hang on a while yet, and returned that same evening with Philip Turnor, the HBC surveyor who had just arrived from Hudson Bay. "Samuel, you were right!" Turner said to him. "Your readings were not nearly as far off as Dalrymple would have wished."

"No passage runs out of Hudson Bay?"

"No passage, Samuel. As you demonstrated."

A short while later, forced by the pain to take an extra large dose of opium, Samuel Hearne felt engulfed by a wave of joy. As an explorer, he stood vindicated. Wales would see that his book would be published. He had said goodbye to Wales, the dearest friend a man ever had, and had thanked him from the bottom of his heart.

Hearne remembered his other great friend, who had emerged out of a swirling snowstorm to save his life. Without the peerless Matonabbee, he would never have reached the mouth of the Coppermine. He refused to dwell upon Bloody Falls, and thought instead of Mary Norton, the only woman he had ever loved. Hearne chose to remember the good times, when with his beloved wife he would stride out of Prince of Wales Fort to hunt geese, carrying his musket on his shoulder. He remembered loving Mary Norton in the blazing light of the aurora borealis. In November 1792, as at age forty-seven he passed away, Samuel Hearne remembered loving Mary Norton.

13

LIFE AFTER DEATH

FOR ADMIRERS of Voltaire, as for skeptics, dissenters, non-conformists, existentialists, and unbelievers of all varieties, the history of *A Journey to the Northern Ocean* constitutes the saga of Samuel Hearne's life after death. It's a narrative that echoes with contention and controversy—though certain facts remain beyond dispute. During his unprecedented three-year odyssey, Hearne travelled more than 3,500 miles, mostly on foot, occasionally by canoe, mapping territory unknown to Europeans. He did so not as a native person, for whom such journeys were commonplace if difficult, but as a visitor from another world, an alien creature who managed to adapt and survive and eventually to communicate what he learned to others of his kind.

Samuel Hearne demonstrated that to survive in the north, Europeans would have to apprentice themselves to the native peoples. He was the first explorer to reach the Arctic coast of North America and so to discover the southern channel of the Northwest Passage, that quintessentially European conception. He did pioneering work in ethnology, zoology, and botany. And he built the Hudson's Bay Company's first inland trading post, inaugurating a new chapter in the history of the Company, and so of the northern part of the continent. Yet outside a small circle of fur-trade historians, these accomplishments, all beyond dispute, remain unacknowledged.

At the same time, *A Journey to the Northern Ocean* has sparked ferocious arguments. Besides the geographical wrangling that arose before the book appeared, experts have contended over Hearne's precise routes, over his decision to surrender Prince of Wales Fort, and over the credibility of key sections of his book. Contributors to this acrimonious, two-hundred-year debate include geographers, historians, and literary critics. Among them are cartographer David Thompson, naval officers John Richardson and George Back, and scholars Richard Glover and Ian S. MacLaren.

Some of the earliest commentary came from France. In 1782, as a prisoner aboard the *Sceptre*, Samuel Hearne had promised the comte de La Pérouse that, once released back to England, he would soon publish his journal. Yet the volume did not appear in print until 1795, three years after his death. By then, the translator of La Pérouse's *Voyage Round the World* had appended an introductory note seconding the opinion of the French editor of that work: "There is little doubt . . . but that Mr. Hearne would readily have fulfilled his engagement to la Perouse, as the publication could not have failed to have been profitable to himself, had he not been prevented by the Hudson's Bay Company, as [the editor] Mr. Milet-Mureau conjectures."

Laws of copyright remained undeveloped. But the HBC, as Hearne's

In 1792, the surveyor Philip Turnor vindicated the mapping of Samuel Hearne, proving once more that no Northwest Passage runs west out of Hudson Bay. This painting by Lorne Bouchard is called Turnor Surveys Lake Athabasca.

original sponsor, certainly had the power to veto publication. Judging from internal evidence, Hearne did not revise or amend the work after 1791. By then, essentially, he had been ready to publish for years. Why the delay? For years the HBC could offer a ready excuse: Alexander Dalrymple had attacked details of Hearne's maps, and so the Company required geographical confirmation. Yet when Philip Turnor vindicated Hearne in 1792, still the HBC procrastinated. The Company was engaged in a fierce competition with the Montreal-based fur-traders, and Hearne's *Journal* contained information that these "pedlars" might find useful. So though the HBC would circulate the work within trusted circles, like those of Alexander Dalrymple, it saw no reason to encourage wider availability.

Finally, in 1795—over two decades after Hearne completed his trek, by which time his opus revealed no secrets—the HBC allowed the book to appear. Strahan and Cadell published *A Journey from Prince of Wales's Fort in Hudson's Bay to the Northern Ocean* as a large quarto volume of 502 pages (xliv + 458), complete with five maps and four full-page illustrations.

The market for such a work had been well established. In southern England, for example, where the Bristol Library kept extensive records, books in the eclectic category of "history, travel, and geography" accounted for over 45 per cent of all borrowings in the decade ending in 1784, and also for six of the ten most popular books. Throughout Europe, the appetite proved similarly voracious. Foreign editions and translations of *Journey* appeared almost immediately—Irish in 1796, Dutch in 1798, French in 1799. This last opened with an effusive note apostrophizing the late comte de La Pérouse, declaring that all of Europe remained indebted to that voyager: "In returning [the manuscript] to its author on the express condition that he have it printed and published, never has a victor exercised more fruitfully his right of conquest, or imposed upon the vanquished a more honourable condition."

Reviews of the book, long and laudatory, appeared in 1796 in the *Gentleman's Magazine,* the *Analytical Review,* and the *Monthly Review,* and the following year in the *Critical Review.* These reviews offer more summary than analysis, but they do identify the themes and motifs that would dominate later discourse. So, in the *Gentleman's*

Magazine, we read, "Among the principal adventures of the route are the dreadful massacre of the unoffending Esquimaux by the Indians; a particular account of the Indians, their conjuring doctors, and the servile laborious offices performed by the women. . . . The Moose deer and the beaver are treated of at large, and the errors concerning them corrected."

This review quotes Hearne to the effect that his journey "has put a final end to all disputes concerning a North-west passage through Hudson's Bay." It suggests that he has answered critics who contended that the H B C had been slow not only to explore but to expand trade. It praises the explorer's detailed portrait of the Dene, and judges the work "a valuable addition to the discoveries which the enterprising spirit of our countrymen lends them to make."

The *Monthly Review* article runs over five pages, three of which transcribe the description of the massacre at Bloody Falls. The anonymous reviewer mentions Hearne's dispute with Alexander Dalrymple, suggests that the book paints, "in a plain unadorned style, such a striking picture of the miseries of savage life, accompanied with so many minute incidents copied faithfully from nature, that it is impossible to read it without feeling a deep interest, and without reflecting on, and cherishing, the inestimable blessings of civilized society."

Alluding to the style, the reviewer writes, "Mr. H. is not acquainted with the graces of composition: but he relates his adventures with plainness and sufficient perspicuity; and often with those simple touches of nature, which, in truth, are preferable to all ornaments of art." He suggests that "lovers of natural history will be pleased with the description of the principal quadrupeds and birds," and inadvertently reveals the racist prejudices of the times: "Throughout this work, Mr. Hearne speaks with a proper mixture of indignation at the brutalities, and of compassion for the miseries, of those wretched savages. . . . We were particularly pleased with chapter ix, containing a short description of the northern Indians, their country, manufactures, and customs. The gratification of a liberal curiosity respecting such objects is indeed the main benefit resulting from Mr. H.'s toilsome and dangerous undertaking."

As a pioneering anthropologist and naturalist, Hearne would be recognized down the decades without much argument. Early in the twentieth century, the fur-trade historian J.B. Tyrrell would introduce a new edition of *A Journey to the Northern Ocean*, noting that he considered the work invaluable "not so much because of its geographical information, but because it is an accurate, sympathetic, and patently truthful record of life among the Chipewyan Indians at that time. Their habits, customs, and general mode of life, however disagreeable or repulsive, are recorded in detail, and the book will consequently always remain a classic in American ethnology."

Without much equivocation, scholars have also accepted that *Journey*'s authoritative descriptions of plant, bird, and animal life make it a landmark volume. Present-day naturalist C. Stuart Houston contends that Hearne was a century ahead of his time in describing the habits of the arctic ground squirrel, the arctic hare, and the ruffed grouse. Hearne was also the first to give recognizable descriptions of the Ross goose, the muskox, and the wood buffalo, and to elucidate the nesting of the white-crowned sparrow. But Richard Glover summed up best when he asserted that Samuel Hearne showed himself "head and shoulders superior to every other North American naturalist who preceded Audubon."

Following the lead of Alexander Dalrymple, a few critics have denigrated Hearne's geography and attacked his navigational skills. But most recognize that given the inadequacy of his equipment, the explorer worked miracles in achieving what he did. Discussion continues over what precise route Hearne followed during his trek with Matonabbee, and also about whether, at the climax of his journey, he dipped his fingers in the Arctic Ocean or viewed it from a hilltop. Yet even the grudging concede that Hearne was the first European to travel overland to the Arctic coast of North America. At the mouth of the Coppermine River, he established a first point along the only Northwest Passage navigable by ships of his own century and the next.

Geographical disputation aside, Samuel Hearne has survived three concerted assaults on his reputation. The first began with David Thompson, that prudish and judgmental cartographer who, while travelling, would insist on reading an English translation of the Bible to French-speaking voyageurs after a long day of paddling. Late in 1784, a fourteen-year-old Thompson had arrived at Fort Churchill to spend several months working under the direction of the worldly Hearne. Decades later, with only a cursory nod in the direction of truth, the accomplished mapmaker would write, "Mr. Hearne was a handsome man of six feet in height, of a ruddy complexion and remarkably well-made, enjoying good health; as soon as the Hudson's Bay Company could do without his services they dismissed him for cowardice."

That last assertion is ludicrous—and worse was to come. Thompson had been a schoolboy in short pants in 1782 when La Pérouse arrived in Hudson Bay. Yet he wrote, as if with eyewitness authority, "The men in the Fort begged of Mr. Hearne to allow them to mow down the French troops with heavy guns loaded with grape shot, which he resolutely refused; and as they approached he ordered the gates to be opened and went out to meet them and surrendered at discretion."

This is fictitious. By the time the French marched on the fort, the three dozen men inside—no soldiers, but mostly labourers, clerks, and tradesmen—well understood that they would need far greater numbers to defend the fort even for a day. And they knew it because the well-experienced Hearne had called them into the courtyard and explained the situation.

Turning to other matters, Thompson noted that a Sunday sermon would customarily be read to the HBC men in the governor's quarters, the only comfortable room at Churchill Fort: "One Sunday after the service, Mr. Jefferson, the reader, and myself staid a few minutes on orders; he [Hearne] then took Voltaire's *Dictionary* and said to us, here is my belief and I have no other." Thompson concludes his word-portrait by airily observing, "In the autumn of 1785 [Hearne] returned to England, became a member of the Bucks Club and in two years was buried."

Hearne did not return to England until 1787. He never joined the Bucks, and he lived until November 1792. The careless hostility of Thompson's word-portrait, not published until 1916, has undermined Thompson's own reputation. In the mid-twentieth century, Richard Glover produced a scintillating essay entitled *The Witness of David Thompson*, in which he observes, "It is quite astonishing to find how much falsehood and prejudice Thompson was able to pack into the page and a half or less that he devotes to Hearne." Glover demonstrated that Thompson was wrong to charge Hearne with cowardice for avoiding a meaningless battle that could only have cost innocent lives, and attributed the geographer's dislike to the fact "that Hearne was a disbeliever with no use for the rather narrow evangelicalism that served Thompson for religion."

Perhaps, in addition, Thompson bore a grudge because Hearne paid him little attention. In *The Present State of Hudson's Bay*, published in 1790, the disgruntled Edward Umfreville depicted the lamentable state of a lonely orphan apprenticed to the HBC:

The Governor is quite indifferent about him. . . . The boy associates with the common men, forms connections with them, and becomes habituated to their customs, which his tender years are not able to guard against. . . . His employment consists in cleaning the Governor's knives and shoes, running on errands for the cook, and cutting down and carrying heavy logs of wood, much beyond his years and strength. In the mean time, no care is taken to inculcate the precepts of religion and virtue in his mind, or even preserve those principles and knowledge he may have brought in the country.

When Thompson arrived in Churchill, Hearne was still grief-stricken and sorrowing over Mary Norton, still struggling with the arbitrariness of human existence. The unsophisticated Thompson registered him only as a godless eccentric who kept a menagerie of wild animals. Later, resenting the recognition accorded Hearne following the posthumous publication of his book, the skilled mapmaker proved unable to transcend his boyhood misconceptions.

THE SECOND ASSAULT on Hearne's reputation developed out of a book by George Back, a midshipman who travelled down the Coppermine River with John Franklin from 1819 to 1822. Back's superior officer, John Richardson, contributed a chapter-length "Digression concerning Hearne's Route," in which he mistakenly asserted that Bishop John Douglas had edited *A Journey to the Northern Ocean*.

In 1951, more than a century later, Richard Glover responded, observing that Hearne's opus "tells one of the greatest of all stories of Canadian exploration, yet it is a book that lies under a cloud." He charges that Richardson's allegations "have thrown a large doubt over both the authenticity of Hearne's text and the accuracy and motives of his statements, and, secondly, they have formed, either in whole or in part, the basis of most subsequent opinions expressed on the *Journey to the Northern Ocean.*"

Glover demonstrates that the bishop had little to do with Hearne's book, and repudiates the claim that the work was revised by anyone except the explorer himself. As evidence, he cites the "author's constant, and rather untidy, habit of using footnotes to append corrections and afterthoughts to a text he was, perhaps, too indolent to rewrite himself."

Certainly, William Wales made suggestions, and possibly added a few inconsequential footnotes. But the internal evidence, including inconsistencies, inaccuracies, and omissions, demonstrates clearly, as Glover notes, that "the book's blemishes and qualities both are Hearne's." At this time, copy editing for consistency was virtually unknown. Certainly, no editor worthy of the name would have allowed "Thelewey-aza-yeth" to appear four times in four different spellings, or failed to integrate numerous crucial footnotes into the text. Glover concludes that *A Journey to the Northern Ocean* was published almost exactly as Hearne wrote it, and pronounces it "one of the classics of Western Canada's past, a mine of information for the anthropologist, naturalist, and historian of the fur trade, let alone any value it may have for the geographer or as one of the great adventure stories of the world."

THE THIRD ASSAULT on Hearne began late in the twentieth century. It grew directly out of the second—specifically, out of a suggestion by George Back. In his journal of the first Franklin expedition, later published as *Arctic Artist*, Back described his own arrival at Bloody Falls and attempted to rename that historic site:

We were now at Massacre Rapid—celebrated in Hearne's voyage for the shocking scene that occurred there—the most interesting part of which I imagine to be unfounded—as one of our guides had accompanied him—said that he [Hearne] was two days march from them at the time of their (the Indians) attacking the Esquimaux. The havoc that was there made was but too clearly verified—from the fractured skulls—and whitened bones of those poor sufferers—which yet remained visible.

A close reading of Back's journal reveals that, initially, only one of nine accompanying natives claimed to have travelled with Hearne fifty years before. This was a man called Humpy, identified as the older brother of the Dene leader Akaitcho. The paragraph above, however, refers to a younger brother, White Capot, who apparently claimed a similar history. How old were these travellers in 1821? The warriors with whom Hearne trekked north along the Coppermine had left behind all women and children. By the time George Back arrived fifty years later, White Capot would have had to be at least sixty-five, while Humpy would be closer to seventy—and this in a world so challenging that people of forty-five or fifty found it difficult to survive.

According to the narrative of John Franklin, yet another Dene, a man named Rabbit's Head, also claimed to have travelled with

The Dene leader Akaitcho as depicted by Robert Hood, one of the Royal Navy men who lost his life while travelling overland with John Franklin. Akaitcho was appalled at the "slow mode of traveling" of the naval party, whose approach contrasted starkly with that of Samuel Hearne. Where Hearne had adapted to the demands of the harsh environment, apprenticing himself to the native peoples, Franklin sought to impose a way of life developed in more forgiving climes—with disastrous results.

Hearne. Obviously, making this assertion increased a guide's status with the credulous Englishmen. The cleverest of the Dene deduced that challenging Hearne's version of events—asserting, for example, that the HBC man had not even witnessed the massacre—would enhance his own prestige still further. Yet even Hearne's earliest surviving field notes put him at Bloody Falls, while Back's claim of discovering skulls has itself been challenged as fictional.

In recent decades, literary theorists have challenged "the truth" of the work of numerous explorers and "winterers." Ian S. MacLaren argues that eighteenth-century editors and publishers did not always associate veracity with facts, and that editorial involvement, and indeed "corruption," was common in both scientific works and travel narratives.

Turning to Hearne's *Journey*, and having taken his cue from George Back, MacLaren analyzes the development, through several drafts, of the narrative of the massacre at Bloody Falls. He notes that Hearne's rough field notes make no mention of the memorable "young girl, about eighteen years of age," who dies at the traveller's feet, "twining and twisting round the spears like an eel," nor of the subsequent death of a half-blind old woman. MacLaren suggests that such details are fabricated, entirely fictional, and that the young woman in particular is drawn from the conventions of the Gothic novel.

Other contemporary scholars start from the premise that Hearne helped to construct contrasting images of the violent Indian and the peaceful Inuit—and that those images are false. In an attempt to exonerate the Dene warriors and to justify their act of aggression, they have argued that the massacre was probably committed in retaliation for some previous attack. Some have suggested that Hearne witnessed no massacre, and contend that, although John Franklin and others later reported seeing evidence, probably they were lying. But why would Franklin lie? He was no friend of Hearne. On the contrary, he would have revelled in declaring that he could discover no evidence of any massacre. Wishful thinking to the contrary, Franklin and his men reported what they saw: bones and broken skulls.

Where Glover argued that Hearne's most important and surprising achievement was the writing of his book, MacLaren suggests that the explorer did not write key sections of *A Journey to the Northern Ocean*. Here, he goes beyond any previous commentator—and here, almost certainly, he goes wrong. MacLaren contends that another writer, some more literate soul, created the massacre scene that has helped inscribe *Journey* as a literary classic. If not John Douglas, then William Wales; if not Wales, then some anonymous third party—anybody but Samuel Hearne. In support of this contention, MacLaren cites the letter the mariner wrote from his deathbed advising his publisher that "anything in reason shall be allowed to the person that prepares the Work for the Press."

He also quotes a historian who warned that Cook's *Third Voyage*, extensively rewritten by John Douglas, can be read as an exercise in hero-making but not as an explorer's account of his experience. Yet even a cursory comparison of Cook's *Voyage* and Hearne's *Journey* explodes the analogy. The first book is coherent, well integrated, highly literate; the latter is a pioneering work of immersion reporting, and crucial because it emerges out of a vanished world. It is also awkward, uneven, and littered with footnotes that howl for integration. The contrast would be incomprehensible, except for one difference: *Voyage* was edited and revised by a well-educated professional; *Journey* was the product of a single idiosyncratic mind.

Those who question the explorer's authorship of the massacre at Bloody Falls have forgotten how Hearne resolved the mystery of the James Knight expedition. As demonstrated in the book *Dead Silence*, Hearne created an unforgettable image of two final survivors, "the most haunting vision of failed discovery in the pageant of Arctic exploration." If this born storyteller could create one memorable fiction, why could he not generate a second? When describing the massacre, Hearne pushed "the truth" beyond what today is regarded as acceptable limits. But he did precisely the same when writing about Knight. And he was toiling more than two centuries ago. Literary conventions and boundaries were less clearly demarcated than they would be even one hundred years later. Not only that, but Hearne was working without models, developing a new genre. The eighteenth century had no shortage of travel writers—tourists with notebooks. But few indeed were the authors who had immersed themselves in a foreign culture and then made literature out of the experience. As a storyteller, Hearne blazed his own trail. If, in retrospect, he appears to have crossed one river too many, surely that is neither surprising nor unforgivable.

OVER THE CENTURIES, Samuel Hearne and *A Journey to the Northern Ocean* have inspired not just analytical but also creative responses. These include profiles in magazines and anthologies, juvenile novels in French and English, a fictionalized first-person account of the trek to the Coppermine, and a 1963 biography, *Samuel Hearne and the Northwest Passage.*

The first to respond creatively, however, was Samuel Taylor Coleridge. That early Romantic poet would call attention to Samuel Hearne's influence on his literary ballad "The Three Graves," the development of which is well documented. In 1797, when reviews of *Journey* were still appearing, Coleridge and William Wordsworth were living as neighbours in northern Somerset, not forty miles from Beaminster. Wordsworth began drafting a ballad about the laying on of a curse. He stalled and turned the work over to Coleridge, who wrote a "humble fragment" published as "The Three Graves."

Later Wordsworth would observe, "I gave him the subject of his *Three Graves*; but he made it too shocking and painful, and not sufficiently sweetened by any healing views. Not being able to dwell on or sanctify natural woes, he took to the supernatural, and hence his *Ancient Mariner* and *Christabel.*"

The supernatural effects that Wordsworth disliked were precisely those inspired by Samuel Hearne. "The Three Graves" dramatizes the unfolding of a curse pronounced by an English widow scorned in love. Two decades after writing it, Coleridge would recall the mariner's influence:

I had been reading Bryan Edwards's account of the effect of the Oby witchcraft on the Negroes in the West Indies, and Hearne's deeply interesting anecdotes of similar workings on the imagination of the Copper Indians (those of my readers who have it in their power will be well repaid for the trouble of referring to those works for the passages alluded to) and I conceived the design of showing that instances of this kind are not peculiar to savage or barbarous tribes, and of illustrating the mode in which the mind is affected in these cases, and the progress and symptoms of the morbid action on the fancy from the beginning.

In *The Road to Xanadu,* a landmark investigation of Coleridge's creative processes, John Livingston Lowes reports that the poet owned a copy of the 1796 Dublin edition of Hearne's *A Journey to the Northern Ocean*: "It contains in Coleridge's hand a long note on pp. 343–45, which gives evidence of the care with which he had read the volume." Hearne's "deeply interesting anecdotes" include the one about Matonabbee's imploring him to lay a curse on an implacable enemy. Hearne drew an evocative picture featuring two figures, a fatal stabbing, and a watching eye. Matonabbee's enemy, a vigorous warrior, no sooner learned of the curse than he wasted away and died.

In developing "The Three Graves," Coleridge changed the setting and characters, but developed the supernatural theme along identical lines: an aggrieved party lays a curse, and the intended victims, learning of it, weaken and die for no discernible reason. As Coleridge attested, the psychology of the poem—and also, in his view, its chief merit—owed much to Samuel Hearne.

Still more intriguing is the genesis of *The Rime of the Ancient Mariner*. On November 13, 1797, during a protracted hike in northern Somerset with Wordsworth and his sister, Dorothy, Coleridge suggested composing a literary ballad that the poets could then sell to defray expenses. That night, Wordsworth withdrew from the project—although later he would claim several contributions.

In truth, that November ramble provided "little more than the setting of a match to a fire already laid," as Lowes observes. Several determining factors in the poem's action fell into place, but the skeleton ship and the narrator, whom Coleridge originally called "the Old Navigator," were already at work in the poet's mind: "A tentative Navigator in Coleridge's brain is feeling about for a story to fit him."

Lowes devotes pages to tracing the literary antecedents of that narrator. He demonstrates that the Ancient Mariner is "an archetypal figure"—a primordial character who surfaces repeatedly, in various guises, down through the ages.

A question then arises: Which real-life individual activated this Eternal Wanderer in the unconscious mind of the gifted Coleridge? Who caused it to become "numinous" or gravitational, and to attract secondary material in a creative process that lasted years? Who inspired *The Rime of the Ancient Mariner*?

Lowes advances no theories, but academics have since proposed a couple of candidates. One such candidate is Fletcher Christian, the

This 1875 depiction of the Ancient Mariner by Gustave Doré captures the
transcendent, archetypal nature of the figure. Like Hearne, Doré
grew up in a town (Strasbourg) awash in history; like Hearne,
he lost his engineer-father at an early age.

gentleman first officer who in 1789 led the mutiny on HMS *Bounty*. According to this theory, Christian did not die on Pitcairn Island as history declares, but instead returned as a fugitive to England. There, he secretly related his sensational story to William Wordsworth, who subsequently shared the tale with Coleridge—although neither poet ever thought to mention it. More serious scholars have ridiculed this thesis as preposterous.

The second candidate, less easily dismissed, is William Wales— Hearne's best friend. Wales sailed with Captain James Cook on his second great voyage, and Coleridge, in creating his masterpiece, certainly drew on that adventure for colour and detail, just as he borrowed a description of the aurora borealis from *A Journey to the Northern Ocean*. But Coleridge perceived Wales as "a man of uncommonly clear head," while others described the schoolmaster as "a good man, of plain simple manners, with a large heavy person and benign countenance." In composite, Wales emerges as an avuncular, goodnatured, clear-headed man, happily married, comfortably situated— not an outsider who puts one in mind of the Ancient Mariner.

Another individual, however, a loner who settled into London in the late 1780s, bears an uncanny psychological resemblance to that archetypal figure. In *His Brother's Keeper: A Psychobiography of Samuel Taylor Coleridge*, author Stephen M. Weissman argues that the Ancient Mariner's sense of guilt and punishment are wildly disproportionate to his symbolic crime—killing an albatross—and that the narrator can best be understood as suffering from "survivor guilt." Haunted by some harrowing ordeal, the Old Navigator compulsively tells his tale to anyone who will listen.

Consider Samuel Hearne in 1791: a born storyteller, a sometime navigator haunted by horrific memories and guilt feelings, Hearne was best friends with Wales at precisely the time when Coleridge was the foremost student at Christ's Hospital. Hearne's friendship with Wales, Coleridge's published citation, the distinctive psychology of the mariner figure—all the evidence points in the same direction.

Who launched Samuel Taylor Coleridge on a literary adventure that would culminate in the greatest poem he ever completed, sparking an archetypal blaze in the poet's unconscious mind? Was it the profoundly familiar William Wales? Or was it Samuel Hearne, that tormented mariner, who turned up at the Blue Coat School as a visitor from a distant world, a wanderer, strangely driven, telling tales of horror and the supernatural?

In writing "The Three Graves," Coleridge took one of Hearne's anecdotes and transposed it into a different key. In creating the Ancient Mariner, he worked the same transformative magic on the old navigator himself. Anybody seeking the original mariner should look to Samuel Hearne.

RICHARD GLOVER observes that, in his maturity, Hearne "gives hints of varied reading, and his clear intelligence expressed itself in very clear, natural English, enlivened with a gentle irony that most professional writers might envy." He cites the way Hearne demolishes an unscrupulous author's fanciful description of beavers by observing that little remains to be added "beside a vocabulary of their language, a code of their laws and a sketch of their religion."

More evidence that Hearne became a voracious reader surfaces in the footnote-eulogy he devoted to Mary Norton, in which he communicated that she had been his beloved wife by quoting poetry. The notion that Hearne was semiliterate derives from the 1797 obituary that speaks of his boyhood distaste for studying. This was based on information provided by someone who knew Hearne as a child but who did not begin to appreciate his adult accomplishments.

The informant did not witness Hearne's intellectual evolution and lacked the experience or wisdom to imagine it. Awakening as a midshipman to the great wide world, Hearne set about educating himself with a passion. By the time he arrived back at Prince of Wales Fort after his epic trek, Andrew Graham would write of him as "Mr. Samuel Hearne, a young gentleman of a good education."

As a stylist, obviously, Hearne does not compare with James Boswell, his privileged contemporary. Even so, with *A Journey to the Northern Ocean*, the first book about the hinterland written for a wide audience, he put northwestern North America on the literary map. To judge his literacy by his rough field notes and journals, intended for nobody but himself and his Company bosses, is patently unfair. Even great stylists revise and revise and revise again. Often, their original notes resemble scribblings.

In 1970, in an introduction to yet another edition of Hearne's book, historian Leslie H. Neatby wrote, "There is no sign in Hearne's finished work of the supposed deficiencies of his early education. His style is clear, modest and has that blend of simplicity with a touch of dignity and elegance which is the hallmark of the eighteenth-century author." His lucid narrative, applauded by contemporaries, has qualities "which preserve it as a classic in our own time." These derive from the author's personality: "Hearne was observant, inquisitive, amiable and void of prejudice. Though representing a culture that was advanced and still acutely class-conscious, he moves among the Indians as a sympathetic equal. Nothing repels him except cruelty and the oppression of the weak."

But what of truth? Did Samuel Hearne tell the truth?

As a naturalist, he displayed what one scholar rightly characterized as a "scrupulous concern for accuracy." In the eighteenth century, an age of generalists, such a concern could coexist comfortably with an active literary imagination. In *Enduring Dreams: An Exploration of Arctic Landscape*, critic John Moss argues that any story is shaped by the desires of the author, the imperatives of his sponsors, and the conventions of narrative. Samuel Hearne wrote his field notes for himself and the Hudson's Bay Company. Later, addressing a wider readership, he added anecdotes, clarifications, and detailed descriptions of plants, animals, native culture and the landscape. The result, Moss writes, is one of the great works of Arctic literature, "a work of imagination which, in many respects, overshadows the author's achievements as an explorer, naturalist, anthropologist, and agent of commercial enterprise."

Historian Daniel Francis notes that "writers have always leavened their facts with generous portions of dramatic license, working and reworking material, sometimes employing the devices of fiction not to convey information, but to share experience with readers." In recreating the massacre at Bloody Falls, one of the most famous incidents in the history of northern exploration, Hearne was not the first author to shape and polish his raw material. He was striving to create an effect—something akin to what he experienced in reality. He was seeking to communicate a truth beyond facts, and perhaps went beyond facts to communicate it.

A Journey to the Northern Ocean has survived over two hundred years. Two centuries from now, when most of today's award-winning novels have been consigned to the dustbin of literary history, readers will still be debating this classic work. They will still be arguing about Samuel Hearne, who was recognized as a natural storyteller by such literate contemporaries as William Wales and the comte de La Pérouse.

The ultimate testimonial is that of Samuel Taylor Coleridge. In 1791, the young poet could only listen, rapt and riveted, as the strange visitor to his school—tall, blue-eyed, otherworldly—spoke of an odyssey that had culminated in a massacre. Coleridge would forget details, recalling some of them only later, when he perused the published *Journey*. But the legacy went beyond specifics. At some level, when he encountered Hearne, Coleridge registered the spell-binding visitor as an Eternal Wanderer. And when, six years later, having read and digested countless contributory works of literature, he began to write *The Rime of the Ancient Mariner,* the poet gave expression to an archetypal figure called forth by the haunted stranger.

Coleridge gave voice to an Old Navigator awakened by Samuel Hearne.

Epilogue

TRACKING THE MARINER

In August 2001, I travelled north to explore Prince of Wales Fort and Sloop's Cove, where over two centuries before, Samuel Hearne had etched his name in a large, flat rock. I ended up pounding across the Churchill River in a sixteen-foot motorboat with Len McPherson, a Swampy Cree man in his mid-twenties who came originally from York Factory. He carried a twelve-gauge shotgun and warned me to keep an eye out for polar bears. We had roared out of the harbour at sunrise because this late in the year, the end of August, the wind would rise steadily through the morning, creating waves that by noon would capsize a small boat.

I had flown north from Winnipeg after spending several days in the Hudson's Bay Company archives. No road runs north as far as Churchill. I had originally hoped to ride the long, slow train that winds through the sparsely wooded countryside, but time did not permit. Come September, the water turned rough and risky, and tour operators with large boats stopped crossing the river to the fort and the cove. If I hadn't arrived in late August, I would have had to wait until the following spring.

Countless writers have created superb biographies and narrative non-fictions without visiting key locations, but I like to see a primary locale—to feel it, breathe it, smell it. Samuel Hearne had been based in Churchill for two decades, and that put the site at the top of my list.

Since arriving a few days before, I had talked with Parks Canada people and watched hard-to-find videos in an amphitheatre. At the public library, I had deposited an inscribed copy of my book about explorer John Rae, who had passed this way in the nineteenth century.

I had taken photos of Hearne Street, which is not noticeably different from several other dusty streets in the almost treeless town. At the controversially named Eskimo Museum, I had bought an Inuit carving and examined a cannon, one of the original forty-two mounted at Prince of Wales Fort. Over 260 years old, it weighed 3,710 pounds and could once have delivered a direct hit at a distance of 1,000 yards—at least, theoretically.

Acting out of necessity and against the advice of locals, who warned that the polar bears had begun their annual invasion, I had hiked a couple of miles along a rocky path to Cape Merry—wary, watchful miles—dubiously armed with a walking stick. At the cape, a battery of guns still points across the Churchill River. Twenty or thirty metres beyond the guns, I found an underground shelter and a sign warning, "This powder magazine is structurally unsafe. It is dangerous to enter or climb on top of it."

I stood in the salty breeze, as Hearne must have done, listening to the wheeling gulls and staring across the choppy, slate grey river to Prince of Wales Fort. The previous day, I had happily joined a whale-watching tour that called in there. I had enjoying sitting in the big-windowed motorboat, its dual engines silent, as we bobbed above a school of white whales—belugas—all of whom, judging from the shrieks and squawks transmitted by an underwater microphone, delighted in communicating.

The high outer walls of Prince of Wales Fort have been damaged by repeated freezing and thawing, yet they look much as they did in the late 1770s, when Hearne supervised the northern fur trade for the Hudson's Bay Company. Parks Canada warden Ray Girardin led the way through the wooden front gate. Beyond it we found a ruin of crumbling stone walls, although a visitor could still climb onto the ramparts and examine the rusting cannons. From the ramparts, the layout of the fort remains visible in outline: here the governor's quarters, there the masonry shop, over there a fireplace shared by baker and blacksmith.

Before anybody had been allowed to debark from the boat, a second ranger had used a three-wheeled all-terrain vehicle to scout for polar bears. In the centuries since Hearne, the bears have taken seasonal control of Eskimo Point, on which the fort stands. While we rambled around the ruins, this second ranger—McPherson, carrying his twelve-gauge shotgun—kept watch and patrolled. We exchanged friendly words, but I didn't expect to see him again.

Having visited the fort, I began seeking a way to reach Sloop's Cove, where on July 1, 1767, Samuel Hearne had chiselled his name. Since then, because of isostatic rebound, the rising of land after the passing of a glacier, the cove had become a rocky meadow, but it remained three miles up the Churchill River on the north side, the same side as the fort. In the present-day town, I had to find someone willing to take me across the river despite the winds. I asked around in restaurants and hotels. Two best bets came to nothing.

Walking the dusty streets, increasingly worried, I ran into Girardin, the park warden who had shown me around the fort. He led me to McPherson, who owned a motorboat. As a government employee, McPherson could do nothing. As a private citizen, he would swing past my hotel next morning in his half-ton. To beat the wind and the waves, we would leave at 5:30 a.m.

Next morning, not surprisingly, I found nobody on duty in the hotel lobby. Outside remained dark and I saw no sign of a truck. From a shelf of travel books, I plucked a guide called *North Canada*. Lately I had been thinking about visiting the Northwest Territories—specifically, Bloody Falls. I was feeling the need to make a gesture honouring Samuel Hearne, and was toying with the idea of erecting a memorial plaque, as I had done once before to honour John Rae.

But the area around Bloody Falls has been turned into a historic park. The site is well known, accessible—by northern standards, practically overrun. Every summer, adventure travellers paddle down the Coppermine River; workers and tourists fly into the town of Kugluktuk (Coppermine) at the river mouth and hike out to the site. Bloody Falls had been overdone. And in Churchill, this town of sixteen thousand, I had not only seen plaques commemorating Hearne, but had strolled along a street that bore his name.

I flipped to a potted history of the north. The author cited Hearne as one of two men (the other being Alexander Mackenzie) who stood out from the crowd of early explorers, suggesting that these two "wrote the book for future fur-trading exploration and at the same time mapped completely uncharted territory." He described Hearne as "a natural explorer: resourceful, mild mannered, a teetotaler, a self-taught artist, a lover of birds and animals and, above all, a zealous hiker."

In summarizing Hearne's trek with Matonabbee, the writer makes a few small errors. But then he writes, "Hearne's little party reached the banks of the Coppermine River on July 13, 1771, where, after a minor altercation (Hearne called it a massacre) with a local Inuit group, his party followed the river down to the Arctic Ocean."

Little party? Minor altercation? The author adds of Hearne, "He had been retired from his position as head of the Hudson Bay Company in Canada in 1782, for being too timid in the face of overwhelming odds (the French forced him to surrender Fort Prince of Wales when a 74-gun battleship blew the fort to bits and took Hearne prisoner)."

In that single sentence, I counted four errors. Hearne was never the head of the H B C in Canada; he was not retired, he resigned; he did so not in 1782 but five years later; finally, he was not timid but wise and humane as well as courageous. The fort had been indefensible. And during the Seven Years War, Hearne had spent six years sailing and fighting with the Royal Navy—over half a decade that attested to his bravery, utterly forgotten.

The writer of the travel guide was not alone in his lack of awareness. Over the centuries, North American scholars—both fur-trade historians and English professors—have written much about Hearne's remarkable trek to the Arctic Ocean. They have analyzed his relationship with Matonabbee, discussed his attitudes toward women, debated the identity of particular lakes he visited—but always in the context of his northern adventuring. They have treated his sailing with the Royal Navy in summaries, footnotes, and cursory asides, and likewise his other voyaging, his whaling, and his piloting of an overcrowded sloop across the Atlantic to Stromness.

Out front of the motel, headlights pierced the darkness: Len McPherson in his half-ton truck. Down at the dock, as daylight broke, I helped him drag the boat into the water, then climbed into it. We puttered out of the harbour past giant storage containers, but then came open water, and McPherson cranked the engine. Soon we were slapping across the Churchill River, with the sun rising and Prince of Wales Fort shining in the middle distance. That's when it came to me, there in mid-river, with the cold wind blowing: instead of visiting

Bloody Falls, I might better serve my book, and Hearne himself, by travelling to London, Portsmouth, and Beaminster.

McPherson ran the boat onto a sandy beach near Sloop's Cove. He insisted on going ashore first, and disappeared over a hill carrying his twelve-gauge shotgun. Someone had reported seeing polar bears in the vicinity, and he'd brought along the gun to scare them off. Discovering none, he quickly returned. Together, we picked our way along a rocky path. We climbed a rise and suddenly, amazingly, there it was: Hearne's Rock. Two hundred and thirty-four years before, at age twenty-two, Samuel Hearne had chiselled twelve-inch letters into the black stone: "Sl Hearne, July ye 1 1767."

Other men had scratched their names into that rock, some of them preceding Hearne. But none of the other etchings showed anything like the same resolve to engrave letters that would endure. Hearne had come to the New World determined to make a mark—and here it was, the first indication. As I traced those letters with my fingers, I wondered, did the Old World realize?

Len McPherson, a Swampy Cree man who grew up near York Factory, scouted around for polar bears before letting a visitor come ashore at Sloop's Cove. Had he spotted any of the lumbering mammals, he would have fired his twelve-gauge shotgun into the air to scare them off.

England has an absolute passion for its heroes. Perhaps in Portsmouth or Beaminster, people had erected a statue of Samuel Hearne. Given the magnitude of his achievement, not only as explorer but as naturalist and author, such a monument would be no more than appropriate. I would have to investigate further. But I suspected that, if I wished to make a real-world gesture on Hearne's behalf, I was moving in the right direction.

Later that morning, as we downed pancakes at a favourite breakfast site called Gypsy's Bakery, the boat safely stowed, Len McPherson said, "As a writer, you must do a lot of travelling."

"Not enough," I said. "But I'm thinking of England."

EXCEPT FOR landmarks such as Westminster Abbey, St. Paul's Cathedral, and the Tower of London, and tourist attractions such as the houses of Samuel Johnson and William Hogarth, Samuel Hearne's London has vanished. The evening I arrived, I walked to Leigh Street, not far from my hotel, hoping that I might discover the building in which the ailing sailor had lived out his final days. The street looked far too new, and yet too old to have been rebuilt after the Second World War. In a nearby pub, I rousted a local who confirmed that the area had been developed early in the nineteenth century, decades after Hearne had gone to his grave. Clearly, this Leigh Street, the only one in London, was not the roadway I sought.

Fenchurch Street proved equally disheartening—all brisk and shiny and uptown bustle. Of the Hudson's Bay Company headquarters, where Hearne had spent hours sifting journals and records, not a trace remains. And Christ's Hospital, the Blue Coat School on Newgate Street in which Hearne had riveted the attention of Samuel Taylor Coleridge, is today represented only by a plaque on a stone wall.

Fortunately, much that has vanished from the streets endures in the libraries and museums. In the British Library, I spent days perusing documents: the so-called Stowe manuscript, neatly handwritten on unlined, foolscap-size paper; the publishing contract with Andrew Strahan, swirling with legalese and demonstrating that Hearne himself never received a penny for his book, payment being deferred until three months after publication, by which time the mariner was three years dead; and, finally, the last letter Hearne wrote, not incidentally to Strahan, on October 3, 1792, from Nº 8 Leigh Street, Red Lion Square—a missive he neatly folded, sealed with red wax, and dispatched by hand.

The Museum of London proved another treasure house. It dramatizes the devastation of the Great Fire of 1666 and the subsequent development of the city as, between 1700 and 1800, the population grew from 490,000 to 950,000. The museum also evokes the waterfront Hearne knew, where 1,800 ships would sometimes be forced to moor in space for 500, and where several thousand watermen earned their living transporting passengers at fixed rates. A small exhibit on the New River Company, which in the seventeenth century had begun drawing water from the Islington Reservoir, shows how workers joined wooden water pipes, sharpening one end of each like a pencil and inserting it into the next.

In the museum bookshop, I discovered a volume of old maps of London. Having flipped to one depicting the city of the late eighteenth

Red Lion Square remains an oasis of green in central London. Samuel Hearne lived at Nº 8 Leigh Street, now called Dane Street, which runs into this square at the left.

century, I located Red Lion Square—and then could scarcely believe my eyes: running directly out of that square, clearly marked, was Leigh Street—the street in which Hearne had lived his last days. I took out my contemporary map and, comparing, realized what had happened: Hearne's Leigh Street had been renamed Dane Street.

Late that afternoon, I visited Red Lion Square—a small oasis of green, now encircled by development, in which the plant-and-greenery-loving Hearne would have spent many hours. Around the square, no early buildings remain standing. Reconstruction following the Second World War has changed not just street names but also the numbering. However, on the wall of a brick building on the corner of Dane Street, a memorial plaque recalls the clockmaker John Harrison, "who lived and died in a house on this site."

Harrison, the relentless genius who solved the problem of calculating longitude, died in 1776. Eleven years later, Hearne moved into the same street, and possibly into the same house, number eight on the corner. Eventually, he too died in Red Lion Square. I found myself thinking, surely Samuel Hearne, the first European to visit the Arctic coast of North America and the author of a classic work of exploration literature, deserves as much as Harrison to be remembered with a plaque?

To VISIT Beaminster is to travel backward in time to the eighteenth century. This is a town with two hundred "listed," or protected, buildings, some dating from the fourteenth century. Even in the 1800s, houses were built along ancient, winding streets, originally footpaths that followed streams, using traditional methods and the honey-coloured ham-stone available in the area. Block for block, building for building, Beaminster is one of the oldest towns in England.

The afternoon I arrived, having driven for the better part of a day, I parked in a central square, which Hearne once knew as "the Fore Place," and stood soaking up the atmosphere, ignoring the occasional pedestrian and vehicle. An attractive pub dominated the square from one corner, and I decided that after I checked into my bed and breakfast, I would eat at Pickwick's Inn. Now, with darkness falling, I ventured a preliminary stroll down the narrow street that wound past

TOP *The graveyard at Netherbury memorializes numerous Hearns and Hearnes.*

ABOVE *As a boy, Hearne would have attended church services in the Congregational Chapel; today, the building houses the Beaminster Museum.*

St. Mary's Church. Everywhere I looked, I saw old stone houses—clearly sixteenth- and seventeenth-century, some of them. No question about it, I realized: Samuel Hearne would still recognize this place.

During the next few days, I explored not only the town itself, but relevant locations nearby: in Mosterton, the Admiral Hood Inn; in Dorchester, the public records office; in Netherbury, the graveyard containing the remains of numerous Hearns and Hearnes. I drove through Bridport to Lyme Regis, where an antiquarian bookseller sold me a hard-to-find copy of *A History of Beaminster* by Marie de G. Eedle.

To the Beaminster Museum, located in a stone building that Samuel Hearne would have known as the Congregational Chapel, spiritual home of dissenters and non-comformists, I had donated a facsimile edition of *A Journey to the Northern Ocean*, complete with illustrations and fold-out maps. I had pasted a bookplate inside the work, highlighting Hearne's connection with Beaminster and encapsulating his remarkable story—his naval service, his extraordinary trek, his authorship of an exploration classic.

Obviously, I was hoping that this would engender local interest in the forgotten mariner. I had settled on making this gesture while still in Canada, after I telephoned the museum and spoke with the woman who had spearheaded its founding, the above-mentioned Eedle. I asked her if she had ever heard of Samuel Hearne. She recognized the surname, quite common around Beaminster, but admitted to drawing a blank. In her 1984 history, Eedle had not mentioned Hearne. But after our initial telephone conversation, I learned when I visited, she had turned up a two-page entry on him in a 1914 book by Richard Hine.

That afternoon in the local library, I laid hands on a copy of *The History of Beaminster* and discovered, to my intense disappointment, that the salient entry consisted of a rehashing of the 1797 profile of Hearne that had appeared in *The European Magazine and London Review*—a document well known to scholars.

As I examined Hine's book, however, I discovered its particular merits. Where Eedle had crafted her history into a readable narrative for a broad general audience, Hine's book—which later, at the library in Portsmouth, I would peruse at leisure—proved more a source work, a tome bristling with facts and figures that would serve family, local, or specialist historians . . . or itinerant storytellers like myself.

TOP *For centuries, this establishment—currently known as "Pickwick's Inn"—served as the main coaching house for Beaminster. When Samuel Hearne left to join the Royal Navy, he boarded the stagecoach out front.*

ABOVE *Inside the former coach house, beset by strong drink, a visitor might find himself regretting that Beaminster has forgotten the remarkable boy who grew up here—the boy who, after serving in the Royal Navy, would not only become the first European to reach the Arctic coast of North America, but would write a classic work about that adventure, and go on to inspire one of the greatest poems in the English language.*

Together with Eedle's history, Hine's book would provide a wealth of useful information.

But I did not anticipate that on my final evening in Beaminster it would spark a Hearne-related epiphany. When I retreated out of the drizzle into Pickwick's Inn, I anticipated no discoveries, no revelations. With the fire crackling and rain pattering at the window, I sat quaffing and scribbling notes. After polishing off a second pint of dark ale, I headed upstairs to the men's room. In my journal, I had been complaining about scholars of English literature—specifically, that they had failed to recognize Hearne as a literary pioneer, an author who, while advancing no claims as a stylist, had nevertheless produced one of the earliest examples of "immersion reporting" or creative non-fiction in literature.

Upstairs at Pickwick's Inn, despite these roiling thoughts, I recalled that I might not pass this way again and took a moment to snoop. A large room at the front, dim-lit and deserted, obviously functioned on busier nights as the inn's main dining room. Like the pub below, it was decorated with prints of red-coated fox hunters riding horses, blowing horns, and hollering at dogs. For a moment I stared out the front window at the Fore Place, imagining how the square had looked to young Hearne.

As I started back down the stairs, I noticed a piece of paper tacked to the wall of the stairwell and stopped to read. The photocopied text presented snatches of history of Pickwick's Inn, originally called the King's Arms. From the format and typeface, I recognized them as coming from *The History of Beaminster*. I stopped scanning and, with growing excitement, began to read carefully.

The establishment in which I stood had existed since the 1600s. Over the centuries, it had served not only as Beaminster's principal inn, but as the town's chief hostelry and coaching house. In the mid-eighteenth century, anybody travelling out of this village would take the stagecoach from here. This was it, I realized—the place from which Samuel Hearne had departed to join the Royal Navy. This was the coaching house from which, in 1757, the twelve-year-old boy had caught the stage to Dorchester, Portsmouth, and the world beyond.

Back downstairs, gazing around with a new vision, I remembered visiting the nearby Admiral Hood, a public house dedicated to the memory of a ferocious old sailor. Looking around Pickwick's, I wondered whether Samuel Hearne might one day be similarly celebrated in this establishment. As I pulled on my coat, I imagined the perfect future, the pub transformed—no more fox hunters, no more hounds. The walls would be adorned with pictures of sailing ships and the Arctic, with Hearne's maps and sketches, and with portraits of Matonabbee, Wales, and Coleridge. Dominating all else, positioned above the fireplace, would hang the sole surviving likeness of Samuel Hearne, the original Ancient Mariner.

Beaminster might be a history-oriented town, I reflected, moving toward the door, but its oldest, most significant pub showed no sense of history. Pickwick's Inn, indeed. The name had prompted me to ask historian Marie Eedle whether the author of *The Pickwick Papers* had ever lived in Beaminster. Embarrassed, she admitted to having determined that the answer was no: Charles Dickens had never so much as visited.

At the front door, taking one last look around, I thought, this place should be called the Samuel Hearne. But no: here in England, Hearne's name lacked resonance. I would have to do better.

From behind the bar, the owner of the pub said, "Everything all right?"

That's when it came to me: "The Ancient Mariner!"

The pub owner regarded me warily: was this chap daft?

"Great name for a former coach house." I gave him a cheery thumbs-up, adjusted my rain hood, and stepped into the night.

ILLUSTRATION CREDITS

Images not otherwise credited are taken from the author's or other private collections.

ORIGINAL MAPS BY DAWN HUCK:
Pages 8, 74, 80, 132, 192

COURTESY OF THE HUDSON'S BAY COMPANY ARCHIVE/
MANITOBA PROVINCIAL ARCHIVES:
Pages v, 61, 83, 91, 99, 119, 124, 136, 161, 169, 173, 188, 189, 200, 205, 209, 219, 246, 254, 280, 287

COURTESY OF THE NATIONAL ARCHIVES OF CANADA:
Pages 103 (Charles William Jefferys/National Archives of Canada/ C-070250), 107 (Peter Rindisbacher/National Archives of Canada/ C-1917), 155 (George Back/National Archives of Canada/ C-102852)

PHOTOS BY KEN MCGOOGAN:
Pages 10, 15, 22, 87, 227, 301, 305, 307

PHOTOS BY PAUL VANPEENEN:
Pages 157, 160

PHOTO BY JAY ZVOLANEK:
Page 143

BIBLIOGRAPHY

Abel, Kerry. *Drum Songs: Glimpses of Dene History.* Montreal and Kingston, Ont.: McGill-Queen's University Press, 1993.

Analytical Review. 1796, Pt. 1.

Ashton, Rosemary. *The Life of Samuel Taylor Coleridge: A Critical Biography.* Oxford: Blackwell, 1996.

Beattie, Owen, and John Geiger. *Dead Silence: The Greatest Mystery in Arctic Discovery.* Toronto: Viking, 1993.

Belyea, Barbara, ed. *A Year Inland: The Journal of a Hudson's Bay Company Winterer.* Waterloo: Wilfrid Laurier University Press, 2000.

Berton, Pierre. *The Arctic Grail: The Quest for the North West Passage and the North Pole, 1818–1909.* Toronto: McClelland & Stewart, 1988.

———. "Samuel Hearne's Epic Trek." In *My Country: The Remarkable Past.* Toronto: McClelland & Stewart, 1976.

Binnema, Theodore, Gehrard J. Ens, and R.C. MacLeod, eds. *From Rupert's Land to Canada: Essays in Honour of John E. Foster.* Edmonton: University of Alberta Press, 2001.

Blanchet, Guy H. "Thelewey-aza-yeth." *The Beaver* (September 1949).

Boswell, James. *The Life of Samuel Johnson.* Hertfordshire, UK: Wordsworth Editions, 1999.

Bowen, Frank C. *Men of the Wooden Walls.* London: Staples, 1952.

Brand, M.J. "Samuel Hearne and the Massacre at Bloody Falls." *The Polar Record*, 28, no. 166 (July 1992).

Brewer, John. *The Pleasures of the Imagination: English Culture in the Eighteenth Century.* New York: Farrar Straus Giroux, 1997.

Brody, Hugh. *Living Arctic: Hunters of the Canadian North.* Vancouver: Douglas & McIntyre, 1987.

313

Carter, Sarah. *Aboriginal People and Colonizers of Western Canada to 1900.* Toronto: University of Toronto Press, 1999.

Charnock, John. *Biographia Navalis; or, Impartial Memoirs of the Lives and Characters of Officers of the Navy of Great Britain.* London: R. Faulder, 1798.

Chatteron, E. Keble. *The Mercantile Marine.* Boston: Little Brown, 1923.

Clarke, John. *The Life and Times of George III.* London: Weidenfeld & Nicolson, 1972.

Coleridge, Samuel Taylor. *The Complete Poems.* Ed. William Keach. London: Penguin, 1997.

Coutts, Robert. *On the Edge of a Frozen Sea: Prince of Wales' Fort, York Factory and the Fur Trade of Western Hudson Bay.* Ottawa: Parks Canada, 1997.

Cranston, Maurice. *The Noble Savage: Jean-Jacques Rousseau, 1754–1762.* Chicago: University of Chicago Press, 1991.

Critical Review. 1797.

Csonka, Y. "Samuel Hearne and Indian-Inuit hostility." *The Polar Record,* 29, no. 169 (April 1993).

Davis, Richard C., ed. *Lobsticks and Stone Cairns: Human Landmarks in the Arctic.* Calgary, Alta.: University of Calgary Press, 1996.

Defoe, Daniel. *A Tour Through the Whole Island of Great Britain.* Harmondsworth, UK: Penguin, abridged 1971; first published 1724–26.

———. *Robinson Crusoe.* London: Oxford, 1998. First published London: William Taylor, 1719.

Eedle, Marie de G. *A History of Beaminster.* Chichester, UK: Phillimore, 1984.

Ellingson, Ter. *The Myth of the Noble Savage.* Berkeley: University of California Press, 2001.

Francis, Daniel, ed. *Imagining Ourselves: Classics of Canadian Non-Fiction.* Vancouver: Arsenal Pulp Press, 1994.

Franklin, John. *Narrative of a Journey to the Shores of the Polar Sea, in the Years 1819, 20, 21, and 22. . . .* London: John Murray, 1823.

Fraser, Antonia. *Kings and Queens of England.* London: Cassell, 1998. First published London: Weidenfield & Nicolson, 1975.

French, Gerald. *The Martyrdom of Admiral Byng.* Glasgow: MacLellan, 1961.

Fuller, W.A. "Samuel Hearne's Track: Some Obscurities Clarified." *Arctic,* 52 (September 1999).

Fumeleau, Rene. *Denendeh: A Dene Celebration.* Yellowknife, NWT: Dene Nation, 1984.

Gates, William G. *Portsmouth in the Past.* Portsmouth: S.R. Publishers, 1926.

Gentleman's Magazine. 1796.

Glover, Richard. "Cumberland House." *The Beaver* (December 1951).

———. "A Note on John Richardson's 'Digression Concerning Hearne's Route.'" *Canadian Historical Review* (September 1951).

———. "La Pérouse on Hudson Bay." *The Beaver* (March 1951).

———. "The Witness of David Thompson." *Canadian Historical Review,* 31 (1950).

Hanson, Lawrence. *The Life of Samuel Taylor Coleridge: The Early Years.* New York: Russell & Russell, 1962.

Harrison, Keith. "Samuel Hearne, Matonabbee, and the 'Esquimaux Girl': Cultural Subjects, Cultural Objects." *Canadian Review of Comparative Literature,* 22, nos. 3–4 (1995).

Hayes, Derek. *First Crossing: Alexander Mackenzie, His Expedition across North America, and the Opening of the Continent.* Vancouver: Douglas & McIntyre, 2001.

Hearne, Samuel. *Cumberland House and Hudson House Journals, 1775–1782.* Edited by E.E. Rich. London: Hudson's Bay Record Society, 1951.

———. *A Journey from Prince of Wales's Fort in Hudson's Bay to the Northern Ocean, 1769, 1770, 1771, 1772.* Edited with an introduction by Richard Glover. Toronto: Macmillan, 1958. First published London: Strahan and Cadell, 1795.

Hearne, Samuel, and Philip Turnor. *Journals of Samuel Hearne and Philip Turnor.* Toronto: Champlain Society, 1934.

Henday, Anthony. *A Year Inland: The Journal of a Hudson's Bay Company Winterer.* Edited by Barbara Belyea. Waterloo, Ont.: Wilfrid Laurier University Press, 2000.

Hill, John Spencer. *A Coleridge Companion: An Introduction to the Major Poems and the Biographia Literaria.* London: Macmillan, 1983.

Hine, Richard. *The History of Beaminster.* UK, 1914.

Holmes, Richard. *Coleridge: Early Visions.* Hammondsworth, UK: Viking Penguin, 1989.

Home, Gordon. *Old London Bridge.* London: Bodley Head, 1931.

Hood, Dorothy. *The Admirals Hood.* London: Hutchinson, 1935.

Hopwood, Victor. "Explorers by Land to 1867." In *Literary History of Canada,* 2nd ed., Vol. 1. Edited by Carl F. Klinck. Toronto: University of Toronto Press, 1965.

Houston, C. Stuart, ed. *Arctic Artist: The Journal and Painting of George Back, Midshipman with Franklin, 1819–1822*. Commentary by I.S. MacLaren. Montreal and Kingston, Ont.: McGill-Queen's University Press, 1994.

———. "Samuel Hearne." *Picoides* (Fall 1989).

Huck, Barbara. *Exploring the Fur Trade Routes of North America*. Winnipeg, Man.: Heartland, 1999.

Inglis, Alex. *Northern Vagabond: The Life and Career of J.B. Tyrrell—The Man Who Conquered the Canadian North*. Toronto: McClelland & Stewart, 1978.

Innis, Harold A. *The Fur Trade in Canada*, revised edition. Toronto: University of Toronto Press, 1956.

Inwood, Stephen. *A History of London*. New York: Carroll & Graf, 1998.

Ireland, Bernard. *Naval Warfare in the Age of Sail: War at Sea 1756–1815*. New York: HarperCollins, 2000.

King, J.C.H. *First Peoples, First Contacts: Native Peoples of North America*. London: British Museums Press, 1999.

Lamb, Charles. "Recollections of Christ's Hospital." In *The Complete Works and Letters of Charles Lamb*. New York: Random House, 1935.

Lambert, Andrew. *War at Sea in the Age of Sail: 1650–1850*. London: Cassell, 2000.

Lambert, Richard S. *North for Adventure: How Sam Hearne Crossed the Arctic Desert*. Toronto: McClelland & Stewart, 1952.

La Pérouse, J.-F. G. *A Voyage Round the World Performed in the Years 1785, 1786, 1787, and 1788*. London: Robinson, Edwards & Payne, 1799.

Leech, Samuel. *A Voice from the Main Deck: Being a Record of the Thirty Years' Adventures of Samuel Leech*. Boston: Whittemore, Niles & Hall, 1857.

Lewis, Michael. *England's Sea Officers: The Story of the Naval Profession*. London: Allen & Unwin, 1948.

———. *A Social History of the Navy, 1793–1815*. London: Allen & Unwin, 1960.

Lowes, John Livingstone. *The Road to Xanadu: A Study in the Ways of the Imagination*. Boston: Houghton Mifflin, 1927.

Lovette, Leland P. *Naval Customs: Traditions and Usages*. Annapolis, Md.: U.S. Naval Institute, 1939.

Marcus, Geoffrey. *Heart of Oak: A Survey of British Sea Power in the Georgian Era*. London: Oxford University Press, 1975.

———. *Quiberon Bay*. Barre, Mass.: Barre Publishing, 1963.

Martin, Peter. *A Life of James Boswell*. New Haven and London: Yale University Press, 1999.

Masefield, John. *Sea Life in Nelson's Time*. Greenwich, UK: Conway Maritime, 1905.

Mason, Hadyn. *Voltaire: A Biography*. Baltimore, Md.: Johns Hopkins University Press, 1981.

MacLaren, I.S. "Exploration/Travel Literature and the Evolution of the Author." *International Journal of Canadian Studies* (Spring 1992).

———. "Samuel Hearne and the Printed Word." *The Polar Record*, 29, no. 169 (April 1993).

———. "Samuel Hearne and the Landscapes of Discovery." *Canadian Literature*, 103 (Winter 1984).

———. "Samuel Hearne's Account of the Massacre at Bloody Falls, 17 July 1771." *Ariel: A Review of International English Literature* (January 1991).

MacIver, Angus, and Bernice MacIver. *Churchill on Hudson Bay*. Churchill, Man.: Churchill Ladies Club, 1982.

McGrath, Robin. "Samuel Hearne and the Inuit Oral Tradition." *Studies in Canadian Literature*, 18, no. 2 (1993).

McMillan, Alan D. *Native Peoples and Cultures of Canada: An Anthropological Overview*, 2nd ed. Vancouver: Douglas & McIntyre, 1995.

Monthly Review. 1796, Pt. 11.

Morse, Eric. "Was This Hearne's Thelewey-aza-yeth?" *The Beaver* (Winter 1971).

Moss, John. *Enduring Dreams: An Exploration of Arctic Landscape*. Concord, Ont.: House of Anansi Press, 1994.

Mowat, Farley. *Coppermine Journey: An Account of a Great Adventure, Selected from the Journal of Samuel Hearne*. Toronto: McClelland & Stewart, 1958.

Newman, Peter C. *Company of Adventurers*. Toronto: Penguin/Viking, 1985.

Nuffield, Edward W. *Samuel Hearne: Journey to the Coppermine River, 1769–1772*. Vancouver: Haro Books, 2001.

O'Brian, Patrick. *H.M.S. Surprise*. Glasgow: Collins, 1973.

———. *Men-of-War*. London: Norton, 1976.

Poliquin, Daniel. *Samuel Hearne: Le marcheur de l'Arctique*. Montreal: XYZ, 1995.

Payne, Michael. *The Most Respectable Place in the Territory: Everyday Life in Hudson's Bay Company Service: York Factory, 1788 to 1870*. Ottawa: Minister of Public Works, 1989.

———. *Prince of Wales' Fort: A Social History, 1717–1782*. Manuscript Report 371. Ottawa: Parks Canada, 1979.

Pelly, David F. *Thelon: A River Sanctuary*. Merrickville, Ont.: Canadian Recreational Canoeing Association, 1996.

Picard, Liza. *Dr Johnson's London: Life in London, 1740–1790*. London: Weidenfeld & Nicolson, 2000.

Pope, Dudley. *At 12 Mr. Byng Was Shot*. London: Weidenfeld & Nicolson, 1987.

———. *Life in Nelson's Navy*. London: Unwin Hyman, 1989.

Pottle, Frederick A. *James Boswell: The Earlier Years, 1740–1769*. New York: McGraw-Hill, 1966.

Pritzker, Barry M. *A Native American Encyclopedia: History, Culture, and Peoples*. New York: Oxford University Press, 2000.

Ralfe, J. *The Naval Biography of Great Britain*. London: Whitmore & Fenn, 1828.

Ray, Arthur J. *Indians in the Fur Trade: Their Role as Trappers, Hunters, and Middlemen in the Lands Southwest of Hudson Bay, 1660–1870*, 2nd ed. Toronto: University of Toronto Press, 1998.

Rich, E.E. *The Fur Trade and the Northwest to 1857*. Toronto: McClelland & Stewart, 1967.

———. *Hudson's Bay Company, 1670–1820*. Glasgow: Macmillan, 1960.

Roberts, J.M. *The Making of the European Age: The Illustrated History of the World*. Volume 6. *The Age of Revolution*. New York: Oxford University Press, 1999.

Russell, Dale R. *Eighteenth-Century Western Cree and Their Neighbours*. Hull, Que.: Canadian Museum of Civilization, 1991.

Schwartz, Richard B. *Daily Life in Johnson's London*. Madison: University of Wisconsin Press, 1983.

Smith, Bernard. "Coleridge's Ancient Mariner and Cook's Second Voyage." *Journal of the Warburg and Courtauld Institutes*, 19 (1956).

Smollett, Tobias George. *Roderick Random*. London: J.M. Dent, 1927.

Speck, Gordon. *Samuel Hearne and the Northwest Passage*. Caldwell, Ida.: Caxton Printers, 1963.

Thompson, David. *David Thompson's Narrative, 1784–1812*. Edited by R.G. Glover. Toronto: Champlain Society, 1962.

Tunstall, Brian. *Admiral Byng: And the Loss of Minorca*. London: Philip Allan, 1928.

Tyrrell, J.W. *Across the Sub-Arctics of Canada: A Journey of 3200 Miles by Canoe and Snowshoe through the Barren Lands*. London: T. Unwin, 1898.

Van Kirk, Sylvia. *Many Tender Ties: Women in Fur-Trade Society in Western Canada, 1670–1870*. Winnipeg, Man.: Watson & Dwyer, 1981.

Voltaire. *Candide and Philosophical Letters.* New York: Bobbs-Merrill, 1961. First published 1759.

———. *Philosophical Dictionary.* Translated by Theodore Besterman. London: Penguin, 1972. First published 1764.

———. *Voltaire's England.* Edited by Desmond Flower. London: Folio Society, 1950.

West, Richard. *The Life and Strange Surprising Adventures of Daniel Defoe.* London: HarperCollins, 1997.

Wales, William. "Journal of a Voyage, Made by Order of the Royal Society, to Churchill River. . . ." *Philosopical Transactions,* 60 (1770).

Wales, William, and Joseph Diamond. *Observations on the State of the Air, Winds, Weather, Etc. Made at Prince of Wales's Fort.* London, 1769.

Waller, Maureen. *1700: Scenes from London Life.* London: Hodder & Stoughton, 2000.

Ward, Donald. *The People: A Historical Guide to the Frst Nations of Alberta, Saskatchewan and Manitoba.* Saskatoon, Sask.: Fifth House, 1995.

Warkentin, Germaine, ed. *Canadian Exploration Literature in English: An Anthology.* Toronto: Oxford University Press, 1993.

Webb J., S. Quail, P. Haskell, and R. Riley. *The Spirit of Portsmouth: A History.* Chichester, UK: Phillimore, 1989.

Weissman, Stephen M. *His Brother's Keeper: A Psychobiography of Samuel Taylor Coleridge.* Madison, Wisc., and Conn.: International Universities Press, 1989.

Wilson, J. Tuzo. "New Light on Hearne." *The Beaver* (June 1949).

ACKNOWLEDGEMENTS

A GOOD EDITOR tells an author what's wrong with a manuscript—
what is not working the way it should. A great editor does that, but
also perceives unrecognized potentialities: "Perhaps you should
develop this further?" Phyllis Bruce is one of Canada's great editors.
She made this book better. Phyllis is my "point person" at Harper-
Collins Canada, where Kevin Hanson, vice-president of sales and
marketing, has also gone far beyond the call of duty in supporting
and, indeed, contributing to *Ancient Mariner*.

Having worked with a variety of book publishers over the years, I
am sincerely thrilled to find myself toiling with a group of consum-
mate professionals, among them Rob Firing, Noelle Zitzer, Alan
Jones, Neil Erickson, Roy Nicol, Ann Echlin, Akka Janssen, Shona
Cook, and freelance editor Stephanie Fysh.

My literary agent, Beverley Slopen, who brought me to Harper-
Collins, demonstrates continually why she is regarded as one of the
best in the business; in New York City, during a post-theatre crush,
she even managed to get our party into Sardi's.

Another early reader of this work—the author, editor, and fur-
trade aficionado Barbara Huck—made many valuable suggestions;
she also helped induce Dawn Huck, an award-winning book designer,
to contribute the stellar maps. These two lead the Winnipeg contingent, which also includes the helpful people who care for the national
treasure trove that is the Hudson's Bay Company archives, among
them Maureen Dolyniuk; nor can the fine work of the HBC's Judith
Hudson Beattie, broadcast on CBC Radio, go without citation and thanks.

Farther north, in Churchill, Manitoba, Raymond Girardin and Len McPherson helped make my research trip both successful and fun.

In England, the British Library in London allowed me to peruse important documents; in Portsmouth, the Norrish Central Library surprised me with its extensive collections; and in Beaminster, historian Marie de G. Eedle proved a walking encyclopedia of local lore. As well, in sorting out Samuel Hearne's naval career, British researcher R.W. O'Hara led me through a multitude of arcane records that I would otherwise still be deciphering.

Others to whom I am indebted include Peter St. John, Robert Bragg, William Barr, Annalee Greenberg, Doug Whiteway, Paul vanPeenen, David Butts, Tom Keyser, Victor Ramraj, Dave Obee, Cameron Treleaven, John Geiger, Michael Payne, Jim Taylor, and Shannon Oatway. Above all, without the constant support and encouragement of my wife, Sheena Fraser McGoogan, this book would not exist. The errors and infelicities are my own.

Finally, as an author who writes full-time, I wish to thank the Pierre Berton Writers' Retreat, the Alberta Foundation for the Arts, and the Canada Council for the Arts. The financial support of these institutions has proved crucial to me, as it has to so many writers.

KEN MCGOOGAN

INDEX

Page numbers in *italics* indicate maps and illustrations.

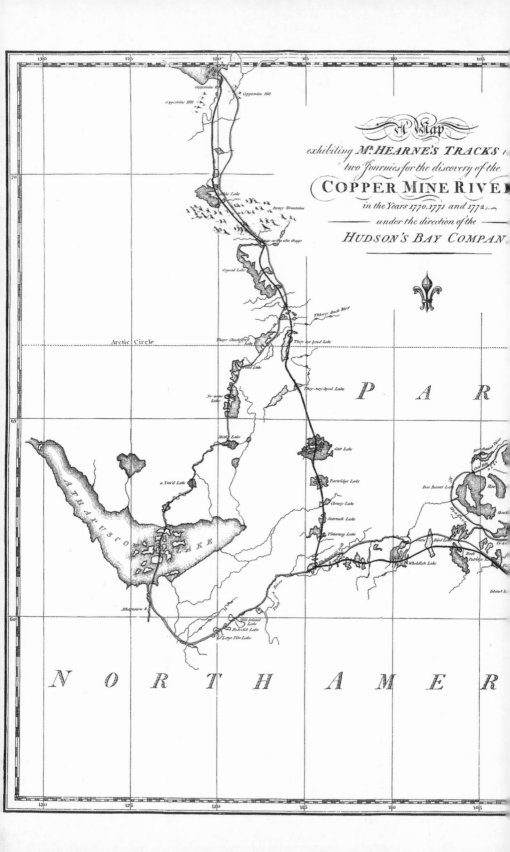

A Map

exhibiting Mr HEARNE'S TRACKS in two Journies for the discovery of the COPPER MINE RIVER in the Years 1770, 1771 and 1772 under the direction of the HUDSON'S BAY COMPANY

Coppermine R.
Coppermine Hill
Coppermine Hill

Noble Lake

Snowy Mountains

lake or the who chago

Copead Lake

Thence duck River

Arctic Circle

Thye Chuckefford Lake

They tye tyud Lake

Peint Lake

They-ney-byed Lake

Xe name Lake

P A R

Methy Lake

a Xow'd Lake

Catt Lake

Partridge Lake

Doo Baunt Lake

Clowey Lake

Saterack Lake

Titterney Lake

Wheldfish Lake

Bird Lake

Rock Partridge

A T H A P U S C O W   L A K E

Island L.

Athapuscow R.

Thel   River

Hill Island Lake
Bedondisi Lake

Large Pike Lake

N   O   R   T   H   A   M   E   R